RIVALS FOR POWER

PRESIDENTIAL-CONGRESSIONAL RELATIONS

SIXTH EDITION

Edited by

JAMES A. THURBER
American University

JORDAN TAMA
American University

ROWMAN & LITTLEFIELD
Lanham • Boulder • New York • London

Executive Editor: Traci Crowell
Assistant Editor: Mary Malley
Senior Marketing Manager: Karin Cholak
Marketing Manager: Deborah Hudson
Cover Designer: Chloe Batch
Cover Art: AP Photo/Susan Walsh

Credits and acknowledgments for material borrowed from other sources, and reproduced with permission, appear on the appropriate page within the text.

Published by Rowman & Littlefield
A wholly owned subsidary of The Rowman & Littlefield Publishing Group, Inc.
4501 Forbes Boulevard, Suite 200, Lanham, Maryland 20706
www.rowman.com

Unit A, Whitacre Mews, 26-34 Stannary Street, London SE11 4AB, United Kingdom

British Library Cataloguing in Publication Information Available

Library of Congress Cataloging-in-Publication Data
Names: Thurber, James A., 1943– editor. | Tama, Jordan, editor.
Title: Rivals for power : presidential-congressional relations / edited by James A. Thurber, American University Jordan Tama, American University.
Description: Sixth edition. | Lanham : Rowman & Littlefield, [2018] | Includes bibliographical references and index.
Identifiers: LCCN 2017015842 (print) | LCCN 2017021838 (ebook) | ISBN 9781538100998 (electronic) | ISBN 9781538100974 (cloth : alk. paper) | ISBN 9781538100981 (pbk. : alk. paper)
Subjects: LCSH: Presidents—United States. | United States. Congress. | United States—Politics and government—20th century.
Classification: LCC JK585 (ebook) | LCC JK585 .R59 2018 (print) | DDC 320.973—dc23
LC record available at https://lccn.loc.gov/2017015842

For Claudia, Mark, Lissette, Kathryn, Greg, Tristan, Bryan, and Kelsey

For Julia, Amos, and Jesse

Contents

Figures and Tables

FIGURES

TABLES

Preface

With Donald Trump's election to the presidency and the maintenance of Republican majorities in the Senate and House of Representatives, Republicans control two of the three branches of the US government. One might assume in this context that this book's title—*Rivals for Power*—has become an inapt description of the relationship between the president and Congress. Indeed, there were clear indications as Trump took office in January 2017 that his relationship with the Republican majority in Congress would be more cooperative than the relationship between President Barack Obama and the Republican congressional majority during the preceding years. Yet it also quickly became clear that President Trump's relationship with Capitol Hill would be strained in important respects. Within the first few weeks of Trump's presidency, disagreements and tensions emerged between Trump and congressional Republicans on a number of major issues, including the repeal and replacement of the Affordable Care Act ("Obamacare"), infrastructure spending, trade agreements, relations with Russia, and immigration and refugee policy. These interbranch conflicts prevented Trump from achieving a major legislative accomplishment during his first one hundred days in office.

For those thinking about adopting or purchasing this book, this edition brings together the knowledge of leading scholars and scholar-practitioners to explain the complex political dynamic between the president and Congress in new chapters. One of the main themes of the book is that the executive and legislature regularly compete and clash with each other, whether the White House and Congress are controlled by the same party or by different parties. The book focuses on the political polarization in our democracy, so clearly shown in the 2016 election campaigns. It also includes ample evidence of both conflict and cooperation between the two branches. The book analyzes the structural, political, and behavioral factors that shape the relationship between the president and Congress, while showing how and why rivalry has tended to intensify when different parties control the two branches. The book's evidence spans a range of eras in US history, with particular attention to developments under recent presidents, including Trump and Obama. Although Trump's presidency remains too young to offer many definitive judgments of it as of this writing, the book considers his emerging relationship with Congress and assesses how his relationship with Congress is likely to play out going forward.

The book is intended for students, scholars, public officials, the media, and the general public. While it presents and draws on original cutting-edge research, it is written in language designed to be accessible to readers who do not possess a political science degree. This sixth edition is also quite different from past editions of the book. Five of the book's contributors—including one of its coeditors—are contributing to the book for the first time, and the chapters of returning contributors feature extensive new material.

The book is clearly a collective effort. We thank all of the contributors for their dedication to the project and for the high quality of their chapters. We have learned immensely from their scholarship, as well as from the dozens of authors in the previous five editions. Collectively, all of these scholars have given us a better understanding of the president and Congress and their interaction.

We are also grateful to Traci Crowell, Janice Braunstein, Mary Malley, and the rest of the Rowman & Littlefield team, who not only made the book's publication possible, but also enhanced it through their expertise and care. We thank, too, the peer reviewers of the book's previous edition, who gave us helpful ideas for improving the book, and we thank Balazs Martonffy for excellent research assistance.

We remember with great fondness our dear friend and mentor, Barbara Sinclair, a contributor to past editions of *Rivals for Power*, who passed away in March 2016. Barbara was a giant among scholars of Congress. Her outstanding research continues to inform this book.

Jim enthusiastically welcomes Jordan as a coeditor. He has enjoyed working with Jordan for the last six years at the Center for Congressional and Presidential Studies (CCPS). Jordan has added his fresh and careful scholarship on Congress, the presidency, and foreign policy to this edition. Their perspective as APSA Congressional Fellows (years apart) and their work with former Congressman Lee Hamilton has added immeasurably to this book. As founder and former director of CCPS and a former congressional staff member, Jim thanks the hundreds of former students and friends who are working or have worked in Congress or the White House for sharing their wisdom and knowledge about American politics and government. First among these is Professor Patrick Griffin, who has closely worked with Jim at CCPS for the last eighteen years and has brought a combination of scholarly research and insights from years on the Hill, in the White House, and as a leader in the Washington advocacy community. As editor of *Congress and the Presidency*, Jim thanks the hundreds of authors and reviewers of manuscripts who have contributed to his knowledge about the two institutions.

Jim thanks his close friend and colleague, former dean of the school of public affairs, former provost, and recently former president of American University (AU), Neil Kerwin. Neil has never failed to understand the importance of AU's relationship with our government institutions and has been an unfailing supporter of CCPS and Jim's scholarship. He also thanks Candice Nelson, interim director of CCPS, for her friendship and support.

Jim thanks his wife, Claudia, for her many years of love, support, and encouragement. Her careful scholarship and wisdom as a lawyer with years of government service has taught Jim much, especially about the importance of the regulatory process. She has kept Jim balanced in his continuing assessments of the political landscape.

Jim dedicates this book to his family. He is thankful for the joy and love given to him every day by Claudia, Mark, Lissette, Kathryn, Greg, Tristan, Bryan, and Kelsey.

Jordan thanks Jim for bringing him on board as coeditor of this edition, integrating him into the work of CCPS, and providing him with generous mentorship. He is also grateful for Jim's leadership over a period of several decades in advancing the study of congressional-presidential relations in many ways. Jordan is grateful, too, for the support, mentorship, and friendship of James Goldgeier, dean of AU's School of International Service; AU professors Philip Brenner, Daniel Esser, Jonathan Fox, Tammi Gutner, Miles Kahler, Nanette Levinson, Shoon Murray, Sarah Snyder, and Sharon Weiner; and other colleagues who are too numerous to name.

Jordan also thanks the American Political Science Association for the opportunity to learn about Congress firsthand through its Congressional Fellowship program. He further thanks former US Representative Lee Hamilton, US Representative James McGovern, Cynthia Buhl, and Janice Kaguyutan for teaching him much of what he knows about how Congress works and modeling how Congress can act in a bipartisan manner to advance US interests and universal human rights.

Jordan is grateful for the love and support of his parents, Phil, Lanni, and Ellyn; his grandparents, William, Elsa, and Joseph; his aunts, Jillian, Rachel, and Julie; his sister, Gabriela; and the rest of his family. He dedicates this book to his wife, Julia, and his sons, Amos and Jesse, with deep thanks for their love and support and for the joy that they bring into his life.

CHAPTER 1

An Introduction to Presidential-Congressional Rivalry

James A. Thurber and Jordan Tama

After one of the most divisive, consequential, angry, nasty, and bizarre presidential campaigns in the history of the United States, President Donald J. Trump and a Republican-dominated Congress must govern. President Trump must show that he can make good on his promise to "cut through gridlock and get things done."[1] Congressional Republicans must do the same thing, having won both chambers of Congress in 2016. The outcomes of elections do not guarantee power in the American political system, but voters hold presidents accountable if they fail to keep their promises. Yet Trump quickly found after taking office that it is complex and difficult to translate campaign promises into legislation and especially difficult to do so rapidly in Congress. Remarkably, despite having fellow Republicans in command on Capitol Hill, Trump struggled mightily during his first months as president to enact into law any of his top legislative priorities.

As presidential candidates, both Donald Trump in 2016 and Barack Obama in 2008 promised to change the way Washington works. This promise proved to be elusive for President Obama. After eight years in office, the relationship between the White House and Congress seemed to be broken and incapable of compromise and getting much done. The congressional Democrats under President George W. Bush adopted a strategy of denying the Republican Party any meaningful legislative victories. The congressional Republicans perfected that game in the last six years of the Obama presidency. Will the Democratic congressional leadership continue this tradition under President Trump? Will the next few years bring more gridlock or will they feature compromise and bipartisanship?

In his 2017 inaugural address, Trump leveled sharp criticism of the ways of Washington, stating, "For too long, a small group in our nation's Capital has reaped the rewards of government while the people have borne the cost."[2] At the same time, he promised in a more positive vein to "heal our

1

divisions" while making America "great again."[3] A few days later, Trump spoke of developing a "beautiful relationship" with congressional leaders, announcing his intention to make "big" deals with them.[4]

In his 2013 State of the Union address, President Barack H. Obama stated in a more consistently positive spirit, "Mr. Speaker, Mr. Vice President, Members of Congress, fellow Americans, fifty-one years ago, John F. Kennedy declared to this chamber that 'the Constitution makes us not rivals for power, but partners for progress.'"[5] For Obama, this notion of a partnership for progress proved to be wishful thinking. The relationship between the president and Congress, often conflictual even in less polarized eras, became very far removed from Kennedy's model during Obama's last six years in office. Does Trump have any greater prospect of developing an effective partnership with Congress?

FROM CAMPAIGNING TO GOVERNING

Election campaigns and strategies to get votes in Congress for presidential initiatives have similar dynamics and complexities. Well-run campaigns and successful governing strategies start with a clear plan and message, make good use of resources, and address liabilities. They both also take into account factors such as the candidate's or president's personality/charisma, key constituencies in the nation and on Capitol Hill, the mood of the broader electorate, the strength of party organization and leadership, and the nation's economic situation.

Donald Trump ran an unconventional presidential campaign. While he proved to be highly attuned to the mood of a sizable portion of the electorate, his personality, tweets, and unpredictable actions made it difficult for his campaign to have a clear and consistent strategy. These factors have also complicated his ability to govern by generating uncertainty about some of his positions and making it difficult for his administration to stay on the same page consistently with congressional Republicans.

The journey from the battles of campaigning to the enterprise of governing is always quick for newly elected presidents, who have just ten weeks to transition from the campaign to the presidency. This journey appeared especially rapid for Trump following his election in November 2016. Trump started the process of governing even before taking office through numerous policy tweets and meetings with congressional and world leaders. A journalist noted several weeks after the election: "Stylistically, Trump seems to be charting a different course toward lawmakers than President Obama, who was criticized for his seemingly aloof personal relations with them. Trump is embracing a more hands-on approach—one that has played out in rapid-fire phone calls, text messages, and highly publicized visits to Trump Tower."[6]

Party loyalty in Congress has been the norm for the past few decades under both unified government, in which the same party controls the presidency and both chambers of Congress, and divided government, in which the presidency and both chambers of Congress are not controlled by the same party. This tendency of party loyalty has led Congress as a whole to defer to the presidency more under unified government than under divided government.

Following the 2016 election, there were some signs that Trump's oft-expressed hostility to the Republican establishment and policies that fell outside of the mainstream might cause party loyalty to dissolve to some degree. Indeed, some of Trump's key policies—on issues from infrastructure spending to trade—cut across orthodox partisan lines.[7] Moreover, Trump's pattern of making pronouncements that deviate from the priorities of congressional Republicans has generated frustration among many of his party allies on Capitol Hill.[8] However, Trump signaled an early cease-fire with the Republican leadership in Congress in an attempt to bridge the separation between the White House and the Hill, and congressional Republicans retained strong incentives to band together with the president on most issues.[9] Congressional Democrats, for their part, faced a dilemma: should they resist Trump at every turn or break ranks and compromise?[10] Thus far, they have mainly done the former.

President Barack Obama's journey from campaigning to governing was also quick. While the 2016 campaign was excessively negative, ugly, and often more about personalities than policy, the 2008 and 2012 Obama campaigns might have been the best-run presidential campaigns in the history of the United States. *Washington Post* veteran reporter David S. Broder declared the 2008 campaign to be the "best campaign I've ever covered."[11] The passage of the $787 billion economic stimulus bill three weeks into Obama's first term and his introduction of a transformational $3.6 trillion budget one month into his administration were also swift and historic, as was a federal government fiscal crisis faced by Obama and Congress soon after his reelection in 2012.

Campaigns and governing do not happen in a vacuum, and they are not fully predetermined by economic or political circumstances. Successful campaigns usually develop a clear message and strategy that mobilizes groups of voters that will help the candidate win—that is, the party loyalists ("the base") and the swing voters (often moderates who fall in the middle of the ideological spectrum). President Obama sought support in Congress during his first term in the same way: he built a solid base of votes from his party and then tried to reach out for votes from moderate Republicans. But he failed to persuade congressional Republicans to support his policy agenda.

Throughout his presidential campaign, President Trump promised to change the way Washington works and to repeal and replace many of the

Obama policies. From his own first day in office, President Obama attempted to use his "political capital" from his successful election campaign to work with Congress. The size of his election victory (53 percent of the popular vote), his popularity as shown in early high poll ratings (mid-60 percent job-approval ratings during his first month in office), and the natural strength of partisan support in unified government (solid Democratic majorities in the House and Senate) helped him build a strong relationship with Congress during his first two years in office.[12] However, this important presidential reserve, "political capital," is often an intangible and transient force, as shown by its rapid decay after a burst of remarkable productivity at the outset of Obama's presidency.

Obama's first two years as president were exceedingly successful in terms of legislative accomplishments, but that productivity was effectively stopped after the 2010 election. During 2009–2010, Democrats controlled both chambers of Congress with large majorities. Between July 7, 2009, and February 4, 2010, they even held a filibuster-proof supermajority of sixty votes in the Senate.[13]

By contrast, although the Republicans controlled both bodies in Congress after the 2016 election, Trump lacked a filibuster-proof majority in the Senate and faced a fractured Republican Party on key issues. For instance, Republicans on the Hill were sharply split within weeks of the election over whether to endorse Trump's call for tariffs on goods sold by companies that move production overseas or Trump's charge that the US intelligence community lacked strong evidence of Russian hacking of Democratic e-mail accounts during the election.[14] Disagreement also quickly emerged among Trump and congressional Republicans over proposals to repeal the Patient Protection and Affordable Care Act (the health-insurance reform popularly known as Obamacare), resulting in their failure to achieve their top legislative priority during Trump's first one hundred days in office.[15]

Obama used the advantage of unified party government during his first two years in office to enact a bevy of major legislation, including the American Recovery and Reinvestment Act (a major economic stimulus program), the reauthorization and funding of the Troubled Asset Relief Program (a program to purchase troubled private sector assets), Obamacare, and the Dodd-Frank Wall Street Reform and Consumer Protection Act (a major financial system reform).[16]

This period of legislative productivity in part inspired a conservative "Tea Party" backlash in the 2010 midterm elections. The Republican Party gained control of the House with the election of eighty-seven new members and narrowed the Democratic majority in the Senate. During the 112th Congress (2011–2012), divided government led to gridlock in Congress. Tensions came to a head in May 2011 when Republicans objected to raising the debt ceiling without instituting a plan to reduce the deficit. This impasse resulted in a downgrade of the nation's credit rating and the creation of a special congressional committee (the "super committee") to recommend a deficit-reduction plan, which failed to resolve the issue.[17]

How to address looming fiscal deadlines became a primary theme of the 2012 campaign and the major agenda of the president and Congress. In the November 2012 election, Republicans retained control of the House, Democrats retained control of the Senate, and President Obama was reelected to a second term, thus guaranteeing continued conflict over the federal budget and other pressing policy issues. The period following the 2012 election was challenging for President Obama; there was no honeymoon in his second term, only continued conflict with a highly partisan and divided Congress. President Trump also faced an abbreviated honeymoon during his first year in office.

President Obama's political momentum and relations with Congress were also undermined by the relatively slow pace of America's economic recovery from the great recession and the unified political opposition of the Republican congressional leadership to his policy agenda. Obama's influence in Congress only diminished further after the Republican Party gained control of the Senate in the 2014 midterm election, thereby placing the Republicans in charge of both chambers of Congress.

In this context, Obama's second term was marked by relatively few major legislative achievements, though he did manage in 2015 to reach a deal with congressional leaders that lifted tight caps on federal spending—known as "sequestration"—that had been imposed after Republicans took control of the House in 2011. This deal allowed Obama to gain congressional approval of some modest spending increases to fund important priorities during his last two years in office.[18] On the whole, however, Obama focused more during his final years in office on policy initiatives—such as nuclear talks with Iran, international climate change agreements, gun control regulations, and actions to protect lands and waters subject to environmental dangers—where he could take consequential actions without congressional approval.[19]

DRIVERS OF RIVALRY

Upon taking office, Presidents Trump and Obama called for a change in the way Washington works. President Obama hoped for bipartisanship and reached out to the Republicans in Congress. In an unprecedented act, he met with Republican congressional leaders on the Hill during the first week of his presidency in an attempt to build a bipartisan coalition to support his historic $787 billion economic stimulus package. He ended up getting only three Republican senators to support the bill and no Republican votes in the House. Trump has faced similar difficulties in building a working relationship with the Hill. Even before he was inaugurated, his opposition to Obama's retaliation against Russia's cyberattacks and his criticism of US intelligence agency assessments that Russia tried to influence the US election immediately pitted him against the hawkish wing of the Republican Party. At the same time, Trump's calls for Congress to repeal and replace Obamacare swiftly, without providing Congress with a clear replacement plan, generated frustration among Republicans on the Hill and led to the embarrassing episode of Republican congressional leaders pulling a repeal bill from the House floor due to a shortage of support for it.[20]

Indeed, all recent presidents have had to deal with a long-seated rivalry between the branches of government, tough partisanship, and the difficulty of building coalitions around their policy initiatives. Whether under unified or divided government, the president and Congress are separated and prone to rivalry and find it hard to find "partners for progress." Where does this conflict come from? What are the roots of the rivalry between the president and Congress? Why does the president's success with Congress vary over time?

"The relationship between Congress and the presidency has been one of the abiding mysteries of the American system of government," according to Arthur M. Schlesinger Jr.[21] In this introduction, we examine several root causes of the rivalry between the president and Congress: the constitutional design with its formal presidential and congressional powers; different electoral constituencies for the president, representatives, and senators; varying terms of office among these elected officials; increased partisanship and polarization within Congress; narrow majorities in both chambers; congressional individualism; the permanent election campaign; the impact of a polarized electorate and media (especially cable television and the Internet) in the twenty-four-hour, seven-days-a-week news cycle; and the nature of interest groups and American pluralism.

Constitutional Design

The framers of the Constitution bequeathed to Americans one of the most enduring rivalries in government, that between the president and Congress.[22] The Constitution separates the three branches of government (legislative, executive, and judicial) but combines their functions, creating conflict and shared powers.[23] As Richard Neustadt observed, the Constitution created a government "of separated institutions sharing powers," which makes it difficult for presidents to bridge the constitutional gap even in the best of political circumstances. In his study of the president and Congress, Charles S. Jones concludes, "A separated system is a bulwark against major change, as the history of reform efforts demonstrates."[24]

The Constitution gives the president and the Congress different powers, and each is jealous of the other's constitutional prerogatives regardless of context. Article II of the Constitution gives the president only four legislative responsibilities: (1) to inform Congress from time to time on the state of the union, (2) to recommend necessary and expedient legislation, (3) to summon Congress into special session and adjourn it if the two houses cannot agree on adjournment, and (4) to exercise a qualified veto. The Constitution invests Congress with "all legislative Powers" (lawmaking), but it also authorizes the president to recommend and veto legislation. Congress must pass legislation and can override vetoes. If the president vetoes a bill, "it shall be reposed [overridden] by two-thirds of the Senate and the House of Representatives" (Article I, Section 7).

Because it is so difficult for Congress to gain a two-thirds vote, presidential vetoes are usually sustained. Through 2016, presidents had used the veto 2,572 times; 1,067 of these were "pocket vetoes" not subject to congressional override.[25] Congress overrode presidential vetoes 7 percent of the time (110 times) when it had the opportunity to vote on them. President Obama used the veto only twice in his first six years in office and only twelve times altogether—thereby tying President George W. Bush for the fewest vetoes of any president since President Warren Harding. Only one of Obama's vetoes was overridden by Congress.[26]

This record shows that it is easier to stop legislation than it is to pass it. President Bill Clinton embraced that notion in his historic budget battle in 1995 when he said: "This is one of those moments in history when I'm grateful for the wisdom of our Founding Fathers. The Congress gets to propose, but the president has to sign or veto, and that Constitution gave me that authority and one of the reasons for the veto is to prevent excess. They knew what they were doing and we're going to use the Constitution they gave us to stand up for what's right."[27]

On the other hand, the constitutional need to achieve the approval of sixty senators in order to overcome a filibuster generally makes it quite difficult for presidents to gain congressional approval of their policy proposals—even when their party is in the majority in Congress.

The president and Congress also share power in the legislative process in other ways. Presidents are expected to propose and promote policies, setting the agenda for Congress. But Congress has the power of the purse—that is, the power to authorize and appropriate funds for the president and executive branch agencies. Presidents may propose budgets for the federal government, but Congress has the final say on spending. This creates an automatic rivalry over spending and taxing, which dominated President Obama's relationship with Congress during his final six years in office. Rivalry over taxes and spending also quickly emerged under Trump, as most congressional Republicans were reluctant to support Trump's call for major national investments in infrastructure.[28] In another economic area, Congress also has the power to regulate foreign and interstate commerce. On foreign commerce, pro-trade presidents have often clashed with more protectionist Congresses and struggled to achieve congressional approval of trade agreements. However, Trump's staunch anti-trade positions have changed the interbranch politics of this issue, making the president more protectionist than most members of Congress.

The powers to declare war, to provide for a militia, and to adopt laws concerning bankruptcy, naturalization, patents, and copyrights are also bestowed on Congress. The interpretation of presidential and congressional war power has changed over time as presidents have frequently deployed the military without congressional authorization, creating another common contemporary source of conflict. In addition, Congress has the authority to establish or eliminate executive branch agencies and departments—as it did in creating a new Department of Homeland Security in 2002 and a new Director of National Intelligence and National Counterterrorism Center in 2004—and to oversee their operations.

In other powers, the Senate must approve cabinet nominees, ambassadors, and Supreme Court and federal judicial appointees before they can take office. The president also cannot enter into a binding treaty with a foreign government without the treaty's approval by a two-thirds vote of the Senate, though all modern presidents have sometimes circumvented this requirement by signing international accords as "executive agreements," which do not require Senate ratification, rather than as treaties. All of these constitutional congressional and presidential powers force both institutions to confront each other in governance, which more often than not creates rivalry and conflict. Congress also has the more informal powers of deliberation concerning presidential proposals and education of the American people.

A dramatic but rarely employed check on the president is impeachment. The president and executive branch officials can be impeached (formally accused) by a majority vote in the House and tried in the Senate. If two-thirds of the senators vote to convict, the official is removed from office. Only Presidents Andrew Johnson and Bill Clinton have been tried on impeachment charges. The vote fell one short of the number required to convict Johnson and the Senate did not come close to convicting Clinton. The House Judiciary Committee recommended that Richard M. Nixon be impeached for transgressions in connection with the Watergate burglary involving the Democratic National Committee offices and the ensuing cover-up. Nixon, however, resigned the presidency before a full session of the House could vote on the impeachment issue. The threat of impeachment

establishes an important check on the president and executive branch officials, limiting the power of the president.

The framers of the Constitution deliberately fragmented power between the national government and the states (creating a system known
as federalism) and among the executive, legislative, and judicial branches
(creating the separation of powers at the federal level).[29] They also divided
legislative powers by creating two coequal houses of Congress with different constituencies, which further magnifies rivalry and conflict. Although
divided in two, Congress was designed to be independent and powerful,
able to check the power of the executive and to be directly linked with
the people through popular, periodic elections. The framers wanted an
effective and powerful federal government, but they also wanted to limit
its power in order to protect personal and property rights. Having experienced the abuses of English monarchs and their colonial governors, the
framers were wary of excessive executive authority. They also feared "elec-
tive despotism," or excessive legislative power, something the Articles of
Confederation had given to state legislatures.

The framers created three branches of government with none having a
monopoly over their most important functions. This separation of powers
restricted the power of any one branch, and it required cooperation among
the three in order for them to govern effectively. Today, as then, political
action requires cooperation between the president and Congress. Yet the
Constitution, in the way that it divided power between the two branches,
created an open invitation for conflict.[30] In sum, in creating a separated
presidency and two equal legislative chambers, the framers guaranteed
checks and an ongoing rivalry between executive and legislative power.

Nevertheless, ultimately legislative-executive relationships are not ze-
ro-sum games. If one branch gains power, the other does not necessarily
lose it. Threats like the terrorist attack on the United States on September
11, 2001, and the great recession of 2008–2009, can contribute to the policy-making power of both the president and Congress. The war on terrorism,
the wars in Iraq and Afghanistan, the economic crisis, and large budget
deficits have led to new administrative (and legislative) powers expanding
the scope of both branches. Even these crises, however, have not eliminated
the rivalry between the two institutions and the two parties.

Different Electoral Constituencies

James Madison in "Federalist No. 46" described the greatest source of
conflict between the president and Congress, their different constituencies.
The US system of government, unlike parliamentary systems throughout the
world, elects the executive and members of the legislature independently.

The president is elected from a vastly broader national electoral coalition than are representatives or senators. Representatives tend to have particularly narrow and homogeneous constituencies, but even the constituencies of senators are not as broad as the president's. Members of Congress, even those who belong to the president's party or hail from his or her home state, therefore represent specific interests that can conflict with the interest of the president in representing the nation as a whole. In short, rivalry is built into the election system for the president and members of Congress. Presidents must build a broader electoral coalition in order to win their office than any member of Congress. Congress has difficulty representing the nation as a whole, but represents narrow state and local interests well.

James Madison well understood this dichotomy of interest as an important source of conflict between the president and Congress. In the *Federalist Papers*, he wrote: "The members of the federal legislature will be likely to attach themselves too much to local objects. . . . Measures will too often be decided according to their probable effect, not on the national prosperity and happiness, but on the prejudices, interests, and pursuits of the governments and the people of the individual States."[31] Moreover, today's members of Congress often live in discrete communities and cleverly drawn noncompetitive House districts favoring one party or the other, but especially favoring incumbents. Only eighteen House seats were competitive in 2016.[32] Those incumbents who run for reelection are overwhelmingly successful, as reelection rates are in the mid-90th percentile for House members and mid-80th for senators.

The trend toward ticket splitting between presidential and congressional candidates further exacerbates already strained relations between the president and Congress. Election returns for Congress have increasingly diverged from national presidential returns. During the past forty years, as the power of political parties to control the recruitment of candidates has declined significantly, there has been a corresponding rise in individualistic candidacies for the presidency (especially Trump), the Senate, and the House, as revealed by the Republican Tea Party movement and the Freedom Caucus, which brought into office representatives who challenged the traditional Republican establishment during Obama's presidency. Fewer and fewer members of Congress ride into office on the electoral "coattails" of the president. This has led to the election of presidents who find it difficult to translate electoral support into governing support. Short or nonexistent presidential coattails by Trump in 2016 (and Obama in 2008 and 2012, Bush I in 1988, Clinton in 1992 and 1998, and Bush II in 2000 and 2004) lead to the conclusion that "the emperor has no clothes." With the decline of presidential coattails, strong-willed, independent-minded members of Congress are largely beyond the president's control. They are often more responsive to district and specialized interests than to the national agenda of the president.

Varying Terms of Office

The interaction of Congress and the president is shaped not only by their different constituencies and electoral competitiveness, but also by their different terms in office. Differences in the length of terms of presidents and members of Congress create different legislative incentives and strategies, often causing conflict between the two branches. The constitutional structure of US government, which separates the Congress and the president, sets different terms of office for representatives (two-year terms), senators (six-year terms), and the president (four-year terms) and ensures they will be chosen from different constituency bases. Presidents have only four years, possibly eight, in which to establish their programs. Presidents know their tenure is short and do not want to waste time in the adoption of their policies before an anticipated decline in popularity. President Trump was no exception to this motivation to rapidly push his legislative agenda in his first one hundred days in office.

Reelected presidents, such as Obama, George W. Bush, and Clinton, no longer need to worry about elections and can focus during their second terms on their legacy—protecting their successes and pushing new public policy in an effort to secure an honored place in history. By contrast, the drive for reelection is always a top priority for members of Congress, since term limits do not exist for them.[33] Legislators, then, are often reluctant to allow their workload and policy preferences to be dictated by a president who has different objectives. They are often driven by the short-term motivation to be reelected rather than the long-term policy goals of a president.

Presidents seek rapid change, as did Trump upon taking office, but Congress moves more slowly; it is deliberative and inefficient primarily because it represents a vast array of local interests. Congress passes new laws slowly and usually reviews old ones carefully. The decision-making pace of Congress is especially sluggish when the president is not of the same party.

President Trump promised and then pushed for major changes in health-care policy (Obamacare), infrastructure spending, taxes, and trade. Confronted with major economic problems and two wars, President Obama also pursued an ambitious policy agenda in his first term. He did not back off his campaign promises in 2008 of withdrawal from Iraq, quick action to turn the economy around, health-care reform, financial reforms, and new policies to address climate change. However, Congress had its own pace and its own ideas on most of these issues. In some cases, such as Obamacare and the Dodd-Frank financial reform, Congress did ultimately approve major legislation during Obama's first two years in office, after an extended process of deliberation and debate. In other cases, such as climate change, Congress failed to generate the agreement needed to act.

Political Parties

Another factor influencing the relationship between the president and Congress is the role of political parties. The federal system of state-based political parties contributes to the independence of members of Congress from the president. The president must work with decentralized political party organizations that often exercise little control over the recruitment of candidates, mete out weak discipline, and hold particularly weak leverage over members of Congress. Senators and representatives usually run their own races with their own financing.

The way members of Congress respond to state and local conditions also has little to do with national party platforms or presidential politics. Members often freely pursue their own interests without fear of discipline from the president. Independence from political parties and the president allows legislators to seek benefits for their own constituents and to serve specialized interests.

Intraparty harmony can be even more difficult to achieve when the president stakes out policies that do not represent the positions of the party's establishment, as has been the case under Trump. Indeed, Trump ran against the Republican establishment and is not identified with many long-standing Republican policy priorities. For these and other reasons, many Republican politicians criticized and avoided Trump during the 2016 campaign, though they had to work with him once he was elected president.

On the other hand, there is a continuing strong trend in the House and Senate toward greater ideological and party loyalty, as the two parties in Congress have become more homogeneous and unified over the past several decades. Congressional party discipline and leadership often overcomes the decentralization of party organization outside of government. An analysis of congressional "party unity" votes, defined by *Congressional Quarterly* as votes where a majority of one party votes against a majority of the other, shows that congressional voting has been characterized by record levels of polarization in recent years. Whereas a majority of Republicans aligned against a majority of Democrats only about one-third of the time in the early 1970s, that alignment characterized nearly two-thirds of congressional votes during the Obama administration (see figure 1.1). Moreover, in such party unity votes, the average percentage of representatives and senators voting with their party's majority increased from about 60 percent to more than 85 percent during that time (see figure 1.2). In short, congressional parties have grown much more ideological and polarized, leading to more policy gridlock and legislative difficulties for presidents.

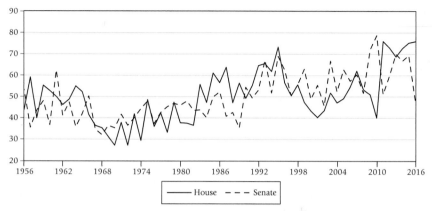

Figure 1.1. Percentage of Party Unity Votes in Congress, 1956–2016

Note: Party unity votes are those roll call votes on which a majority of Democrats aligned against a majority of Republicans. This graph depicts the percentage of roll call votes that represented party unity votes in each chamber in each year. The 2016 data are based only on votes prior to the November 2016 election.

Sources: "2015 Vote Studies: Party Unity Remained Strong," *CQ Weekly*, February 8, 2016; "CQ Vote Studies: 2016 Party Unity," *CQ Weekly*, October 17, 2016.

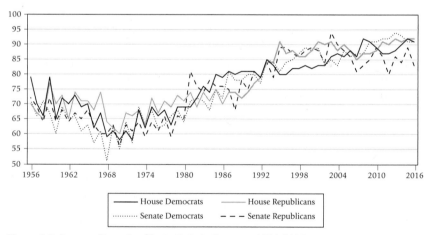

Figure 1.2. Average Strength of Party Unity in Congress, 1956–2016

Note: The scores depicted in this graph represent the average percentage of Democratic or Republican lawmakers in each chamber who voted with their party's majority in party unity votes for each year. The 2016 data are based only on votes prior to the November 2016 election.

Sources: "2015 Vote Studies: Party Unity Remained Strong," *CQ Weekly*, February 8, 2016; "CQ Vote Studies: 2016 Party Unity," *CQ Weekly*, October 17, 2016.

Party Control of Government

Whether or not the same political party controls the presidency and both chambers of Congress also influences greatly the relationship between the president and Congress, as legislative-executive cooperation tends to be greater under unified government than under divided party government. Unified government returned to America for the outset of President Trump's administration and for President Obama's first two years in office, while divided government characterized the final six years of Obama's presidency.

From 1901 through 2018 (118 years), we have had unified government for sixty-nine years (58 percent of the time) and divided government for forty-nine years (42 percent of the time). (See table 1.1.) Yet the pattern of the last fifty years has been quite different from the pattern of the previous seven decades. From 1901 to 1968, divided government occurred during only fourteen years (21 percent of the time), but from President Richard Nixon's first year in office (1969) through the first Congress of the Trump administration (2018), it occurred during thirty-five years (70 percent of the time). Although President George W. Bush had unified government most of the time and Presidents Obama and Trump had unified government for the first two years of their presidencies, divided government is the norm in modern US politics.

Presidents are more likely to be successful with their legislative agendas with unified government than with divided government. This has been especially true since the post-1980 resurgence of party-line voting and party cohesion in Congress. This tendency is evident in "presidential support" scores, which measure the frequency with which a majority in Congress votes in accord with the president's stated position on legislation.[34] As shown in figure 1.3, President Obama's presidential support score of almost 97 percent during his first year in office under unified government

Table 1.1.　Unified and Divided Party Control of Government, 1901–2018

Years	Party Control	Number of Years	Percentage of Years
1901–1968	Unified	54	79
	Divided	14	21
1969–2018	Unified	15	30
	Divided	35	70
All (1901–2018)	Unified	69	58
	Divided	49	42

Note: Unified party control exists when the presidency and both chambers of Congress are controlled by the same party. Divided party control exists when the presidency and both chambers of Congress are not controlled by the same party. The table assumes that the presidency and both chambers of Congress will remain controlled by the Republican Party for the remainder of the 115th Congress.

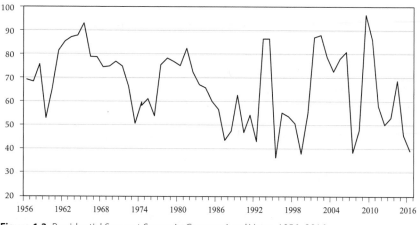

Figure 1.3. Presidential Support Scores in Congressional Votes, 1956–2016

Note: This figure represents the percentage of votes in the House and Senate for a given year in which the outcome of the vote corresponded to the president's position, out of all votes on which the president took a clear position. The 2016 data are based only on votes prior to the November 2016 election.

Sources: "2015 Vote Studies: Presidential Support Hits Low for Obama," *CQ Weekly*, February 8, 2016; "CQ Vote Studies: 2016 Presidential Support," *CQ Weekly*, October 17, 2016.

set a record since measuring such scores started with President Eisenhower, but Obama's support score dropped to 39 percent by his final year in office under divided government. Overall, Reagan and Bush had low presidential support scores in Congress because of divided government. Clinton's scores during his first two years (1993–1994) in office averaged over 86 percent, and dropped to 36 percent in 1995 after the Republicans captured the Congress. President Trump's resolve to bring quick change to Washington by increasing spending on infrastructure, repealing and replacing Obamacare, reforming immigration policy, and reforming tax policy is dependent upon Congress. Notwithstanding Trump's early legislative struggles, unified party government should make it easier for him to advance these goals.

However, unified party control of government does not mean the two branches will work closely together consistently, as tensions between Trump and some congressional Republicans have revealed during the 115th Congress. Conversely, divided government does not always mean that the two branches will fight. David Mayhew found that when it comes to passing major legislation or conducting investigations, it "does not seem to make all that much difference whether party control of the American government happens to be unified or divided."[35] However, it is generally easier for presidents to govern during periods of unified government. Under unified government, Trump and congressional Republicans are likely to experience less tension and more legislative victories than

Obama experienced during his last six years in office, but an underlying rivalry and sharp differences on certain issues will still exist.

Political Polarization and the Missing Middle

President Trump inherited extreme partisan polarization that has now been on the rise for several decades, which is making it more difficult for him to gain broad support for his policies.[36] It dominated the 2016 campaign and has become a fact of life in twenty-first-century American politics. In Congress, overwhelming evidence demonstrates clearly that our two major parties are ideologically as far apart as at any point in the past 150 years (see figure 1.4).[37] And at the voter level, there are strong disagreements based on race, gender, age, region, and urban-rural-suburban values that make up an important part of the foundation of partisan polarization facing the president and Congress.[38]

A fundamental reason for gridlock and dysfunctionality is the disappearance of the moderates or what some have called the vital center in Congress. There has been a steady decline in the number of moderates voting together in Congress since the 1970s. Four decades ago, there was a vigorous middle

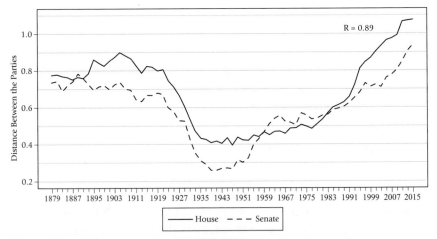

Figure 1.4. Party Polarization in Congress, 1879–2015

Note: This graph depicts the size of the average difference in voting patterns between Republican and Democratic lawmakers in each chamber for each year from 1879 to 2015, on votes that can be mapped on a left-right ideological scale labeled by scholars as the DW-NOMINATE first dimension. For more information on this measure, see Nolan McCarty, Keith T. Poole, and Howard Rosenthal, *Polarized America: The Dance of Ideology and Unequal Riches*, second edition (Cambridge, MA: MIT Press, 2016). *R* is a measure of the correlation between the two lines in the graph.

Source: Keith T. Poole and Howard Rosenthal, http://voteview.com/political_polarization_2015.htm. Used with permission from Poole.

in Congress. Both parties spanned the ideological divide that exists today. Indeed, for much of the twentieth century, each party had a large liberal wing and a large conservative wing. On divisive issues such as civil rights, liberal Democrats and moderate northern Republicans would join forces against conservative southern Democrats and conservative Republicans from other regions. Getting the votes needed to stop a filibuster required a coalition of senators from both parties, and the ideological diversity of the parties often made it feasible to create such coalitions. However, today the Democratic Party is thoroughly associated with liberalism and the Republican Party is thoroughly associated with conservatism, making the formation of bipartisan coalitions much more difficult.

Figure 1.5 illustrates this decline in moderates as measured by the percentage of representatives and senators whose voting patterns overlap with at least one member of the other party—that is, Republicans whose voting patterns fall to the left of a Democrat or Democrats whose voting patterns

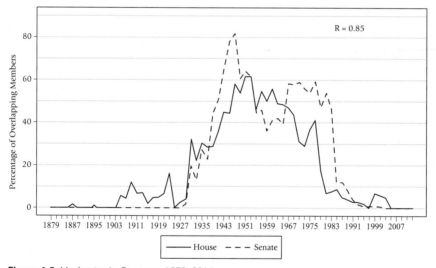

Figure 1.5. Moderates in Congress, 1879–2014

Note: This graph depicts the percentage of lawmakers in each chamber whose voting patterns overlap on an ideological spectrum with at least one lawmaker in the other party. For Republicans, such an overlap involves a voting pattern that is more liberal than the voting pattern of at least one Democrat. For Democrats, such an overlap involves a voting pattern that is more conservative than the voting pattern of at least one Republican. The measure is based on the DW-NOMINATE first dimension. For more information on this measure, see Nolan McCarty, Keith T. Poole, and Howard Rosenthal, *Polarized America: The Dance of Ideology and Unequal Riches*, second edition (Cambridge, MA: MIT Press, 2016). *R* is a measure of the correlation between the two lines in the graph.

Source: Keith T. Poole and Howard Rosenthal, http://voteview.com/political_polarization_2014. htm. Used with permission from Poole.

fall to the right of a Republican on a left-right ideological spectrum.[39] Whereas about half of all members of Congress could be considered moderates based on this measure during the presidencies of Dwight Eisenhower, John F. Kennedy, Lyndon Johnson, and Richard Nixon, none met this standard for centrist voting during Barack Obama's presidency.

Related to the lack of the middle in each party is the movement of both parties to more extreme partisanship, which has also helped to create congressional dysfunction. Polarization has reduced the frequency of consensus in the House and reduced legislative productivity in the Senate.[40] In addition, the movement of former House members into the Senate has contributed to increased partisan polarization in the upper chamber.[41]

Not only does the decline in centrist members increase polarization, but high levels of polarization have driven some centrists out of Congress in frustration. The decision to forgo running for reelection by a number of moderate members of Congress in 2014 and 2016 was in part a result of the polarized atmosphere in the Senate.

Interest Groups and Pluralism

Candidate Trump ran against interest groups and lobbyists with his call to "drain the swamp" and clean up the "corruption and special interest collusion in Washington, DC."[42] This was also a theme of candidate Barack Obama in 2008. Both Trump and Obama promised to change the way Washington works. President Obama was unable to do so and President Trump has also found it difficult to reform our pluralist system.

Public opinion surveys clearly show an increase over the past ten years of those who believe lobbyists have too much influence and a decline in those who think they have too little.[43] A major theme of the Trump campaign (and the Bernie Sanders presidential campaign) was to attack the cozy vested interests "controlling" Washington. President Trump played into the negative public attitudes about lobbying, as did President Obama. In his 2008 campaign, Obama promised: "I intend to tell the corporate lobbyists that their days of setting the agenda in Washington are over, that they had not funded my campaigns, and from my first day as president, I will launch the most sweeping ethics reform in US history. We will make government more open, more accountable and more responsive to the problems of the American people."[44] He later said, "We are going to change how Washington works. They will not run our party. They will not run our White House. They will not drown out the views of the American people."[45] President Trump promised to "Make America Great Again" by reducing the power of special interests and their lobbyists.

Despite these promises by Obama and Trump, the passage of their ambitious legislative agendas has depended greatly upon the input and support of interest groups and lobbyists. When a president's policy agenda is proposed, especially through his or her budget, there is a mobilization of interests for and against the thousands of policy decisions and proposals embedded in the fiscal plan, as shown in the intense lobbying surrounding President Trump's first budget in 2017. This competition among a variety of interests has often produced deadlock and stalemate on the nation's most pressing problems, but it has also contributed to the enactment of major reforms. Interest groups play a central role in the relationship between the president and Congress. Without the help of well-organized groups, the president and Congress cannot easily enact legislation. With them against the president, it is exceedingly difficult to bring about reform.

Pluralism in the form of group-based politics limits (or enhances) the power of the president and Congress to pursue their own agendas and thereby increases the competition between them. Policy-making gridlock often comes from competition among organized interests in society, not simply from polarization and divided party control of government. Deadlock over the budget, tax reform, debt and deficit reduction, entitlement reform, immigration, gun control legislation, clean air policy, energy policy, health-care policy, and education, along with the tendency toward "government by continuing resolution," represent the consequences of conflict and a lack of agreement among organized groups outside Congress. Unified party government under President Trump has mitigated, but not solved, this gridlock problem.

The constitutional First Amendment rights, especially freedom of speech, freedom of assembly, freedom of the press, and freedom to petition government for grievances, are the foundation of pluralism in US politics. The decay of centralized political party organizations in the last forty years in the United States has contributed to the growth of pluralism.[46] As political parties have lost power to recruit and elect candidates who are loyal to party leaders in government, interest groups and factions within the parties (e.g., the Tea Party movement and Bernie Sanders progressives) have gained political power. The United States is experiencing extreme competition among groups, "hyperpluralism," that makes it almost impossible to define the public good in terms of anything other than the collection of special narrow interests.[47] Hyperpluralism intensifies the rivalry between the president and Congress and often leads to deadlock by making it difficult to make the necessary compromises between the national interests of the president and the parochial interests of members of Congress.[48] However, crises and presidential leadership can break the deadlock, as happened under President George W. Bush after the attacks of September 11, 2001, and under President Obama following his election at a time when the economy was failing. President Trump may also find the deadlock in Congress and conflict with the White House lessened if the nation faces a crisis.

FROM PROMISES TO PERFORMANCE

Candidate Trump promised considerable changes in the way Washington works as well as in specific policies. His one-hundred-day action plan to "Make America Great Again" was outlined during his campaign in "a contract between myself and the American Voter."[49] He promised to begin by "restoring honesty and accountability, and bringing change to Washington."

Trump's "contract" included six measures to clean up the "corruption and special interest collusion in Washington, DC":

1. A constitutional amendment to impose term limits on all members of Congress
2. A hiring freeze on all federal employees and reduction in the federal workforce through attrition (exempting military, public safety, and public health)
3. A requirement that for every new federal regulation, two existing regulations must be eliminated
4. A five-year ban on White House and congressional officials becoming lobbyists after they leave government service
5. A lifetime ban on White House officials lobbying on behalf of a foreign government
6. A complete ban on foreign lobbyists raising money for American elections

Trump also promised seven actions to "protect American workers":

1. Renegotiating NAFTA or withdrawing from the deal under Article 2205
2. Withdrawing from the Trans-Pacific Partnership
3. Directing the secretary of the treasury to label China a currency manipulator
4. Directing the secretary of commerce and US trade representative to identify all foreign trading abuses that unfairly impact American workers and direct them to use every tool under American and international law to end those abuses immediately
5. Lifting the restrictions on the production of fifty trillion dollars' worth of job-producing American energy reserves, including shale, oil, natural gas, and clean coal
6. Lifting the Obama-Clinton roadblocks to vital energy infrastructure projects, like the Keystone pipeline
7. Canceling billions in payments to UN climate change programs and using the money to fix America's water and environmental infrastructure

Trump further promised five actions to "restore security and the constitutional rule of law":

1. Canceling every unconstitutional executive action, memorandum, and order issued by President Obama
2. Beginning the process of selecting a replacement for [Supreme Court] Justice [Antonin] Scalia, who will uphold and defend the US Constitution
3. Canceling all federal funding to sanctuary cities
4. Beginning to remove the more than two million criminal illegal immigrants from the country and cancel visas to foreign countries that won't take them back
5. Instituting "extreme vetting" and suspending immigration from terror-prone regions where vetting cannot safely occur

President Trump acted quickly through executive orders to carry out some of these promises—such as his pledges to order a government-wide hiring freeze and withdraw from the Trans-Pacific Partnership—during his first days in office. On some other issues, such as labeling China a currency manipulator, Trump's own position changed after he took office and became more attuned to the downsides of certain actions.

At the same time, on issues where legislation is needed to act, Trump's desire to move fast collided with the much slower pace of Congress and the challenge of forging consensus among hundreds of legislators. Moreover, proposing policies without thorough analysis and political preparation can be deadly. Indeed, as Trump urged congressional Republicans early in 2017 to act quickly to repeal and replace Obamacare, some Republicans on Capitol Hill presciently cautioned that it would be unwise to repeal the health-care legislation without first reaching agreement on a sensible plan for replacing it.[50] More generally, without strong congressional Republican support and the help of some congressional Democrats, Trump's ambitious policy agenda will be difficult to pass and implement.

In 2008, candidate Obama promised to reduce rivalry between the two branches and to "change the way Washington works." He urged Congress to fix the breakdown in the budget process and to stop passing large omnibus spending bills well after the start of the fiscal year.[51] President Obama also said he would reduce the polarization and would improve the comity and civility between the president and Congress. Thus far, there is little evidence that Trump will be more successful with his promises to bring change to the nation's capital than his predecessor.

OVERVIEW OF THE BOOK

How should presidents and Congress be evaluated on their basic governing functions? How much of a president's success and failure is shaped by Congress? How do polarization, partisan pressures, elections, and interest groups affect the behavior of the president and Congress? How do presidents seek to build support for their legislative agenda, and how do congressional leaders approach their relationships with the president? To what extent can presidents use unilateral action or regulatory authority to shape policy without congressional approval? What are the effects of congressional investigations of the executive branch? What has been the impact of presidential-congressional relations on judicial appointments, domestic policy, and foreign policy? What forces shaped Obama's relationship with Congress? How are presidential-congressional relations likely to evolve under Trump, and how will they be affected by Trump's distinct personality, policy preferences, and political style? These are some of the important questions addressed in this book.

This edition of the book represents a collaboration of academics and practitioners who have written chapters that focus on the causes, character, and consequences of conflict and cooperation between the president and Congress. The book's authors draw on a wide range of research and employ a variety of policy and political perspectives in analyzing this fundamental relationship. No single analytic approach or dominant ideology reigns.

In chapter 2, Sarah Binder assesses presidential-congressional relations in an era of polarization. She explains that high levels of polarization make gridlock more common in Washington because they make it harder for elected officials to forge the large, bipartisan coalitions that are needed to institute major policy changes. Moreover, today's closely divided electorate often gives the opposition party a greater incentive to criticize the majority party than to cooperate with it in the making of public policy. Binder shows that the share of salient public issues characterized by legislative deadlock has increased considerably in recent decades—on both domestic and foreign policy—reaching record-high levels during the divided government years of the Obama administration. Binder illustrates the difficulties of governing in a polarized era through a discussion of the legislative and political strategies of congressional Republicans during the Obama years. She also considers the extent to which legislative productivity will increase with the return of unified government under Trump, cautioning that increases in productivity are likely to be limited by continued polarization, Trump's low levels of public popularity, and significant policy differences among Republicans.

Campaigns, elections, and voters have a fundamental impact on the president and Congress. In chapter 3, David Jones examines how electoral incentives often lead members of Congress to act in ways designed to boost the public reputation of their party and tarnish the public reputation of the opposing party. As he explains, these incentives exist because individual representatives and senators are more likely to get reelected if their party's brand is more popular than the other party's brand. Moreover, a more favorable brand for a member's own party or a less favorable brand for the other party increases a member's ability to attain influence within Congress and achieve his or her public policy goals. Jones illustrates these patterns through a discussion of the behavior of members of Congress in Obama-era debates over defunding Obamacare, combating the Ebola epidemic, and authorizing the use of military force against ISIS. He also considers how concerns about party reputations are likely to shape congressional-executive politics during the Trump administration, noting that unified government should give Republicans a greater incentive to demonstrate that they can govern competently and give Democrats a greater incentive to draw attention to issues that can be blamed on Republicans.

In chapter 4, James Pfiffner analyzes the uses and abuses of unilateral presidential authority. He outlines key tools available to the president to act unilaterally—including executive orders, presidential memoranda, administrative regulations, and emergency powers—and documents how recent presidents have acted without congressional approval in both domestic and foreign affairs. Pfiffner illustrates the prevalence and importance of presidential unilateralism by discussing executive actions by Presidents Obama and George W. Bush concerning immigration policy, the use of military force, the interrogation and detention of terrorism suspects, intelligence surveillance, signing statements, and drone strikes. Pfiffner argues that while presidential discretion in policy making is necessary, unchecked executive power is dangerous. He places the blame for recent high levels of presidential unilateralism on both the White House and Congress, explaining that congressional gridlock and polarization have made it particularly tempting for presidents to resort to unilateral action.

In chapter 5, regulatory lawyer Claudia Hartley Thurber shows how President Obama accomplished some of his policy objectives without congressional action and how President Trump must move to accomplish his antiregulatory policy goals. She shows that once divided government made it very difficult for Obama to achieve congressional approval of new initiatives, he relied heavily on federal departments, agencies, and commissions to advance his agenda through regulations. Some of this rulemaking implemented the Dodd-Frank and Obamacare financial and health-care reform laws, despite strong opposition to the rules from congressional Republicans. Additional regulations addressed major environmental and safety issues pursuant to the authority granted to departments and agencies in their enabling statutes. Thurber also examines the ability of Congress to check the president's regulatory power by disapproving proposed rules, and outlines the options available to Trump to reverse Obama's regulatory actions. She cautions that getting rid of regulations can be very time-consuming and costly, suggesting that there are limitations to the ability of Trump and the Republican Congress to overturn recent regulations.

A major function of Congress is oversight of the executive branch and the president. In chapter 6, Douglas Kriner analyzes the most high-profile form of oversight: congressional investigations. He shows that investigations provide Congress with a powerful tool for influencing politics and policy making during times of high partisan polarization and institutional dysfunction, since a congressional committee chair can begin an investigation without the broader approval of Congress or the president. Kriner explains that congressional investigations can be consequential in three ways: by spurring legislative initiatives, prompting preemptive presidential actions, or eroding popular support for the president. He illustrates these pathways of influence through case studies of the so-called Church Committee investigation of intelligence abuses in the 1970s and the congressional investigation of the Obama administration's handling of the attack on the US consulate in Benghazi, Libya, in 2012. While the former investigation resulted in preemptive presidential changes to intelligence policies and important intelligence reform legislation, the latter investigation contributed to the defeat of Hillary Clinton in the 2016 election.

In chapter 7, academic-practitioners Gary Andres and Patrick Griffin draw on their extensive experience in the White House, on Capitol Hill, and in the advocacy business to analyze how presidents manage legislative affairs in today's highly polarized age. They argue that presidents have not been immune to the rise in polarization that has affected Congress so dramatically in recent decades. Instead, presidents have responded to increased polarization on the Hill by more systematically and aggressively supporting their own party and seeking to make the other party look bad. Andres and Griffin also present a framework for understanding the president's legislative relations, which explains how the president's relationship with Congress is shaped by the president's institutional constraints and advantages, goals, and political skills. They consider, too, changes outside government that are affecting White House–Congress interactions, including the fragmentation of the media landscape, the proliferation of interest groups, and new technologies. They illustrate their argument with examples from recent presidencies and discuss the congressional challenges and opportunities facing Trump under conditions of unified government and high polarization.

In chapter 8, Ross Baker analyzes the important relationship between congressional leaders and the president. Whereas one might expect the president and the leaders of the president's party in Congress to see eye-to-eye and work hand-in-hand almost all of the time, Baker explains that the relationship between these leaders often represents a "provisional partnership" characterized by both cooperation and conflict. This is in part because the president's desire to leave a major policy legacy during his or her limited time in office provides the president with a stronger incentive than congressional leaders to seek deals with the opposing party. In addition, tension often arises because congressional leaders have a stronger incentive than the president to keep controversial legislation off the floor of Congress in order to protect parts of their diverse caucus from politically difficult votes. Baker illustrates these tendencies through a discussion of the relationship between Obama and Senate Democratic Leader Harry Reid. Drawing on in-depth interviews of senior aides to Reid, he shows that Reid and the White House were not on the same page in some of the most important policy debates of the Obama years.

John Anthony Maltese analyzes the relationship between the president, Congress, and the courts in our separated system of government in chapter 9. He uses the controversy over filling the Supreme Court vacancy left by the 2016 death of Antonin Scalia as a springboard for discussing the highly political nature of judicial appointment debates. Maltese explains that it has been common for members of Congress to block judicial nominees whom they oppose throughout American history, but that partisan polarization and interest group lobbying for and against nominees have made many judicial appointment debates particularly contentious in recent years. The rise in partisanship associated with these debates has also resulted in high numbers of vacancies in US courts under divided government. Remarkably, Congress confirmed only twenty Obama nominees to federal courts in 2015–2016, while failing to act on fifty-two Obama nominees to federal courts during those years. By contrast, Maltese observes that unified government should allow President Trump to achieve higher Senate confirmation rates during his first two years in office.

In chapter 10, James A. Thurber evaluates the relationship between the president and Congress in domestic policy. He explores how the relationship on major domestic issues differs under divided and unified government, and how it is affected by partisan polarization. His analysis focuses on recent battles over the economy, the federal budget, and health-care reform—areas where presidents have had a much more productive relationship with Congress under unified government than under divided government. He gives particular attention to battles over taxes and spending, which concern a fundamental function of government and dominated political debate for much of the Obama presidency. Thurber also assesses the relationship between Trump and Congress, showing that Trump and congressional Republicans share many common domestic policy priorities but also have different approaches to some key issues. He observes that Trump's proclivity to act unilaterally and without consulting Congress closely could lead his relationship with Congress to grow strained in important areas of domestic policy despite the existence of unified government.

Jordan Tama analyzes presidential-congressional relations in foreign policy in chapter 11. While the president is clearly the leading actor in American foreign policy, Tama shows that Congress often constrains the president's ability to achieve important international goals. He also considers the extent to which politics "stops at the water's edge"—as the old adage asserts—in today's highly polarized era. Although it remains more common on foreign policy than on domestic policy for the president to attract bipartisan congressional support, Tama shows that many foreign policy debates are characterized by division between the parties, splits within the parties, or clashes between the two branches of government. He illustrates these patterns by discussing major Obama-era debates concerning military intervention, economic sanctions, international trade, and climate change policy. He also observes that differences in the foreign policy positions of President Trump and congressional Republicans are likely to prevent Trump from obtaining the full support from lawmakers in his party on some key international matters.

CONCLUSION

Congressional-presidential rivalry has a number of deep-seated structural sources, from the Constitution's separation of powers system to the differing electoral incentives of lawmakers and the president. While these sources of rivalry are unlikely to disappear, there are some steps that the president and members of Congress can take to make their relationship more constructive. In particular, they can do more to cultivate relationships that cross institutional and party lines. One common criticism of Obama was that he did not invest a lot of time in the establishment of strong relationships with members of Congress.[52] The creation of an informal presidential-congressional consultative body could help ensure that the president and congressional leaders spend the time together that is needed to build relationships that can serve as a foundation for working through difficult political and policy challenges together. Such a body could consist of the president and the Republican and Democratic leaders of the House and Senate, and could meet once a month without a preset agenda to enable an exchange of views and a discussion of areas of possible cooperation that is not limited to the handling of major crises.[53]

Interbranch relationship building would also be beneficial at less senior levels of the government. To cultivate fewer misunderstandings and greater cooperation between executive branch and congressional staff—as well as between House and Senate staff—key staff from the White House, executive branch agencies, the House, and the Senate could gather annually for an off-the-record daylong retreat. This could bring a better understanding of the people and politics involved in the legislative process to executive branch officials and a better grasp of the impact of legislative actions to senior staff on the Hill. Although there will be significant policy differences among the participants, these gatherings could boost trust and even generate cooperation between the two branches.[54]

We should also keep in mind that congressional-presidential rivalry is not necessarily bad. To the contrary, it can help to ensure that neither the president nor Congress moves government policies in directions that are sharply at odds with the will of the electorate or the interests of the United States. Indeed, the framers created a system hardwired for interbranch rivalry precisely in order to guarantee that checks and balances existed.

Yet rivalry need not—and should not—be equated with hostility, stalemate, or dysfunction. The interests of the American people are not well served when the relationship between Congress and the president is characterized by intense partisanship and stifling gridlock. In recent years, tensions between the branches and parties have been excessive, making rivalry more destructive than constructive. The harsh tone of political discourse during and after the 2016 election makes us all the more concerned about the current direction of American politics.

At the same time, we recognize that there have been many ups and downs in the intensity of political combat in US history, and we remain hopeful that the system designed by our framers will be resilient to the pressures it is facing today. Although powerful forces often push our elected officials to seek to score political points by attacking, rather than cooperating with, each other, we take heart that most Americans continue to want the president and members of Congress to work together to address important national problems. In the end, of course, it will largely be up to the American people to decide whether they will reward or punish our leaders for advancing or blocking initiatives designed to make the United States—in the words of the Constitution—a "more perfect union."

NOTES

1. Steven Pearlstein, "The Democrats' Dilemma: Resist Trump at Every Turn or Break and Compromise," *Washington Post*, December 17, 2016.

2. Inaugural address of Donald J. Trump, available at https://www.whitehouse.gov/inaugural-address.

3. Inaugural address of Donald J. Trump.

4. Jeff Zeleny, "Donald Trump, Home Alone, Puts Out the White House Welcome Mat," *CNN.com*, January 24, 2017.

5. Barack H. Obama, "State of the Union Address," February 12, 2013.

6. Mike DeBonis, "A Détente Early on for Trump, GOP Leadership," *Washington Post*, December 24, 2016.

7. David Brooks, "New Life in the Center," *Washington Post*, November 11, 2016.

8. Mike DeBonis, Kelsey Snell, and Ed O'Keefe, "Hill Republicans Want Answers. On Wednesday, Trump Gave Them Only More Questions—and Fresh Headaches," *Washington Post*, January 28, 2017.

9. DeBonis, "A Détente Early on for Trump, GOP Leadership."

10. Pearlstein, "The Democrats' Dilemma."

11. David S. Broder, "The Amazing Race," *Washington Post*, November 2, 2008.

12. For Obama's approval ratings, see http://www.gallup.com/poll/113980/Gallup-Daily-Obama-Job-Approval.aspx.

13. On July 7, 2009, Al Franken (D) won the contested Minnesota seat, giving the Democrats sixty votes. However, Ted Kennedy's (D) illness kept him away from the Senate from March 2009 until his death in August 2009. Until Paul Kirk (D) replaced Kennedy on September 24, 2009, the Democrats lacked the necessary sixty votes. On February 4, 2010, Scott Brown (R) replaced Kirk in the Massachusetts delegation, dropping the number of seats held by the Democrats to fifty-nine.

14. Rachael Bade, "Top House Republican Won't Back Trump's Tariff Proposal," *Politico*, December 5, 2016; David E. Sanger, "Trump, Mocking Claim That Russia Hacked Election, at Odds with G.O.P.," *New York Times*, December 10, 2016.

15. Kyle Cheney, John Bresnahan, and Rachael Bade, "Republicans Yank Obamacare Repeal Bill," *Politico*, March 24, 2017.

16. James A. Thurber, ed., *Obama in Office* (Boulder, CO: Paradigm Publishers, 2011).

17. See James A. Thurber, "Agony, Angst, and the Failure of the Supercommittee," *Extensions* (Summer 2012), Carl Albert Congressional Research and Studies Center, University of Oklahoma.

18. Julie Hirschfeld Davis, "No Grand Bargain, But Deal Is Still a Victory for Obama," *New York Times*, October 27, 2015.

19. For instance, see Steve Holland, "Obama Warns Divided Congress That He Will Act Alone," Reuters, January 29, 2014.

20. Cheney, Bresnahan, and Bade, "Republicans Yank Obamacare Repeal Bill."

21. Arthur M. Schlesinger Jr. and Alfred De Grazia, *Congress and the Presidency: Their Role in Modern Times* (Washington, DC: American Enterprise Institute, 1976), 1.

22. See James A. Thurber, "Congress and the Constitution: Two Hundred Years of Stability and Change," in Richard Maidment, ed., *Reflections on the Constitution* (University of Manchester Press, 1989), 51–75.

23. For this constitutional basis of conflict, see Richard E. Neustadt, *Presidential Power and the Modern Presidents: The Politics of Leadership from Roosevelt to Reagan* (New York: Free Press, 1990); James L. Sundquist, *The Decline and Resurgence of Congress* (Washington, DC: Brookings Institution, 1981); Steven A. Shull, *Domestic Policy Formation: Presidential-Congressional Partnership?* (Westport, CT: Greenwood Press, 1983); Michael L. Mezey, *Congress, the President, and Public Policy* (Boulder, CO: Westview Press, 1985); Louis Fisher, *Constitutional Conflicts between Congress and the President*, 4th rev. ed. (Lawrence: University of Kansas Press, 1996); Louis Fisher, *The Politics of Shared Power: Congress and the Executive* (Washington, DC: CQ Press, 1993); Charles O. Jones, *The Presidency in a Separated System* (Washington, DC: Brookings Institution,

1994); Charles O. Jones, *Separate but Equal Branches: Congress and the Presidency* (New York: Chatham House, 1999); Charles O. Jones, *Clinton and Congress: Risk, Restoration, and Reelection* (Norman: University of Oklahoma Press, 1999).

24. Jones, *The Presidency in a Separated System*, xiii.

25. US House of Representatives, History, Art & Archives, "Presidential Vetoes: 1789 to Present," http://history.house.gov/Institution/Presidential-Vetoes/Presidential-Vetoes.

26. For veto data, see http://www.senate.gov/reference/Legislation/Vetoes/ObamaBH.htm.

27. Todd S. Purdum, "President Warns Congress to Drop Some Budget Cuts," *New York Times*, October 29, 1995.

28. DeBonis, Snell, and O'Keefe, "Hill Republicans Want Answers."

29. See Jones, *The Presidency in a Separated System*.

30. See George C. Edwards III, *Overreach: Leadership in the Obama Presidency* (Princeton, NJ: Princeton University Press, 2012); George C. Edwards III, *Presidential Influence in Congress* (San Francisco: Freeman, 1980); and Cecil V. Crabb Jr. and Pat M. Holt, *Invitation to Struggle: Congress, the President, and Foreign Policy*, 4th ed. (Washington, DC: CQ Press, 1992).

31. James Madison, "Federalist No. 46," in Clinton Rossiter, ed., *The Federalist Papers* (New York: New American Library, 1961), 296.

32. The Cook Report, December 7, 2016.

33. David R. Mayhew, *Congress: The Electoral Connection* (New Haven, CT: Yale University Press, 1974).

34. *Congressional Quarterly* measures and publishes these scores. CQ and several scholars have advised that the scores "must be interpreted with care" since the president's public positions do not always reflect the president's private positions and there exist many bills on which the president does not take clear positions.

35. David R. Mayhew, *Divided We Govern* (New Haven, CT: Yale University Press, 1991, 2005), 198.

36. James A. Thurber and Antoine Yoshinaka, eds., *American Gridlock: The Sources, Character, and Impact of Political Polarization* (New York: Cambridge University Press, 2015); also see Morris P. Fiorina, *Culture War? The Myth of a Polarized America* (Boston: Longman, 2011) and Laurel Harbridge, *Is Bipartisanship Dead? Policy Agreement in the Face of Partisan Agenda-Setting in the House of Representatives* (New York: Cambridge University Press, 2015).

37. Thurber and Yoshinaka, *American Gridlock*; also see Thomas E. Mann and Norman J. Ornstein, *The Broken Branch: How Congress Is Failing America and How to Get It Back on Track* (New York: Oxford University Press, 2006); and Thomas E. Mann and Norman J. Ornstein, *It's Even Worse Than It Looks: How the American Constitutional System Collided with the New Politics of Extremism* (New York: Basic Books, 2013).

38. Alan I. Abramowitz, "The New American Electorate: Partisan, Sorted, and Polarized," in Thurber and Yoshinaka, *American Gridlock*, 19–44.

39. This measure derives from the commonly used DW-NOMINATE measure of the ideology of legislators. DW-NOMINATE scores are produced by applying a spatial model to roll-call voting in Congress. These scores allow for the comparison of members of different Congresses across time. Keith Poole and Howard Rosenthal, the creators of this measure, argue that the first ideological dimension of this measure, capturing differing views on economic policy, explains most roll-call-

voting decisions. A second dimension, capturing views on race, has diminished in importance since the 1960s. For more information on DW-NOMINATE, see Nolan McCarty, Keith T. Poole, and Howard Rosenthal, *Polarized America: The Dance of Ideology and Unequal Riches*, 2nd ed. (Cambridge, MA: MIT Press, 2016). Data and graphs available at http://www.voteview.com.

40. Barbara Sinclair, "The President and Congressional Party Leadership in a Polarized Era," in James A. Thurber, ed., *Rivals for Power: Presidential-Congressional Relations*, 4th ed. (Lanham, MD: Rowman & Littlefield, 2009), 83–104.

41. Sean Theriault and David Rohde, "The Gingrich Senators and Party Polarization in the U.S. Senate," *Journal of Politics* 73, no. 4 (October 2011): 1011–24.

42. Amita Kelly and Barbara Sprunt, "Here Is What Donald Trump Wants to Do in His First 100 Days," *NPR.org*, November 9, 2016.

43. See, for instance, "Americans' Views of Money in Politics," *New York Times/ CBS News Poll*, June 2, 2015, http://www.nytimes.com/interactive/2015/06/02/us/politics/money-in-politics-poll.html.

44. New Hampshire News, "The City as Infestation," October 9, 2012, http://www.nhpr.org/node/14408.

45. NBC News, "DNC Bans Lobbyist Money," June 6, 2008, http://www.msnbc.msn.com/id/24989468/wid/7468326.

46. See Joel H. Sibley, "The Rise and Fall of American Political Parties," in L. Sandy Maisel, ed., *The Parties Respond: Changes in American Parties and Campaigns* (Boulder, CO: Westview Press, 1994), 3–18.

47. James A. Thurber, "Political Power and Policy Subsystems in American Politics," in B. Guy Peters and Bert A. Rockman, eds., *Agenda for Excellence: Administering the State* (Chatham, NJ: Chatham House Publishers, 1996), 76–104.

48. See Jonathan Rauch, *Demosclerosis* (New York: Times Books, 1994).

49. Kelly and Sprunt, "Here Is What Donald Trump Wants to Do in His First 100 Days."

50. Burgess Everett, "GOP Resistance Grows to Obamacare Repeal Without Replacement," *Politico*, January 7, 2017.

51. See James A. Thurber, "The Dynamics and Dysfunction of the Congressional Budget Process: From Inception to Deadlock," in Larry Dodd and Bruce Oppenheimer, eds., *Congress Reconsidered* (Washington, DC: Sage and CQ Press, 2013), 319–45; and James A. Thurber, "Twenty-Five Years of Deficit and Conflict: Partisan Roles in Congressional Budget Reform," in Nicole C. Rae and Colton Campbell, eds., *New Majority or Old Minority: The Impact of Republicans in Congress* (Lanham, MD: Rowman & Littlefield, 1999).

52. Francine Kiefer, "Obama's Icy Relationship with Congress: Can It Ever Thaw?" *Christian Science Monitor*, February 24, 2014.

53. For a similar proposal in the area of foreign policy, see Lee H. Hamilton, with Jordan Tama, *A Creative Tension: The Foreign Policy Roles of the President and Congress* (Washington, DC: Woodrow Wilson Center Press, 2002), 89–90.

54. Efforts by think tanks and foundations like the Brookings Institution, the Aspen Institute, the William and Flora Hewlett Foundation's Madison Initiative, the Bipartisan Policy Center, to name just a few institutions, bring present and former members of Congress and top-level executive branch officials together to discuss policy and process to help bridge the partisan gap between the parties.

CHAPTER 2

Congress and the President

Legislating in Polarized Times

Sarah Binder

> The single most important thing we want to achieve is for President Obama to be a one-term president.
>
> —Senate Minority Leader Mitch McConnell (R-KY)[1]

Nearly two years after the election of President Barack Obama and a Democratic Congress in 2008, Senate Republican leader Mitch McConnell of Kentucky on the eve of the 2010 midterm elections declared his party's top goal: to prevent Obama from securing a second term. Although McConnell failed to block Obama's reelection, Republicans retook the House in 2010 and the Senate in 2014, and put Donald J. Trump in the White House in 2016. McConnell's strategy—keeping GOP fingerprints off Democratic initiatives—enabled voters to hold Democrats accountable for the government's performance and propelled Republicans back to power.

Obama's relationships with Democratic and Republican Congresses over the course of eight years in office provide a window into the politics of legislating in polarized times. Both reflecting and fueling ideological and partisan polarization, Republicans' bare-knuckles strategy largely undermined Democrats' capacity to govern—producing some of the least productive Congresses since World War II. In this chapter, I review the forces that shape congressional-presidential interactions, explore record levels of stalemate during the Obama years and put them into broader historical perspective, and speculate about legislative prospects under President Trump and the return of unified Republican control of government.

DYNAMICS OF LAWMAKING, IN THEORY

The publication of David Mayhew's *Divided We Govern* in 1991 marks the origins of the contemporary study of congressional-presidential relations and their impact on Congress's legislative performance.[2] Highlighting questions about the effects of political parties on Capitol Hill, Mayhew brought systematic evidence to bear in testing claims about the impact of divided party control on Congress and the president's ability to generate landmark laws. *Divided We Govern* followed decades of work by presidential and legislative scholars perplexed and frustrated by periods of divided party government that prevailed after World War II. Between 1897 and 1954, divided party control of government occurred 14 percent of the time; between 1955 and 1990, two-thirds of the time. As prominent political scientist V. O. Key in the 1960s summed up the state of our knowledge of the impact of party, "Common partisan control of executive and legislature does not assure energetic government, but division of party control precludes it."[3] Decades later, scholars continued to call for a new theory of coalitional government to explain how Congress and the president could secure major policy change in the presence of divided government.[4]

In *Divided We Govern*, Mayhew tackled the challenge by asking a simple question about Congress's performance in the postwar era: "Were many important laws passed?"[5] Mayhew sought to test for the effect of divided party control on the level of lawmaking. He identified landmark laws in a two-stage process that combined contemporary judgments about the significance of Congress's work in each session with policy specialists' retrospective judgments about the importance of legislation. Mayhew then generated a comprehensive list of landmark laws enacted in each Congress between 1946 and 1990, subsequently updated online through 2014. Mayhew then tested whether the presence of divided government reduced the number of major laws enacted each Congress.[6]

Mayhew concluded that party control is inconsequential in shaping a president's legislative accomplishments: not much more gets done under divided party control than when a single party controls both ends of Pennsylvania Avenue. Mayhew absolved divided government as a cause of legislative inaction, and then attempted to disentangle other influences on congressional performance. Some of those forces—including legislators' electoral incentives—pointed toward constancy in the record of lawmaking. But other forces, Mayhew demonstrated, appeared to be important alternative sources of variation in explaining congressional productivity, including shifting public moods or tastes for activist government, presidents' electoral cycles, and issue coalitions that cut across the left-right divide.

Mayhew's counterintuitive finding spawned a healthy debate about the forces that undergird Congress and the presidents' legislative records. One prominent theoretical response to Mayhew's work was Keith Krehbiel's *Pivotal Politics*.[7] Krehbiel introduced a new theoretical framework for conceptualizing the conditions that foster lawmaking by the two branches. Krehbiel's key contribution was the concept of legislative and presidential "pivots" engaged in a "pivotal politics" game—institutional actors endowed with key procedural rights within a stylized legislative game.

Krehbiel's central insight was that constitutional and extraconstitutional institutional rules create "pivotal" players on whom collective choice depends. In the congressional context, the collective choice at stake is the formulation of public law. Focusing on the presidential veto and the Senate filibuster, Krehbiel argued that the cloture and veto pivots were the critical actors for determining whether or not changes to the policy status quo would be adopted. Any existing policy located between these pivots (the "gridlock interval") cannot be changed, assuming that legislative politics have a single dimension and that lawmakers' votes and presidential positions reflect their sincere preferences over policy. In other words, legislative stalemate can occur even in the presence of a president and a congressional majority that favor policy change.

The pivotal politics theory has important implications for understanding the conditions under which Congress and the president will be able to agree to major policy change. Most important, the theory suggests that policy outcomes must be consistent with the views of the supermajority pivots of the legislature. For example, with a conservative president and bicameral congressional majority, efforts to move policy substantially to the right would be blocked by a liberal filibuster pivot. Senate Democrats in 2005, for instance, blocked Republican president George W. Bush's push to privatize Social Security. Threatening to filibuster, Democrats prevented the proposal from moving forward—even though Republicans controlled both branches of government. According to the pivotal politics model, right of center status quos would also remain unchanged when conservatives control both branches: a conservative president would veto any movement left of the policy and the veto would be sustained by the veto pivot. Under the theory, major policy change is likely only when elections alter the alignment of pivotal players or major exogenous shocks make existing policy untenable. Crises—such as the terrorist attacks of September 11, 2001—are a prime example. Despite split party control of Congress in the fall of 2001, President Bush succeeded in securing bipartisan support for most of the legislative measures he sought in retaliation against the perpetrators of 9/11.

Noticeably, political parties do not appear anywhere in the pivotal politics model. Legislators are individual utility maximizers, rather than partisans seeking the party's collective electoral or policy goals. Parties are mere aggregations of individuals rather than players endowed with formal agenda setting or blocking rights. One of the model's nice features is that it helps to explain why unified party control often fails to produce major policy change. Failure to secure the support of the filibuster pivot has hamstrung many a majority party, including Democrats under President Bill Clinton in 1993 when he sought a large stimulus bill and Republicans under President George W. Bush in 2005 when he pushed to privatize Social Security. *Pivotal Politics* also helps to explain the challenges faced by President Obama's Democratic majority in 2010 after the loss of its filibuster-proof Senate majority—requiring compromise with the Republicans, for example, in crafting the landmark Dodd-Frank Act that revamped the financial regulatory system.

The model also suggests that legislative gridlock will occur in periods of divided government, for instance, with a Republican-controlled Congress and a Democrat in the White House. In this scenario, a conservative congressional majority's effort to move policy to the right would be thwarted by a left-side filibuster pivot, as well as a left-side presidential veto. The veto pivot, whose vote would be necessary to override the president's veto, is also unlikely to prefer the conservative majority's proposed policies. For example, Republican efforts in 2015 to repeal Obamacare and Dodd-Frank and to authorize construction of the Keystone pipeline faltered in the face of Democratic threats to filibuster and Obama vetoes.

The broader implication of both the Mayhew and Krehbiel models is that policy change is likely only when large, bipartisan coalitions agree that major change is necessary to resolve public problems. Moreover, Krehbiel's model helps to account for other empirical regularities identified by Mayhew, including the "honeymoon" effect in which new presidents secure major policy change. The pivotal politics model suggests that gridlock would indeed be broken if a new president pushes major change when he or she inherits extreme status quo policies that are out of step with the views of new congressional majorities and the president.

In the nearly two decades since the publication of *Pivotal Politics*, other legislative scholars have challenged Mayhew's and Krehbiel's nonpartisan accounts by building theory that expects party influence over the shape of policy outcomes. In my own work on gridlock discussed below, I suggest that both interbranch and intrabranch conflict—conditioned by partisan and institutional forces—shapes the prospects for major legislative change.[8] First, I show that the degree of partisan polarization matters: ideologically distant, cohesive parties make harder the crafting of large bipartisan majorities and widespread public support necessary for durable policy change. Second, I suggest that intrabranch conflict is a subtle barrier to legislative action, showing that bicameral differences within a party limit Congress's legislative capacity. Other scholars, such as Frances Lee, suggest that policy deadlock ensues in electorally competitive eras: opposition parties have few incentives to negotiate agreements if they believe they will recapture

control of both branches in the near future.[9] Messaging rather than legislating becomes the order of the day. Taken together, such accounts suggest that electoral, partisan, and institutional forces collectively shape the prospects for legislating in polarized times. More often than not, the parties settle on campaigning on issues rather than taking credit for new laws.

PATTERNS IN POSTWAR LAWMAKING

How do we know how productive Congress and the president are in addressing public problems? Mayhew advocates that we count up the number of landmark laws enacted every two years by Congress and the president. I prefer to measure legislative deadlock more directly. In previous work, I isolated the set of salient issues on the nation's agenda and then determined the legislative fate of those issues in each Congress.[10] The result is a ratio of failed measures to all issues on the agenda each Congress. The measure nicely captures past episodes of Congress's legislative performance. For example, according to the measure, Lyndon Johnson's Great Society Congress is the most productive of the postwar period and the 2013–2014 Obama Congress (in which Republicans drove the government to shut down and nearly defaulted on the nation's debt) is the most deadlocked. Such assessments comport with historical and contemporary coverage of Congress and the president's postwar performance.

As I explained in *Stalemate*, I identify every policy issue on the legislative agenda based on the issues discussed in the unsigned editorials in the *New York Times*.[11] Using the level of *Times* attention to an issue in any given Congress as an indicator of issue salience, I locate for each Congress between the 80th (1947–1948) and the 113th (2013–2014) the most salient issues on the legislative agenda. I then turn to news coverage and congressional documents to determine whether or not Congress and the president took legislative action in that Congress to address each salient issue. The measurement strategy produces a denominator of every major legislative issue raised by elite observers of Capitol Hill and a numerator that captures Congress's record in acting on those issues. The resulting gridlock score captures the percentage of agenda items left in limbo at the close of each Congress.

Figure 2.1a displays the size of the policy agenda through 2014, coupled with the number of failed legislative issues in each Congress.[12] Looking first at the smoothed trend line in the overall number of legislative issues mentioned each Congress in the *Times* editorials, the size of the overall agenda increases as expected with the return of large liberal majorities during the mid-1960s and stays at this expanded level through the advent of the civil rights, environmental, and women's movements of the 1970s. Only in recent years do we see a slight increase in the size of the agenda, no doubt

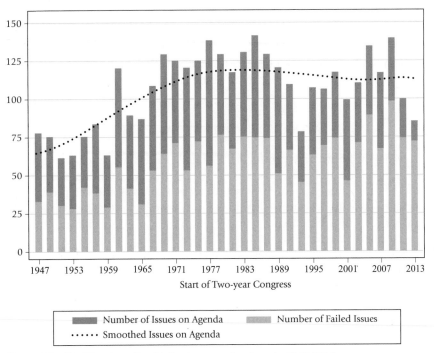

Figure 2.1a. Total Number of Legislative Issues on the Agenda, 1947–2014

reflecting both later efforts to renew the spate of landmark laws of the earlier, activist period and newer issues brought to the fore by the war on terror, global climate change, and so on.

The trend in the number of salient issues (displayed in figure 2.1b) is more eye-catching. The overall size of the agenda increases only incrementally over the most recent decade, but the number of salient issues rises markedly in the most recent Congresses. It is possible that the recent rise in deadlock has helped to fuel expansion of the agenda: big issues remain unsolved and thus recur on the nation's agenda in the following years. Failure to address reform of immigration law, entitlement programs, and the tax code, for example, likely helped to increase the number of salient issues on the agenda during the Obama years. Moreover, a spate of new issues in the past decade likely caught the attention of the *Times'* editorial writers, including homeland security, global warming, cybersecurity, US wars in Iraq and Afghanistan, the onset of financial crisis, and the worst economy since the Great Depression.

Six features stand out in patterns of legislative deadlock on salient issues (figure 2.2). First, the frequency of deadlock rises steadily over time. Perceptions that Congress struggles more today than it did decades ago hit the mark. Second, the direst claims about congressional performance

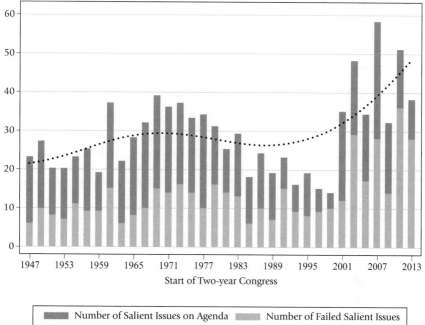

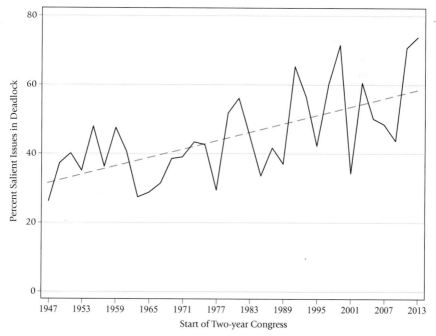

Figure 2.1b. Number of Salient Legislative Issues on the Agenda, 1947–2014

Figure 2.2. Frequency of Legislative Deadlock, 1947–2014

during the Obama administration are true. Despite a remarkably productive Congress in 2009 and 2010 when Obama enjoyed a filibuster-proof, sixty-vote majority in the Senate for several months, most of the Obama years are marked by record levels of deadlock. By this measure, the 113th Congress appears to be the "worst Congress ever"—at least since the series begins after the end of World War II. In fairness, the title should be shared with the last Congress of the Clinton administration in 1999–2000 and with the dismal 112th Congress (2011–2012). In all three Congresses, lawmakers and the president deadlocked on almost three-quarters of the most salient issues on the agenda. No surprise that public approval of the 113th Congress bottomed out at 7 percent when legislative stalemate closed down nonessential parts of the federal government for three weeks.

Third, caution is still in order in comparing recent Congresses. Some of the issues considered "successfully" addressed in recent Congresses might never have been deemed acceptable outcomes previously. For example, Congress and the president traditionally fund federal highway construction for multiyear periods. Following the expiration of highway programs in 2009, however, it took more than thirty short-term extensions of the highway program until the parties finally agreed to a fully funded, multiyear bill late in 2015. Two-week extensions seem like obvious failed efforts to reauthorize highway spending. But what about the multiyear highway bill adopted in 2012, an agreement that funded only a third of a traditional six-year bill? I consider the highway bill as a success, even though the two-year bill failed to ensure the solvency of highway trust funds after two years. Lawmakers did not resolve the financial impasse until late in the fall of 2015 when legislators raided the capital surplus of the Federal Reserve to replenish the highway trust fund.[13] Similarly, Congress and the president reached an agreement to raise the government's debt limit in the summer of 2011 that included creation of a special committee to generate over a trillion dollars in federal savings. I consider the 2011 deficit reduction package a legislative "success," even though the resulting "super committee" eventually deadlocked. Peak levels of deadlock in the Obama years likely underestimate the challenges of legislating in highly polarized times.

Fourth, President Obama's first Congress from 2009 to 2010 (the 111th) was relatively productive compared to Congress's performances over the past decade (with the exception of the 9/11 Congress). But the 111th Congress fell far shy of the records of unified Democratic Congresses under President Johnson's Great Society Congresses. Granted, the 111th Congress was nearly thirty points more productive than the Obama Congresses that followed: The 111th enacted landmark changes to the nation's health-care, financial regulation, and other laws. But the widely heralded 111th Congress still left a hefty list of issues in limbo, including proposals to revamp secondary education programs, reform campaign finance, and address global warming, immigration, and gun control. Even with control of the White House and large Democratic majorities, Obama's party struggled to surmount major barriers to major policy change.

Fifth, a brief look at the 107th Congress's performance in the wake of the attacks of September 11, 2001, is instructive. Overall, the 107th Congress (with unified Republican control of both branches for just a few months early in 2001) was fairly productive, leaving just a third of the policy agenda in 2001 and 2002 in stalemate. But lawmakers' capacity to make deals was directly shaped by the events of 9/11. Eight of the thirty-five salient issues on the agenda in that Congress rose directly from the attacks of September 11. And on those eight issues, Congress and the president mustered a perfect record: they enacted the PATRIOT Act, wrote the Authorization for the Use of Military Force, addressed the needs of 9/11 victims, and more. Even on less salient issues stemming from September 11, congressional deadlock was extraordinarily rare, with just a single issue left in legislative limbo. Still, a cooperative spirit and unity of purpose did not extend to the rest of the policy agenda. If we exclude the issues related to the terrorist attacks, Congress and the president deadlocked on just under half of salient policy issues. Congress appears to have retained the capacity to act swiftly when some crises occur, also evidenced by Congress's October 2008 bailout of Wall Street after the Federal Reserve and Treasury allowed Lehman Brothers to go under just weeks before. However, legislative unity dissipates when Congress turns its attention back to its normal policy agenda. Moreover, not every crisis spurs action. Despite overwhelming majorities in favor of tougher restrictions on gun purchases after the killing of schoolchildren in Newtown, Connecticut, in 2012, Congress failed to act.

Finally, separating the agenda into domestic and foreign policy components offers a glimpse of Congress's broader and relative legislative action in each domain.[14] As figure 2.3 makes plain, foreign policy issues comprise a relatively small percentage of the postwar policy agenda. There was a slight increase in the attention paid to foreign policy in 2013 and 2014, but congressional attention to foreign policy has remained relatively low in comparison to the domestic agenda, averaging about a fifth of the agenda in recent years.

Viewed more broadly, over the postwar period lawmakers are far more likely to deadlock on domestic policy compared to foreign policy (figure 2.4). In just four Congresses since 1947 has foreign policy deadlock outstripped domestic deadlock (during the Vietnam War in the late 1960s and early 1970s, during the Afghanistan war in 2005, and during the most recent Congress in 2013–2014). Still, although foreign policy has been immunized to some degree from the rising polarization that infects the legislative process today, we do see traces of rising partisanship in the realm of defense, trade, and international affairs. Somewhat remarkably, Congress

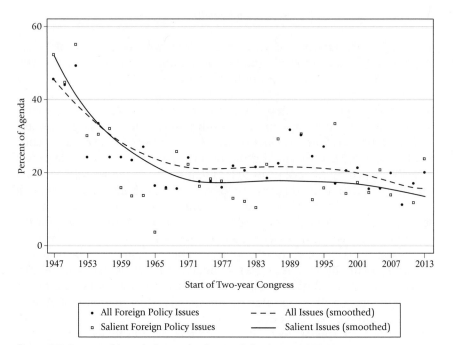

Figure 2.3. Percent of Agenda Devoted to Foreign Policy Issues, 1947–2014

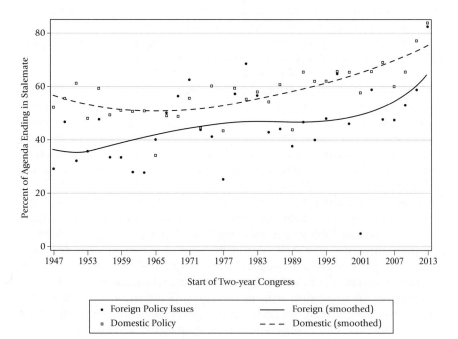

Figure 2.4. Domestic versus Foreign Policy Gridlock (All Issues), 1947–2014

and President Obama stalemated often over domestic and foreign policy in 2013 and 2014. They failed to reach consensus on roughly three-quarters of the most salient issues before Congress during those years. Questions related to negotiating a multination nuclear deal with Iran, sanctioning Russian aggression in the Ukraine and Crimea, addressing the civil war in Syria, the Obama administration's opening of relations with Cuba, and the prospects for new international trade agreements—these and other flash-points inherited the polarized dynamics that infected the domestic policy agenda. Whether this change portends a new pattern for the Trump administration's dealing with Congress or is just an aberration remains to be seen.

EXPLAINING LEGISLATIVE DEADLOCK

In my initial study of legislative stalemate—spanning the Truman through Clinton administrations—unified party control of Congress and the White House significantly reduced the frequency of deadlock. In contrast, split party control of Congress and the White House empowered the opposition party to block policy measures that they opposed, generating higher levels of stalemate in periods of divided party control. Still, I showed in *Stalemate* that party control alone was insufficient to explain variation in Congress and the president's ability to tackle public problems. First, a shrinking political center drove up the frequency of stalemate.[15] The emergence of polarized political parties—even before the Bush and Obama presidencies—complicated the challenge of building coalitions capable of overcoming the veto points institutionalized on Capitol Hill. Second, bicameral policy differences complicated the formation of winning coalitions, even in periods of unified party control.[16] Although electoral and policy differences between the branches tend to garner the most attention in Washington, bicameral policy differences undermined lawmakers' capacity to strike final legislative deals. The 2010 and 2012 congressional elections—handing control of the House to Republicans while keeping the Senate and White House in Democratic hands—generated bicameral conflict that contributed to record levels of deadlock after Obama's first two years in office.

Expanding my purview beyond the initial *Stalemate* study to include the George W. Bush and Obama administrations (through 2014), partisan polarization remains consequential. Declining moderation—controlling for party control and bicameral conflict—still generates more frequent bouts of deadlock. With moderation at barely a tenth of its postwar high, nearly 75 percent of salient issues were mired in deadlock in 2013 and 2014. Regardless of whether we view polarization as a function of ideological differences, strategic disagreement by partisans seeking electoral advantage, or a mix of the two, the results are clear: when ideological or electoral incentives yield intensely partisan behavior, lawmakers and the president struggle to find broadly palatable solutions to the range of problems they face.[17] Counter to the expectations of the American Political Science Association's classic 1951 statement, *Towards a More Responsible Party System*, loyal, cohesive parties undermine rather than facilitate problem solving in Congress.

In contrast, the impact of party control on legislating over the longer period appears attenuated. On average, once we control for the polarized nature of today's parties, unified governments are barely more productive than divided ones. To be sure, unified Democratic control of government after the election of 2008—coupled with a short-lived filibuster-proof Senate majority of sixty Democratic senators—yielded major legislative dividends in 2009 and 2010: Congress and the president crafted the Affordable Care Act, rewired the nation's financial sector in the Dodd-Frank Wall Street Reform Act, advanced major arms control, and dumped the military's "Don't ask don't tell" policy, among other accomplishments. But the impact of unified party control more generally over the longer period is harder to detect.

Why do we observe high levels of deadlock regardless of party control? I suspect that the recent, rising proclivity of opposition party senators to insist on sixty votes for adoption of most amendments and measures has undermined the legislative power of majority parties in periods of unified party control.[18] For example, increased minority party exploitation of its parliamentary rights would help to explain the litany of legislative measures left in limbo after Senate Democrats lost their filibuster-proof majority in the winter of 2010, as well as the heavy load of measures left undone at the close of the Republican-led 108th Congress (2003–2004). Then Minority Leader McConnell's avowal to make Obama a one-term president no doubt helped to undermine the traditional power of unified party control in driving legislative agreements. Refusing to come to the bargaining table undercut the legislative success of the Obama administration.

The results also suggest a weakening of the impact of bicameral differences on the prospects for lawmaking. My measure of bicameral differences (which taps the level of discord when the chambers review the decisions of House-Senate conference committees) is arguably a victim of rising levels of polarization. As shown in figure 2.5, Congress no longer goes to conference to resolve bicameral disagreements. The sharp decline in conferencing partially reflects the overall decline in major lawmaking in Congress. But it also reflects party leaders' and White House staff's proclivity for negotiating deals behind closed doors rather than in the typically more open forum of a House-Senate conference committee.[19] Whatever the reason, the measure no longer offers a robust way to capture the degree of bicameral conflict. In short, the model likely underestimates the impact of bicameral disagreement on Congress's ability to solve problems. After all, we know that the two chambers have taken markedly different approaches to nu-

Figure 2.5. Number of Conference Reports Considered in Both Chambers, 1947–2014

Source: See "Bills Through Conference" section of annual final editions of House Calendars. Calendars for 104th–113th Congresses are available online: https://www.gpo.gov/fdsys/browse/collection.action?collectionCode=BILLS.

merous salient issues in recent years, including climate change, reform of the immigration laws, and repeal of Obamacare and Dodd-Frank. Summed up, electoral, partisan, and institutional forces systematically influence the prospects for major change in Washington, indelibly shaping the legislative interactions of Congress and the president.

LESSONS FROM THE OBAMA YEARS

The relationship between the Obama White House and Congress illustrates the difficulties of governing in a polarized era: the Constitution forces the branches of government to share power, but political and institutional forces today complicate the parties' ability to resolve differences. These lessons offered by the Obama presidency remind us about the power and limits of unified party control of government, as well as the fragility of the concept of bipartisanship in polarized times. Still, the Obama years also remind us that the parties often retain incentives to cooperate despite the intensity of partisan competition in Washington—suggesting a limited but important capacity for deal making, even in a polarized era.

To fully understand the governing challenges faced by the Obama administration, I return to Senator McConnell's vow to make Obama a one-term president. McConnell waited until the fall of 2010 to declare his party's goal. But his party's strategy colored all eight years of Obama's two terms in office. As McConnell stated that fall, "We worked very hard to keep our fingerprints off of these proposals, because we thought—correctly, I think— that the only way the American people would know that a great debate was going on was if the measures were not bipartisan. When you hang the 'bipartisan' tag on something, the perception is that differences have been worked out, and there's broad agreement that that's the way forward." As Ezra Klein of Vox.com summed up McConnell's strategy, "Bipartisanship isn't a function of the ideas in a policy proposal; it's a function of whether the minority party signs on to a policy proposal."[20]

Seeking to prevent bipartisan support for Obama's proposals, House and Senate GOP leaders cajoled rank-and-file Republicans to resist collaborating and negotiating with Democrats on most salient measures.[21] To do otherwise would signal GOP acceptance of Obama's initiatives—if not his presidency. Even on must-pass measures—such as annual spending bills and the periodic requirement that Congress raise the government's legal borrowing limit—GOP leaders stalled until the last minute, hoping (often erroneously) that they would gain leverage by pushing measures to the brink. Moreover, Republican-aligned media (such as Fox News) and other organizations (such as Heritage Action, the activist arm of the conservative Heritage Foundation think tank) pressed Republicans to resist Obama's proposals by highlighting or threatening that lawmakers could face a primary election challenge from their right if they cooperated.

McConnell's strategy paid dividends for Republicans in numerous ways. First, GOP tactics limited the power of unified party control to deliver substantial policy gains to the party in power. During Obama's first two years in office, Republicans largely refused to cooperate in the Democrats' efforts to stimulate the economy in the wake of the worst financial crisis since the Great Depression of the 1930s, to rewire the nation's financial regulatory system, and to revamp the nation's health-care system. Their strategy left Democrats to cobble largely partisan coalitions for the most salient problems on the agenda—exposing them to charges of partisan maneuvering and overreach, even when Democrats adopted proposals that Republicans had previously championed. For example, Democrats based Obamacare largely on "RomneyCare," the health-care model adopted in Massachusetts by future 2012 Republican presidential nominee, Mitt Romney. Similarly, in crafting the Dodd-Frank Wall Street Reform Act, Democrats adopted key proposals from the GOP, including the proposal to force the Federal Reserve to dedicate a steady stream of funding to finance the new Consumer Financial Protection Bureau. Despite their genesis in GOP currents, both programs were relentlessly attacked by Republicans after enactment—leading to legislative efforts to repeal them and legal challenges to their constitutionality.

Second, McConnell's strategy surely contributed to Democrats' loss of the House (2010) and the Senate (2014). Taking advantage of an increasingly partisan electorate—one that often favors Republicans in off-year elections—Republicans recruited a cadre of Tea Party–inspired and other political newcomers who successfully nationalized the midterm elections as referenda on Obama's record. To be sure, fermenting Republican opposition among the electorate also put the party's leadership in the grassroots' crosshairs. Speaker John Boehner (R-OH) and House majority leader Eric Cantor (R-VA) both lost their jobs: Cantor lost his primary election in 2014, and Boehner resigned in the face of a right-wing revolt in his party conference in 2015. Still, the party's opposition to Obama eventually empowered Republicans to take back control of both branches of government, ending a short-lived experiment in Democratic control of government.[22]

Third, McConnell's ploy also empowered Republicans to influence the ideological contour of the Supreme Court even when their party was shut out of the White House. McConnell extended his tactic of resolute opposition to Obama by refusing to allow Senate consideration of the president's pick for the Supreme Court after the sudden death of conservative Justice Antonin Scalia early in 2016. Most Republicans running for reelection in 2016—even those facing voters in states won by Obama in 2012—supported the GOP's refusal to consider or vote on the nomination of US Judge Merrick Garland for the Supreme Court, even though Garland had previously received support from conservative Senate Republicans. Democrats highlighted Republicans' brazen disregard for advice and consent in their widespread unwillingness to even meet with the president's nominee. Although Republicans claimed that the Senate typically refrains from considering Supreme Court nominees during a presidential election year, neutral observers refuted their claims as historically inaccurate and constitutionally suspect.[23] The GOP strategy raised the possibility that future Supreme Court vacancies might only be filled when the president's party controls the Senate.

Still, McConnell's strategy was not entirely cost-free, especially in the realm of advice and consent. Repeated GOP filibusters of executive and judicial branch nominees in 2013 convinced Democrats to curtail filibusters of any nominee save for the Supreme Court—in Senate parlance, known as "going nuclear." The immediate spark was a set of Republican filibusters against three Obama nominees to the DC Court of Appeals in 2013. Some Republicans opposed the nominees on ideological grounds; others admitted that they sought to stop Obama from adding Democratic judges to a circuit evenly balanced with both parties' appointees. More broadly, the battle reflected years of partisan frustration: Democrats added up GOP efforts to block Obama's agenda and his picks for prime appointments and collectively lit the fuse. Democrats went nuclear through a series of procedural motions that created a new interpretation of Senate rules: only fifty-one votes (rather than sixty) would now be required to cut off debate and bring a nomination to an up-or-down vote. McConnell deemed Majority Leader Harry Reid's action a "power grab," calling it "a sad day in the history of the Senate."[24]

By going nuclear, Senate Democrats empowered the president to more fully fill the ranks of the executive branch and the federal courts. Before the Senate went nuclear at the end of 2013, roughly thirty nominees had been confirmed to the federal trial and appellate courts. One year later, nearly one hundred nominees who had either been pending when Democrats went nuclear or nominated afterward were confirmed. Overall, the Senate confirmed 90 percent of the president's judicial nominees in the 113th Congress—a success rate last achieved in the late 1980s. With Republicans back in control of the Senate in 2015 and 2016, confirmation of Obama nominees slowed to a crawl.

Finally, winning back control of the Senate in 2014 led McConnell to revise his playbook for the final two years of the Obama administration. With control of Congress in GOP hands and a wide-open race for the White House approaching in 2016, McConnell adopted a minimally more constructive legislative stance, telling his colleagues that the party needed accomplishments to run on in 2016. "I don't want the American people to think that if they add a Republican president to a Republican Congress, that's going to be a scary outcome. I want the American people to be comfortable with the fact that the Republican House and Senate is a responsible, right-of-center, governing majority," noted McConnell late in 2014.[25]

Toward that end, Republicans in 2015 came to the negotiating table to resolve long-stalemated problems in health, education, and the economy. Among other deal making, the two parties resolved the annual "doc fix" cliffhanger that required changes to Medicare reimbursement formulas, overhauled the long-expired No Child Left Behind education law, negotiated a two-year budget deal to prevent scheduled cuts in domestic and defense funding, and provided long-term funding for federal highway and mass transit programs. In each of these bipartisan bargains, both parties brought to the table their most preferred politics, often crafting "win-win" deals that combined the top priorities of both parties.[26] For example, to finally resolve the "doc fix" stalemate, lawmakers matched Republicans' preference for Medicare cuts with Democrats' desire to expand funding for community health programs. Both parties gained from coming to the negotiating table.

Of course, McConnell encouraged resolution of these long-stalled proposals to ensure that Senate Republicans running for reelection in blue states in 2016 would have a record to run on—confirming as always the power of electoral prospects to condition governing strategies. Although the 2016 elections diminished GOP margins in both chambers, Republicans kept control of Congress and returned the White House to the GOP.

A PREVIEW OF TRUMP AND THE REPUBLICAN CONGRESS

McConnell's strategy no doubt aided the election of Donald Trump in 2016: undermining Obama's legislative accomplishments fueled public dissatisfaction with Washington and with Democrats' capacity to solve public problems. In that sense, McConnell's strategy succeeded: the return of unified GOP control for the first time since 2006 promised Republicans a straight course to achieving McConnell's favored right-of-center agenda, including cutting taxes, repealing Obamacare, and paring back government regulation of the economy. Assisted by Democrats' ban on filibustering most presidential nominations, Republicans stood poised at the outset of 2017 to reverse Obama's policy legacy. And having prevented Obama from filling Justice Scalia's Supreme Court seat, Republicans anticipated solidifying the conservative bent of the nation's highest court.

The election of Trump, however, threw a wrench into McConnell's expectation of a center-right governing majority. To be sure, many of Trump's priorities overlapped with conservatives'—including tax cuts, deregulation, and repeal of Obamacare. But major components of Trump's electoral appeal were ideologically anathema to conservative lawmakers: favoring protectionism over free trade, fiscal stimulus over deficit cuts, saving rather than remaking entitlements, disengagement from rather than proactive leadership of international affairs, and reconciling with rather than challenging despotic Russian leader Vladimir Putin. Over the course of the transition after the November elections, tensions among GOP elites aired publicly as Trump assembled his administration and as some Republicans staked out positions that challenged Trump's priorities. At the same time, most Republicans—particularly in the House—dismissed concerns raised by Democrats and ethics experts: if the Trumps failed to sell off their businesses, conflicts of interest posed by the confluence of the Trump family's private interests and public responsibilities would likely ensue.

How will these tensions shape the relationship between the Trump White House and Congress? Trump's often erratic and unpredictable positions—coupled with a lack of governing experience in his cabinet and White House—make predictions foolhardy. Several reports during the transition, for example, noted that Republican lawmakers feared retribution from Trump and his army of social media supporters should they challenge Trump's agenda.[27] Still, basic electoral and institutional forces are likely to continue to shape Trump's legislative relations. First, although unified party control packs a far less powerful punch than it did before the recent marked rise in polarization, GOP control of both branches should generate legislative dividends for Republicans (especially for measures immunized from filibusters). Second, when Republicans' and Trump's agendas overlap on conservative priorities, we should expect continued partisan polarization, complicating legislative change if Democrats exploit their parliamentary rights to derail majority proposals. So long as polarization is driven by sheer partisan team play—in which the opposition party objects to proposals endorsed by the president—then extreme partisanship will continue to lead to unprecedented levels of deadlock. Third, Trump's often divisive rhetoric and historically weak popular appeal for an incoming president guarantee difficulty in building large bipartisan majorities. Finally, disagreements among Republicans—about how to replace Obamacare, confront Russia, revise taxes, and so forth—almost guarantee bicameral stumbling blocks. Despite new governing majorities, legislative stalemate—even if broken initially in 2017—is likely to remain high.

All that said, could Trump's right-leaning populism—reinforced by several of his key White House advisors—break up ideological divisions in American politics that today reinforce differences between the two political parties? To dissolve that tense partisanship, Democrats would have to find common cause with the Trump White House on a set of policies that lean toward Democrats' policy interests, such as massive new investments in rebuilding the nation's infrastructure. Whether Hill Republicans will buy into the more populist and protectionist issues that Trump campaigned on and whether Democrats could put aside the decidedly illiberal nature of Trump's populism remain to be seen. More likely, the broad-umbrella nature of America's two major political parties can weather a good deal of ideological dissent within each party tent. Moreover, strong party competition for control of Congress and the White House—especially given the GOP's small congressional majorities and Trump's loss of the popular vote by an historic margin—will continue to shape Washington politics. As Frances Lee argues, fierce electoral competition brings control of national institutions within reach for both parties, limiting lawmakers' incentives to compromise with the other party. Party competition in a period of polarized elites is likely to continue to undermine Congress's legislative capacity, even under President Trump.

As we watch the Trump administration and its relationship with Congress take root, we are left in the interim with a national legislature plagued by low legislative capacity. Half-measures, second bests, and just-in-time legislating—or no action at all—are a new norm. Even if President Trump succeeds in getting Washington back on track, Congress's and past presidents' recent difficulties have been costly—both to the long-term fiscal health of the country and to its citizens' trust in government. At the close of the Obama administration, the nation stood at full employment. Regenerating public trust remained a task for the future.

NOTES

1. Glenn Kessler, "When Did McConnell Say He Wanted to Make Obama a 'One-Term President'?" *Washington Post,* September 25, 2012, https://www.washingtonpost.com/blogs/fact-checker/post/when-did-mcconnell-say-he-wanted-to-make-obama-a-one-term-president/2012/09/24/79fd5cd8-0696-11e2-afff-d6c7f20a83bf_blog.html?utm_term=.f268219c39f3, accessed December 25, 2016.

2. David R. Mayhew, *Divided We Govern* (New Haven, CT: Yale University Press, 1991, 2005).

3. See V. O. Key, *Politics, Parties and Pressure Groups* (New York: Ty Crowell, 1964), 688.

4. See James L. Sundquist, "Needed: A Political Theory for the New Era of Coalition Government in the United States," *Political Science Quarterly* 103 (1988–89): 613–35.

5. Mayhew, *Divided We Govern,* 36.

6. See David Mayhew, "Datasets and Materials: Divided We Govern," http://davidmayhew.commons.yale.edu/datasets-divided-we-govern, accessed December 31, 2016.

7. See Keith Krehbiel, *Pivotal Politics* (Chicago: University of Chicago Press, 1998). For a similar approach, see David Brady and Craig Volden, *Revolving Gridlock* (Boulder, CO: Westview Press, 1998).

8. See Sarah A. Binder, "Dynamics of Legislative Gridlock, 1947–2000," *American Political Science Review* 93 (1999): 519–33; and Sarah A. Binder, *Stalemate* (Washington, DC: Brookings Institution Press, 2003).

9. Frances E. Lee, *Insecure Majorities: Congress and the Perpetual Campaign* (Chicago: University of Chicago Press, 2016).

10. Binder, *Stalemate,* chapter 3.

11. Binder, *Stalemate,* chapter 3.

12. I discuss the methodological challenges of updating the dataset in the appendix (pp. 20–22) to Sarah A. Binder, "Polarized We Govern," *Governance Studies Strengthening American Democracy Series,* no. 86 (May 2014), http://www.brookings.edu/research/papers/2014/05/27-polarized-we-govern-congress-legislative-gridlock-polarized-binder, accessed December 27, 2016.

13. Gabe Rubin, "Fed Is a 'Piggy Bank' for Highway Bill," *Morning Consult,* December 2, 2015, http://morningconsult.com/2015/12/fed-is-a-piggy-bank-for-highway-bill, accessed December 27, 2016.

14. I categorize the substantive content of each issue according to the major policy codes developed by the Policy Agendas Project. Any issue touching on international trade, foreign policy, or defense is coded as "foreign policy"; all other

issues are coded as "domestic policy." For policy codes, see http://comparative agendas.s3.amazonaws.com/codebookfiles/Topics_Codebook_2014.pdf, accessed December 30, 2016.

15. To capture legislative moderation, I built a measure of the size of the political center based on voting scores generated by Keith Poole and Howard Rosenthal's NOMINATE system. As detailed in *Stalemate*, I determined the number of "moderate" legislators in each chamber of each Congress, and divided the percentage of moderates by the ideological distance between the two chamber parties. I then averaged both chambers' moderation to create a single moderation score for each Congress. I define "moderate" as a legislator whose first-dimension DW-NOMINATE ideological score places him or her closer to the ideological median of the chamber than to their own party's median. Dividing by party distance helps to distinguish Congresses both by the size and relative location of the political center. For instance, a Congress with a small political center coupled with ideologically proximate parties would score stronger on the "moderation" scale than a Congress with a small political center but ideologically distant parties.

16. To capture the policy distance between the two chambers, I identified all conference reports considered by both the House and Senate in each Congress and determined the percentage of each chamber that voted in support of each report. To measure bicameral policy distance, I calculated the difference in chamber support for each report and generated a mean disagreement score for each Congress. The measure varied from a low of just 2 percent in the early 1950s to a high of over 10 percent in the mid-1990s.

17. On strategic disagreement as a cause of deadlock, see John Gilmour, *Strategic Disagreement: Stalemate in American Politics* (Pittsburgh: University of Pittsburgh Press, 1995).

18. See Steven S. Smith, *The Senate Syndrome: The Evolution of Procedural Warfare in the Modern U.S. Senate* (Norman: University of Oklahoma Press, 2014).

19. The willingness to filibuster the Senate motions needed to go to conference also hamstrings the use of conference proceedings to resolve differences.

20. Ezra Klein, "Obamacare Didn't Pave the Way for Donald Trump. The GOP's Response to It Did," *Vox.com*, March 9, 2016, http://www.vox.com/policy-and-pol itics/2016/3/9/11182590/obamacare-donald-trump, accessed December 30, 2016.

21. For a full treatment of the Republican strategy and its normative and empirical consequences, see Thomas E. Mann and Norman J. Ornstein, *It's Even Worse Than It Looks* (New York: Basic Books, Revised, expanded edition, 2016).

22. The tenure of unified Democratic control was somewhat shorter than historical trends for both parties in the duration of single party control. See Sarah A. Binder, "Ten More Years of Republican Rule?" *Perspectives on Politics* 3, no. 3 (September 2005): 541–43.

23. See, for example, Lauren Carroll, "Mitch McConnell Exaggerates 'Tradition' of Not Confirming Election Year Supreme Court Nominees," *Politifact*, March 22, 2016, http://www.politifact.com/truth-o-meter/statements/2016/mar/22/mitch-mcconnell/ mitch-mcconnell-exaggerates-tradition-not-confirmi/, accessed December 31, 2016.

24. Paul Kane, "Reid, Democrats Trigger 'Nuclear' Option; Eliminate Most Filibusters on Nominees," *Washington Post*, November 21, 2013, https://www .washingtonpost.com/politics/senate-poised-to-limit-filibusters-in-party-line-vote

-that-would-alter-centuries-of-precedent/2013/11/21/d065cfe8-52b6-11e3-9fe0-fd 2ca728e67c_story.html, accessed March 17, 2016.

25. Paul Kane, "New Senate Majority Leader's Main Goal for GOP: Don't Be Scary," *Washington Post*, January 4, 2015, https://www.washingtonpost.com/politics/new -senate-majority-leaders-main-goal-for-gop-dont-be-scary/2015/01/04/80d27196 -9074-11e4-a900-9960214d4cd7_story.html?utm_term=.bf4839e56570, accessed December 30, 2016.

26. On the politics of achieving bipartisan agreements, see Sarah A. Binder and Frances E. Lee, "Making Deals in Congress," in Nathaniel Persily, ed., *Solutions to Political Polarization in America* (New York: Cambridge University Press, 2015).

27. Rachel Bade, "Trump Posse Browbeats Hill Republicans," *Politico*, December 21, 2016, http://www.politico.com/story/2016/12/donald-trump-congress-republi cans-232800, accessed December 31, 2016.

CHAPTER 3

Party Brands, Elections, and Presidential-Congressional Relations

David R. Jones

Often, the behavior of Congress on issues of concern to the White House can be easily explained by a simple but elegant theory: that each member of Congress acts in ways that help strengthen their personal reputation within their constituency. Such behaviors include demonstrating attentiveness to the issue concerns and issue positions of their particular constituents. This theory makes sense, because actions consistent with it are the most likely to guarantee a member's own reelection, while actions that deviate from it in any way run the risk of electoral defeat.

In recent years, however, we see instances of congressional actions that do not seem to be so easily explained. Consider the following three examples of puzzling congressional behavior during the second term of Barack Obama's presidency:

- Why did Republicans, after insisting that Obamacare be defunded as a condition for funding the rest of the government, completely reverse course shortly afterward?
- Why, at a time when the Obama administration's handling of the Ebola virus was a major public concern among both Democratic and Republican constituents,[1] were congressional Democrats significantly more reluctant than Republicans to publicly discuss this issue?
- Why did Republicans, who openly advocated for tougher executive actions against ISIS, refuse to ever schedule a vote to authorize the president's bombing campaign against ISIS in Syria?

While there are certainly many unique factors that help to explain each of these disparate events, it is also true that there is one factor common to them all. In each of these cases, key members of Congress were considering not only how best to burnish their personal reputations; they were also considering how their actions would affect the public reputation of their entire party, or the public reputation of the opposing party. In sum, they were concerned with managing party brands.

This chapter explores the idea that interactions between Congress and the president are often affected by strategies that members of Congress use to boost the favorability of their own party's brand and tarnish the opposing party's brand. The reason that members care about party reputations in addition to their own personal ones is that they recognize that the public's images of the two parties can have important partisan effects in elections. This impacts members directly in their own races, and also indirectly by affecting the chances of their party controlling Congress and the White House. Understanding this dynamic helps explain key interbranch relations in Washington over the past four years pertaining to both domestic and foreign policy issues. It also helps explain the outcomes of the momentous 2014 congressional elections, in which Republicans gained control of the US Senate, and the historic 2016 presidential election, in which Republicans recaptured the White House.

The remainder of this chapter fleshes out these arguments. First, I discuss why party brands affect American elections, and the multiple reasons members have to care about these effects. I also present evidence regarding the electoral effects of party brands, including their impact on the 2014 and 2016 elections. Next, I discuss the major components of party brand reputations, and illustrate how congressional behavior in regard to the executive branch can affect them, using examples from Barack Obama's presidency. Finally, I discuss how the reestablishment of unified party control of government following the 2016 elections is likely to alter how partisan brand management impacts relations between Congress and President Trump.

HOW PARTY BRANDS AFFECT MEMBERS

The Republican Party brand sucks and so people don't want to be a Republican.

—Senator Rand Paul (R-KY)[2]

In seeking to explain congressional behavior, it is important to understand the central goals that motivate members. Congressional scholars generally focus on three such goals that, to varying degrees, each member holds: reelection, influence within Congress, and public policy.[3] If the relative status of the parties' brands had no impact on achievement of these goals, we would have little reason to expect that members of Congress would go out of their way to try to affect these brands. In this section, however, I show that the relative favorability of the public toward the two major party brands does indeed affect the ability of members to achieve these goals. As a result, members have multiple incentives to structure their interactions with the executive branch with an eye to how their actions affect party brand reputations.

I begin with a focus on the reelection goal. The case that parties' overall brand reputations affect individual members' reelection starts with the observation that these elections are not independent of one another. Rather, the electoral fortunes of members of the same party appear to be inexorably linked. In certain election years, for example, Democratic candidates for the House will experience a similar common increase in their vote shares across most districts, and in other years they will experience a common decrease in their vote shares across most districts. The 2014 midterm election was a good example of this phenomenon. Out of all the House seats in which both parties competed in 2012 and 2014, the share of the vote won by the Democratic candidate in 2014 decreased in 84 percent of these districts. This pattern is not unique to 2014. Rather, research suggests it is a regular occurrence.[4]

A main reason that electoral fortunes are significantly shared within a party is that all its candidates share the same party brand label. Political psychologists have found that the image a voter has of a party in turn affects the image that the voter has of any candidate running under that party label, even in the presence of contradictory information about that candidate.[5] This occurs because a party's brand label serves as an "information shortcut" that voters use when assessing candidates.[6] When voters feel more positively about the party generally, this positive feeling transfers to each of that party's candidates. Conversely, when voters feel more negatively about the party, this negativity weighs upon each of that party's candidates. From the perspective of the reelection-oriented member of Congress, the most important scholarly finding is that citizens are more likely to vote to reelect a member of Congress when they are feeling more positively toward that member's party and/or when they are feeling more negatively toward the challenger's party, all else being equal. This finding holds equally true in both House and Senate contests.[7]

The dynamics of the 2014 election illustrate that even over a short period of time, when party brands shift, the vote in the average congressional district shifts in tandem. Specifically, the Associated Press sponsored two election polls during the fall of 2014, one in the last week of September and one three weeks later, in October. Between these two polls, the percentage of Americans with a favorable rating of the Democratic Party dropped from 47 percent to 42 percent. Over the course of these same two surveys, the average reported vote intention in the House race shifted from an even split between the two parties to a six-point Republican advantage.

In addition to reelection, members also desire influence within Congress. There are two main factors that determine how much influence a member has in Congress. One is longevity. While the seniority principle is no longer sacrosanct, in general it is the case that longer-serving members are more likely to ascend to leadership positions within the committee system and within their own party. Of course, the key to longevity in Congress is making sure you continue to get reelected. In this regard, members concerned with influence have the same incentive as reelection-minded members do to care about the status of party brands.

Perhaps more important in determining one's influence in Congress is whether or not one's party is the majority in the chamber. The House of Representatives is so dominated by the majority party that when the Republicans control the House, even the lowliest member of that party probably has more influence over legislation than does the most powerful Democrat. This general pattern of outsized influence for members of the majority party is replicated within the committee system as well. For a significant number of members, a change in which party controls the chamber means the difference between being either the powerful chair of a committee or subcommittee, or the comparatively toothless ranking minority member.

Majority status also affects a member's influence in the Senate, though perhaps to a lesser extent than in the House. A dramatic illustration of this fact took place in May 2001, when Republican Senator Jim Jeffords announced that he would caucus with the Democrats, thereby flipping control of the narrowly divided chamber. Upon hearing the news, Republican Senator Charles Grassley openly wept, because he knew he would lose his chairmanship of the Senate Finance Committee.[8]

These facts demonstrate why members of Congress who care about influence are concerned not only about their own electoral fortunes, but also those of their fellow partisans running for seats in the same chamber. Since each individual member's chances for reelection are influenced by party brands, it is not surprising to find that party brands also affect the overall number of seats a party can expect to win in an election. A study of thirty postwar elections in the House of Representatives finds that a one-point increase in the percentage of Americans with a favorable rating of the Democratic Party produces a gain of about three and a half Democratic seats, and a one-point increase in favorability toward the Republican Party produces a loss of about two Democratic seats.[9] Put simply, parties win more seats in Congress when their party brand is rated more favorably, and when the opposing party's brand is rated less favorably.

In an era of closely divided chambers, the loss of even a handful of seats can mean the difference between majority and minority status.[10] Senate Democrats learned this lesson the hard way during the 2014 election cycle. In early September, survey-based projections of every individual Senate race by HuffPost Pollster showed that Democrats were favored in enough races to retain narrow control of the chamber. But as September turned to October, the poll numbers for many Democratic candidates for Senate around the country began to sink almost in tandem. Within the span of less than two weeks, Democratic leads in Arkansas, Alaska, and Colorado all shifted to tied races, then to Republican leads. Eventually, all three of these key races were won by Republican candidates, flipping control of the chamber from Democrats to Republicans. Many other Democrats in less competitive races saw their poll numbers decline as well. While it is impossible to be certain what the common element in these races was that turned the tide against each Democrat, the timing coincides nearly precisely with a similar decline in overall favorability ratings for the Democratic Party. Polls from the Associated Press, Gallup, Fox News, and ABC/*Washington Post* all showed a drop in public favorability toward Democrats during this election period. In theory, if the Democratic Party had been able to maintain the higher level of favorability that it held in early September, Democrats might have retained control of the Senate majority—and their committee and subcommittee chair positions.[11]

The third goal that members of Congress hold is for government policy to reflect their own views. Members are, of course, more able to shape public policy when they win reelection—thus securing at least a vote on legislation. In addition to this, members who are interested in public policy outcomes also need to be concerned with whether their own party holds a majority in each chamber of Congress. House Speaker Paul Ryan made this point during the 2016 election when he warned of the different reception that budget bills from the House would get in the Senate depending on which party won control of that chamber:

> If we keep control of the Senate in the Republican hands . . . a nice guy named Mike Enzi from Wyoming is the Senate budget chair and he helps us get these budgets to the president's desk, gets these tax bills through. . . . If we lose the Senate, do you know who becomes chair of the Senate Budget Committee? A guy named Bernie Sanders.[12]

Academic studies support this same point about the policy importance of chamber control. In both the House and the Senate, when Democrats have a majority, a greater percentage of the bills that pass would move policy to the left ideologically, and when Republicans have the majority, a greater percentage of bills that pass would move policy to the right.[13] Therefore, anything that affects party control of Congress will also affect the policy output of Congress.

But government policies are not determined by Congress alone. At least equally important is the occupant of the White House. In 2015, congressional Republicans were able to use their majority status to pass bills to approve the Keystone XL pipeline and to repeal Obamacare in both the House and Senate. However, President Obama was able to prevent achievement of these policy goals through the use of his veto power. Furthermore, President Obama was able to use executive actions and orders to implement other policy changes supported by Democrats and opposed by Republicans, including protecting certain undocumented immigrants from being deported, and raising the minimum wage for federal contractors. As these examples show, members of Congress are much more likely to achieve their policy goals when they have a president from their own party.

Because party control of the presidency is crucial for accomplishing policy goals, members of Congress have an incentive to try to affect the outcome of presidential elections. Two years before the 2012 presidential election, the Republicans' leader in the Senate, Mitch McConnell, was very up-front about this fact, stating,

> Some have said it was indelicate of me to suggest that [Senate Republicans'] top political priority over the next two years should be to deny President Obama a second term in office. But the fact is, if our primary legislative goals are to repeal and replace the health spending bill; to end the bailouts; cut spending; and shrink the size and scope of government, the only way to do all these things is to put someone in the White House who won't veto any of these things.[14]

In corresponding fashion, Democrats had an equally strong policy motivation to try to help ensure that President Obama remained in office.

Since members of Congress have a policy incentive to care about presidential elections, this also means that they have yet another reason to care about the popularity of the Democratic and Republican Party brands. Research shows that even after accounting for factors such as individuals' party identification and their evaluation of the nation's economy, the more favorable impression people have of the Democratic Party, the more likely they are to vote for the Democratic candidate for president, and the more favorable impression they have of the Republican Party, the more likely they are to vote for the Republican candidate for president.[15]

Evidence suggests that a drop in the favorability of the Democratic Party brand may have played a role in Hillary Clinton's relatively poor performance in the 2016 presidential election. Four years earlier, in 2012, CNN's final poll before the election showed the Democratic Party with a favorability rating of 52 percent. But in 2016, CNN's final preelection measure found the Democratic Party with a favorability rating of only 47 percent—five points lower than in 2012. This decline in the Democratic Party's favorability rating was reflected in a similar drop in its nominee's popular vote margin: in 2012 the Democratic nominee outpolled the Republican by four points, but in 2016 this margin was cut in half to only two points. Although two points may not seem like a big difference, in this instance the loss of votes was enough that it probably cost Hillary Clinton a victory in the electoral college.[16]

Overall, members of Congress have multiple reasons to care about the public's impression of each party's brand. A more favorable brand for one's own party or a less favorable brand for the opposition party can improve the chances that a member will win reelection, attain more power within the chamber, and achieve cherished policy goals. If there are ways that members can act to affect the parties' brand reputations, we have good reason to expect that they will attempt to do so.

HOW MEMBERS AFFECT PARTY BRANDS

> Our brand's been battered over the past year and a half . . . by a lot of these people [in my party]. . . . They're political amateurs. I had some good friends, good friends, who were at the center of this shutdown strategy. I disagreed with them not because of ideology, just because of dumb tactics.
>
> —Former Congressman Joe Scarborough (R-FL)[17]

The image that Americans have of a party is formed, to a significant degree, by impressions they have of the representatives of that party serving in Congress and (if applicable) in the White House. While some of these impressions are shaped by national and world events that are largely out of the control of these political actors, others are clearly shaped by their own choices. In turn, as noted at the beginning of this chapter, the choices these actors make are sometimes dominated by narrow calculations about the actor's own constituency and personal preferences, but at other times may factor in broader considerations about effects on party brands.

In this section, I focus on two general dimensions of party brands that can be shaped by the choices members of Congress make.[18] First, a party's brand is affected by the degree to which that party seems competent in running the branches of government that it controls. Therefore, parties have an incentive to act in ways that protect their own reputation for competence and impugn that of the opposing party. Second, a party's brand is stronger when the issue positions associated with its representatives in office are more popular among the general public. Therefore, a party has an incentive to promote certain issues and craft specific narratives that give it a relative advantage over the opposing party.

Party Competence

For many Americans, politics is too complicated or uninteresting enough to follow closely. They don't have a well-defined ideology or even strong positions on many issues. In many respects, these Americans may not be interested in *how* government decides to address the nation's problems so much as in *whether* it does so. They want to know: is government effective at its job—in other words, is government competent? Not coincidentally, two variables that best explain variation in party brand favorability are the degree to which Americans approve of the job the president is doing and the job Congress is doing. The president is the most salient representative of his party, and thus plays an outsized role in shaping its brand reputation.[19] Stronger presidential approval helps the favorability of the party in the White House and, to a lesser extent, harms the favorability of the non-presidential party. Reflecting the public's implicit understanding that the majority party largely controls Congress, stronger congressional approval substantially helps the favorability of majority parties, but provides only a minimal boost to minority parties.[20] As such, each party has an incentive to try to maintain a reputation for competence in running the branches of government it controls, and to harm the opposing party's reputation for competence in running the branches it controls.

There are two main clues the public uses to assess competence in government. One is the public's impression of the functional competence of a government entity: can it successfully perform the basic tasks and responsibilities of its job? The other is the public's impression of the outcome effectiveness of government: is society better off or worse off? While these two indicators sometimes go hand in hand, this does not necessarily have to be the case: government can be humming along smoothly, but outcomes nevertheless turn sour; government can be at a standstill, but without serious impact on outcomes.

Research is consistent with the idea that functional competence in government is an important component of party brand reputations. When the president is successful in achieving his legislative goals, public approval of the president increases.[21] Approval of Congress may also increase when a larger portion of the legislative agenda passes.[22] In turn, the functional competence of each branch is likely to affect the brand of the party controlling that branch. For example, when Americans give Congress a low grade for "tackling key issues," they are significantly less favorable toward the majority party in Congress. However, favorability toward the minority party does not decline, indicating that the public does not view the minority as responsible for congressional shortcomings in this regard.[23]

One crucial test of a party's functional competence in office is its ability to pass key legislation to keep the government running. In particular,

Congress is responsible for appropriating funds to pay for government operations, and increasing the debt ceiling (when necessary) to allow such payments to be made. These are minimum requirements for governance, because if they are not done, the government shuts down. Whenever a party that has control over one branch or chamber is viewed as refusing to live up to its responsibility in this area, this has the potential to affect its reputation for competent governance.

A good example of the importance of functional competence for party brands occurred during the government shutdown and debt limit crises of October 2013. Congress faced a deadline of October 1 to either pass regular appropriations bills or a stopgap continuing resolution to fund government operations. It also faced a second deadline of October 17 to raise or suspend the federal debt ceiling; otherwise the government would begin to default on its debt obligations. As the first deadline approached in late September without a regular budget, the Republican-controlled House passed a bill on September 20 to continue spending at current levels, but with an added provision defunding the president's health-care law, the Affordable Care Act (ACA, or "Obamacare"). This House bill was supported by all but one Republican and opposed by all but two Democrats. Immediately, Senate Democrats and President Obama made clear that they would support only a "clean" continuing resolution without any special provisions rolling back Obamacare. On September 27, the Democratic-controlled Senate passed a clean continuing resolution, stripped of the anti-Obamacare amendment. This Senate bill was supported by every Democrat and opposed by every voting Republican. The Republican leadership in the House refused to bring the Senate bill to the floor for an up or down vote. Without any new funding authority, the government entered a shutdown on October 1. All but the most critical federal government operations were forced to stop.

The failure to avert a government shutdown had a dramatic effect on party brands—particularly for the Republican Party. A Gallup poll conducted during the first week of the shutdown found favorable views of the Republican Party had fallen ten points since the month before the shutdown, to 28 percent—the lowest level for either party since Gallup began measuring party favorability in 1992. The Democratic Party's favorable rating also fell during the same period, but only by four points, to 43 percent.[24] The larger impact on Republicans can be attributed to the fact that the Democratic-controlled Senate and White House appeared willing to continue the status quo to keep government operating, while the Republican-controlled House appeared more concerned with its anti-Obamacare position. Accordingly, polling during this period shows that a majority of Americans blamed the shutdown specifically on congressional Republicans.[25]

This negative effect of the 2013 shutdown on the Republican Party brand helps explain why the Republican leadership ultimately reversed course on this issue, despite opposition from its own rank-and-file membership. On October 16, House Speaker John Boehner brought to the floor a bill to fund the government at current levels into early 2014 without any substantial concessions on Obamacare, and to temporarily suspend the debt limit— almost exactly what President Obama had been requesting from the beginning. News coverage of this event made clear that the overriding reason the Republican leadership changed its tune was that it viewed its responsibility not simply as supporting its members' immediate policy positions, but also as protecting the party's overall reputation from further damage.[26] Passing this bill served to minimize the damage by removing the issue from the agenda, allowing Congress to move on to topics that were more favorable for Republicans. Indeed, by early December 2013, Republicans had already gained back half of the drop in favorability that they experienced in the Gallup poll during the shutdown.

So searing was the lesson learned from the shutdown, the Republican leadership was determined to avoid a similar scenario occurring in proximity to a national election. In late October 2015, Speaker Boehner sent to the floor a two-year budget bill that increased spending limits and suspended the debt limit until after the 2016 election. A key Boehner ally, Representative Tom Cole, explained the logic: "The most important thing we can do for the Republican presidential nominee is to . . . make sure we're not talking about government shutdowns and cliffs and crises while the American people are making their final decision on who ought to be the next president."[27] It is impossible to know for certain what effect this strategic decision had on the election. But given how close the results were—and how damaging the 2013 shutdown was to the Republican brand—it seems entirely possible that it did help clear a path for Donald Trump to capture the White House.

Just as functional competence is an important component of party brands, so is outcome effectiveness. This component is particularly important for the president's party. Rightly or wrongly, the American public views the president as the person in government who is most responsible for the nation's well-being, particularly regarding economic prosperity and physical security. When outcomes in these areas are viewed as unacceptable, the president's approval rating suffers, especially on topics that are salient to Americans.[28] Since the president's ratings affect his party's overall brand, members of Congress from the party that does not control the White House have an incentive to raise the public profile of national problems that the president has not been effective in "solving"—regardless of whether or not the president is really responsible for these problems.

The issue of the Ebola virus provides a good example of members of Congress emphasizing problematic outcomes in order to depress the presidential party's brand. On September 30, 2014, the Centers for Disease

Control (CDC) announced the first human Ebola case in the United States. Congressional Republicans and Republicans running for Congress quickly seized on this news and began to mention the issue prominently in their public statements, emphasizing President Obama's failure to keep Americans safe.[29] In turn, research shows that "media coverage increased as candidates commented about Ebola."[30] In contrast, congressional Democrats seemed to hope the issue would go away if they just ignored it. According to a study of congressional newsletters in this period, 82 percent of the newsletters mentioning Ebola came from Republican members of Congress while only 18 percent came from Democrats. The study concluded that "recent Ebola anxiety was driven by partisan politics."[31] A similar partisan pattern emerged in terms of congressional hearing activity. Despite being in the middle of the campaign season—when members typically prefer to be in their districts—the Republican-controlled House of Representatives convened two separate congressional hearings in October to investigate the Obama administration's handling of Ebola. No Ebola hearings were held in the Democratic-controlled Senate until after the election.

Polling data suggest that Republican efforts to promote the idea that Ebola was a grave failure of the Obama administration were effective in damaging Democrats' brand image. Before the deluge of Republican rhetoric and activity on Ebola in October, a September Gallup poll found the Democratic Party with a slight edge in favorability over the Republican Party, 42 to 40 percent. By early November, Gallup reported that favorability toward the Democratic Party had dropped six points to 36 percent—its lowest level ever in Gallup polling. Over the same period, in contrast, the Republican Party's brand favorability edged up two points to 42 percent—the first time in over three years it rated more highly than the Democratic Party's brand. In its analysis, Gallup explicitly cited public perceptions of the Obama administration's handling of the Ebola issue as one clear cause of Democrats' relative decline.[32]

As each of these examples demonstrates, members of Congress strategically adjust their behavior vis-à-vis the president in an effort to try to lower the salience of issues that could damage their party's reputation for competent governance, and raise the salience of issues that could damage the opposing party's reputation for competent governance.

Party Issue Alignment

While it is often easier for Americans to evaluate parties on the basis of functional competence and outcome effectiveness, the public also cares about the actual policy positions advocated by each party. Research shows that the greater the distance between a citizen's ideological position and that of congressional Republicans, the less favorable that citizen is toward them. Similarly, the further a citizen is from congressional Democrats, the less favorable she is toward them.[33] Because most Americans are relatively moderate ideologically, parties that care about the popularity of their brand need to avoid a reputation for ideologically extreme positions. Historical data on party brands demonstrate that since the 1950s, the more conservative the average congressional Republican is, the lower the favorability of the Republican Party; and the more liberal the average congressional Democrat is, the lower the favorability of the Democratic Party.[34] As a result, whenever a policy problem gets onto the public agenda, members of Congress have an incentive to try to ensure that their policy response appears mainstream, at least relative to the opposing party's position.

There are a couple of different ways that parties can affect how reasonable their policy positions, and those of the opposing party, appear to the public. Each of these techniques takes into account the fact that most Americans are not policy experts. The public possesses a limited capacity and desire for learning about and processing nuanced policy arguments.[35] Instead, Americans are more likely to make up their minds about the wisdom of a particular policy option based on simple cues they receive from the parties. Party leaders understand this, and their brand-management strategies account for it. When the parties do battle over policy, they are not simply choosing policy positions, they are also defining for the public what the central issue at stake is, and what each position means in a publicly digestible way.[36]

One way parties can send easily interpretable cues to citizens about the reasonableness of a policy option is to shoehorn the current policy problem into an existing narrative or stereotype that the public already identifies with a party. Each party prefers a narrative that taps into something that the public already likes or trusts about it, or dislikes or distrusts about the opposition.[37] It is possible to illustrate such techniques by returning to the Ebola case discussed earlier.

Once the Ebola issue was firmly on the public agenda in October 2014, each party tried to define the terms of the debate in a way to make its own position seen reasonable and the opposing party's position seem extreme. As their proposed policy solution, Republicans in Congress called on president Obama to impose a ban on all travel between the United States and the West African countries affected by Ebola. This proposal was useful politically because it shifted the focus of the debate to the topic of border security. If the solution to the Ebola problem was securing the border, this would advantage Republicans because the public traditionally views Republicans as more "tough" than Democrats on border security. Indeed, the travel ban's focus on borders put congressional Democrats in the awkward position of either agreeing with the proposal (thus implicitly agreeing that the Democratic president had been too weak), or trying to explain why they were still opposed to stricter border controls even during a possible public health crisis (therefore confirming the existing partisan stereotype). Republican rhetoric explicitly played on this stereotype of Democratic weakness on border security. For example, Representative Louie Gohmert suggested that Democrats opposed the ban because it wasn't "politically correct," stating, "some of my Democratic friends, including this president, they want everyone to feel included. So [they say], 'let's don't quarantine, let's don't close our borders.'"[38]

For their part, Democrats—when they felt compelled to comment at all on this issue—sought to shift the debate away from border security and toward a focus on the importance of federal funding for programs to control and prevent diseases. If the solution to the Ebola problem was funding social programs, this would advantage Democrats because Democrats have a reputation for supporting social spending programs while Republicans have a reputation for cutting them. Accordingly, Democrats in Congress tried to feed into this partisan stereotype by reminding Americans that Republicans were responsible for budgets that reduced funding for both the CDC and the National Institutes of Health (NIH). For example, during a hearing on Ebola, Democratic Representative Henry Waxman cast blame on Republicans by noting that recent cuts to the CDC and NIH were a result of budget sequestration, "and those who allowed that sequestration to happen by closing the government have to answer to the American people."[39]

Ultimately, the parties' political strategies regarding brand management probably had an impact on the actual policies put in place by Congress and the White House. Despite Obama's arguments that travel restrictions were counterproductive, under increasing political pressure from Republicans he eventually imposed some restrictions—for example, requiring passengers originating from affected countries to fly into specific US airports with screening facilities. And, contrary to Republicans' traditional desire to limit spending on foreign aid, after being attacked by Democrats for not putting their money where their mouth was, Republicans eventually approved more than $3.7 billion in funding for the international response to Ebola.[40]

Besides playing to partisan stereotypes, a second way that parties can send easily interpretable cues to citizens about the reasonableness of a policy option is by affecting the level of bipartisan support for that option. Because most Americans do not follow the details of policy debates, it is not always a policy's content that they use to judge how well it represents their preferences. Instead, particularly for more confusing issues, Americans will often form their judgments about a policy based in part on how their elected officials—who presumably know more about these things—line up for or against it. If a policy proposal produces rancor and disagreement between the two parties in Congress, then the public will view it to be controversial, and therefore likely too extreme or unreasonable. On the other hand, if a policy proposal garners the support of members of both parties, the public will assume that it must be a reasonable, moderate policy compromise. Members of Congress understand that this is a cognitive shortcut citizens use. Senator Mitch McConnell himself has noted that "when you hang the 'bipartisan' tag on something, the perception is that differences have been worked out."[41]

Not surprisingly, then, partisan support or opposition to the president's policy proposals affects how favorably the public views the president.[42] When the opposition party signals bipartisan support for the president, the public assumes his positions are reasonable and so his favorability ratings tend to rise. When the opposition party signals strong partisan disagreement with the president, the public assumes his policies are unreasonable, and so his favorability ratings tend to fall. (Interestingly, the opposition party in Congress does not appear to suffer any overall decrease in its favorability rating when it disagrees with the president.) Finally, when some members of the president's own party join the other party in their criticism of the president, signaling bipartisan opposition to the president's position, the public assumes the policy is even more extreme, and his ratings decline even further. In turn, as discussed earlier, since the president is the most salient representative of his party, presidential approval ratings are the most important factor determining his party's brand reputation.

From the perspective of the opposition party, regardless of whether or not they have sincere ideological disagreements with the president or whether they have the numerical strength to defeat his policies, they have an incentive to avoid supporting him so they don't inadvertently improve his party's reputation for having reasonable policies. In cases where the opposition party has difficulty disputing the president's position on its policy merits, it has an incentive to find other nonpolicy reasons for opposing it (e.g., "now is not the time . . ."), or to otherwise suppress that issue from the agenda. From the perspective of the president and his party, every effort should be made to coax the opposition into supporting the president, or, absent an explicit vote to the contrary, claim that bipartisan support exists behind closed doors.

One example of this dynamic took place over the issue of an authorization for use of military force (AUMF) against ISIS. In September 2014, Obama announced that he intended to use air strikes against ISIS in Syria. Significant questions were raised about whether or not the president had the constitutional power to do this based on an old AUMF that predated ISIS. When pressed by reporters about whether new authority was needed, Speaker Boehner originally did not claim otherwise, stating that having Congress vote on a new AUMF "would be in the nation's interest."[43] Obama said he would "welcome congressional support."[44] The question, then, was whether the Republican-controlled House would actually go forward with a vote to explicitly grant him that authority. Based purely on policy considerations, one would expect Republicans to want to do so. Republicans are historically more hawkish on foreign policy than are Democrats, and many Republicans had been repeatedly criticizing Obama for his timidity regarding ISIS.

Despite an AUMF for ISIS seeming to be a good policy fit for Republicans, the Republican leadership steadfastly refused to bring such a measure to the House floor. The stated reasons for this refusal appeared to be somewhat inconsistent. Initially, Boehner said it was not appropriate to do so until the president submitted a formal request to Congress, although having Congress craft its own AUMF was not without precedent. Senate Democrats quickly wrote their own AUMF and reported it out of the Foreign Relations Committee. In February 2015, Obama did submit a draft AUMF request to Congress, just as Boehner had suggested. Even though Boehner had previously stated that Congress had no role to play in determining the language of the authorization, he now said that he would not call for a vote because the request was not written broadly enough. Meanwhile, in the new Republican-controlled Senate, Majority Leader Mitch McConnell justified not holding a vote by stating, "The president does not have a strategy in place. So it'd be hard to figure out how to authorize a non-strategy."[45] Seeming to contradict both himself and Boehner, McConnell later introduced his own broad authorization proposal, but he never brought this bill up for a vote either.

While there are several reasons Republicans might not have wanted to vote on an AUMF for ISIS, one important reason seemed to be a desire to avoid displaying bipartisan support for Obama's ISIS policy. During this time, polls showed "obvious public ambivalence" regarding the wisdom of Obama's course of action.[46] If an AUMF bill came to a vote and received significant Republican support, the public might infer that Obama's ISIS policy was more reasonable than they currently did. Both sides in Washington seemed aware of the importance for Obama and the Democrats to have the appearance of bipartisan support. When Obama began bombing in Syria in September, he tried to gloss over Congress's inaction on AUMF, stating, "I've spoken to leaders in Congress, and I'm pleased that there's bipartisan support for the actions that we're taking."[47] Later, after sending his AUMF request to Congress, he said he was committed to "working with the Congress to pass a bipartisan authorization."[48] On the Republican side, during the same time period in which they were declining to hold a vote on any AUMF, they continued to loudly criticize Obama's policy in the press. This prompted Democratic Representative Marcia Fudge to opine that "the majority doesn't want to take a stand. They want to complain, and tear down, and talk about the president's policy. But they don't want to put forth a policy." Many media accounts agreed that Republicans' desire to maintain the ability to criticize Obama's policy on ISIS played a significant role in the behavior of the Republican leadership regarding AUMF.[49]

This strategy on AUMF appeared to pay dividends for Republicans during the 2016 presidential campaign. Because congressional Republicans were able to avoid putting their party on record with a vote for or against AUMF, most of their candidates vying for the nomination—including three sitting senators and Donald Trump—were able to continue publicly criticizing Obama's ISIS policy, despite the fact that they offered very little in terms of new proposals.[50]

As they interact with the executive branch, members of Congress have multiple ways in which they can influence public favorability toward each party, which in turn impacts elections. As the examples above make clear, competence and issue alignment are two important dimensions of party brands that the public cares about, and that members try to affect.

I conclude this section with a quote illustrating President Obama's recognition of the power that congressional actors have to shape party brands. Following the 2016 election, Obama was asked why he thought that Hillary Clinton and the rest of his party performed so poorly at the polls. He responded,

> The very deliberate strategy that Mitch McConnell and the Republican Party generally employed during the course of my presidency was effective. What they understood was that, if you embraced . . . bipartisan achievement, people feel better. And if people feel better, then they feel better about the president's party, and the president's party continues [to govern]. [But] if it feels broken, stuck, and everybody is angry, then that hurts the president or the president's party.

In Obama's view, then, brand management strategies pervaded his dealings with Congress, colored public perceptions of his presidency and his party, and ultimately impacted the electoral fortunes of his presumed successor, Hillary Clinton.

IMPLICATIONS FOR TRUMP AND THE 115TH CONGRESS

> [F]rom a political standpoint . . . they own it right now. . . . Obamacare is the Democrats' problem. We are gonna take the problem off the shelves for them. We're doing them a tremendous service by doing it.
>
> —President-elect Donald Trump[51]

As of this writing, the winner of the 2016 election, Donald Trump, has not yet been sworn in. Nevertheless, in the remainder of this chapter I speculate about how concern over party brand reputations may affect interbranch relations between Trump and the 115th Congress. In many respects, the fundamentals of party brand management—discussed above—should continue to hold true despite the somewhat new cast of characters. Nevertheless, context also matters. There are several contextual factors that could theoretically affect partisan brand management. These include variables such as how polarized the American public is, how personally popular the president is, and how electorally competitive the two parties are.[52] One contextual factor that may have the biggest effect on partisan brand management in the 115th Congress is the change from divided to unified party control of the legislative and executive branches.

How does a shift from divided government to unified government affect interbranch relations with respect to brand management? One obvious change regards the competence dimension of party brands. Under divided government, the public is more likely to view responsibility for competent governance as being shared between the two parties.[53] The penalty for perceived functional incompetence within Congress on matters such as passing budgets and raising debt limits probably rests somewhat more on the brand of the majority party in Congress—although the president's party can also suffer a bit of a hit as well. Perceived incompetence on outcomes probably rests more on the shoulders of the president and his party's brand, but a president may be able to slough off at least some responsibility for outcomes when his party does not control Congress. In contrast, under unified government, one party controls both the legislative and executive branches. Therefore, any functional or outcome failures are much more likely to be borne by that party alone.

This suggests that in the 115th Congress, the incentives faced by each party will change. In addition to Republicans' continuing need to be concerned about functional competence within Congress, they will now also have to govern in a manner that they calculate is most likely to produce well-received outcomes. And, rather than using their procedural and communications tools to call attention to outcome failures, as they did under President Obama, they will now have an incentive to try to keep any such problems off the public agenda, or otherwise distract from them. Even though President Trump and his fellow Republicans in Congress may not always see eye to eye, they will have an incentive to work together to make government run more effectively. In contrast, Democrats' strategic position will in some ways benefit from being out of the White House. They will finally be unencumbered by the burden of reacting defensively to national problems that appear in the news every day. Instead, they can use their resources—albeit now more limited—to try to draw attention to issues that can be blamed on the Republican-controlled government. When they do so, they can rest assured that any public frustration in this regard is no longer likely to present dangers to the Democratic brand.

Unified government may also affect interbranch relations in regard to the policy-alignment dimension of party brands. On the one hand, unified government means that the president's party largely controls the legislative agenda. As such, it can more easily suppress issues on which the party is at a relative disadvantage. On the other hand, under unified government the president's party in Congress finds it much more difficult to enforce cohesive support for his policy initiatives. This occurs in part because members can get valuable attention from the news media by criticizing a president from their own party. During divided government, in contrast, the president's party is more cohesive because they face an important common threat in the majority party.[54]

This too carries important implications for the behavior of congressional parties in the 115th Congress. Democrats may not have as easy a time as they did during the Obama years raising the salience of issues that advantage their party. This may give them fewer opportunities to draw issue contrasts with Republicans that benefit their own brand or damage that of Republicans. Instead, they will have to hope that events in the news will help get these issues onto the public's radar. For their part, Republicans will face a much greater challenge sticking together as a party. Over the past eight years, Republicans were largely able to define themselves in opposition to Obama without ever having to articulate their own detailed policy positions. Now without a partisan foil in the White House, Republicans will face the choice of either being associated with a specific Trump policy that may sometimes offend large segments of the public, or disagreeing with Trump, thus signaling to the public that certain Republican policies may be too extreme. In contrast, Democrats will be in a position to steal a page from the Republican playbook of 2009–2010. They can begin to adopt the posture of the "party of no"—uniformly opposing nearly every Trump policy initiative, without having to specify exactly what they would do differently. Adopting this strategy would aid them in making Trump's policies appear to the public to be overly extreme, just as Republicans previously did to Obama's agenda.

One policy area in which many of these changes may manifest themselves is Obamacare. In the past, passing stand-alone bills to repeal Obamacare was essentially cost-free for the Republican brand. When Republican leaders put repeal votes on the agenda, this served to remind Americans that healthcare problems still existed in the country, thus making the Democratic president seem ineffective. When Republicans voted to repeal Obamacare, this helped make Democrats' passage of it seem more radical. Forcing Obama to veto such bills reinforced the notion that he and his party must be responsible for national health-care shortcomings. Further, since Obama's vetoes blocked the repeal from taking effect, the public was not confronted with any consequences of a Republican repeal. But with unified Republican government in place, the strategic environment is fundamentally changed. As Donald Trump's quote at the start of this section astutely notes, if the Republican Congress and President Trump actually repeal Obamacare, the Republican Party will begin to "own" health-care outcomes in the United States. If premiums rise, or health-insurance businesses falter, or people lose their health care, it will be the Republican Party's reputation for competence that will suffer, not that of Democrats. From a policy perspective, if Democrats participated constructively in crafting a replacement, this might benefit many of their core constituencies. But from the perspective of party brands, Democrats have no incentive to help Republicans craft a replacement. Unified Democratic opposition to any new health-care replacement proposed by Republicans would hurt only the GOP brand.

Overall, unified government may prove to be a mixed blessing for the GOP. The party is certainly in an enviable position in terms of its ability to shape public policy. But in terms of brand management, unified government also presents some big challenges for Republicans. If congressional Democrats are strategically savvy, although they will lose many policy battles over the next two years, they could succeed in tarnishing the Republican brand. And by doing so, they may help engineer a Democratic Party resurgence in 2018.

CONCLUSION

This chapter has sought to highlight and illustrate a few important observations about how and why party brands affect presidential-congressional relations. First, members have goals besides their own reelection, and this includes an interest in the electability of fellow partisans in their own chamber, in the opposite chamber, and in the Oval Office. Second, members explicitly view their choices in Congress and their interactions with the president in part through the lens of party brands, perceiving the possible effect of these choices on each party's collective reputation for competent governance and reasonable policy stances. Third, members believe they can make strategic decisions regarding their choices—sometimes counter to their core ideology—in an effort to help their party achieve its shared goals. Finally, different political contexts can alter how easy or difficult it is for members of a party to shape party brand images to their benefit. In particular, unified government may in certain respects provide more brand-management problems for the president's party, and greater opportunities for the out-party. What lies ahead under a Trump presidency with Republican control of both houses of Congress remains to be seen. But while the capture of unified control of government by the GOP may be seen as a huge victory by some, in terms of party brand management it may well be a curse.

NOTES

1. According to a YouGov Poll, October 11–13, 2014, 70 percent of all Americans expressed concern about an Ebola epidemic in the United States, including 63 percent of Democrats.

2. Alexander Bolton, "Rand Paul: The GOP Brand 'Sucks,'" *The Hill*, October 29, 2014, http://thehill.com/homenews/222250-rand-paul-gop-brand-sucks.

3. Richard F. Fenno, *Congressmen in Committees* (New York: Little, Brown, 1973), 1.

4. Gary W.Cox and Mathew D. McCubbins, *Legislative Leviathan: Party Government in the House* (Berkeley: University of California Press, 1993), 112–17.

5. Wendy M. Rahn, "The Role of Partisan Stereotypes in Information Processing about Political Candidates," *American Journal of Political Science* (1993): 472–96.

6. Samuel L. Popkin, *The Reasoning Voter: Communication and Persuasion in Presidential Campaigns* (Chicago: University of Chicago Press, 1994).

7. David R. Jones, "Party Brands and Partisan Tides" (paper presented at the annual meeting of the Midwest Political Science Association, Chicago, IL, April 22–25, 2010).

8. Douglas Waller, "How Jeffords Got Away," CNN, May 28, 2001, http://www.cnn.com/ALLPOLITICS/time/2001/06/04/jeffords.html.

9. David R. Jones, "Party Brand Images and Partisan Tides" (paper presented at the annual meeting of the Southern Political Science Association, New Orleans, LA, January 12–14, 2012).

10. Frances E. Lee, *Insecure Majorities: Congress and the Perpetual Campaign* (Chicago: University of Chicago Press, 2016).

11. Polling data and race projections can be found at elections.huffingtonpost.com.

12. Lindsey McPherson, "Ryan Suggests Tax Overhaul Is First Priority of GOP Agenda," *Roll Call*, October 16, 2016, http://www.rollcall.com/news/politics/ryan-suggests-tax-overhaul-first-priority-gop-agenda.

13. David R. Jones, "Partisan Control of Government and Public Policy," in Marjorie R. Hershey, ed., *Guide to US Political Parties* (Washington, DC: CQ Press, 2014), 353–54; Gary W. Cox and Mathew D. McCubbins, *Setting the Agenda: Responsible Party Government in the U.S. House of Representatives* (New York: Cambridge University Press, 2005), 189; Chris Den Hartog and Nathan W. Monroe, *Agenda Setting in the U.S. Senate: Costly Consideration and Majority Party Advantage* (New York: Cambridge University Press, 2011).

14. Michael O'Brien, "McConnell: GOP's 'Only' Option Is to Defeat Obama in 2012," *The Hill*, November 4, 2010, http://thehill.com/blogs/blog-briefing-room/news/127653-mcconnell-gops-only-option-is-to-defeat-obama-in-2012.

15. David R. Jones, "Partisan Polarization and the Effect of Congressional Performance Evaluations on Party Brands and American Elections," *Political Research Quarterly* 68 (2015): 785–801; Jones, "Party Brands and Partisan Tides."

16. If Clinton had performed only one point better in every state, she would have won the electoral college vote, 278–260. If she had performed two points better in every state, she would have won 307–231.

17. Quoted during his appearance on NBC's *Meet the Press*, November 10, 2013.

18. This is not meant to be an exclusive list.

19. See Frances E. Lee, *Beyond Ideology: Politics, Principles, and Partisanship in the US Senate* (Chicago: University of Chicago Press, 2009).

20. Jones, "Partisan Polarization."

21. Charles W. Ostrom and Dennis M. Simon, "Promise and Performance: A Dynamic Model of Presidential Popularity," *American Political Science Review* 79, no. 2 (1985): 334–58.

22. Sarah A. Binder, *Stalemate: Causes and Consequences of Legislative Gridlock* (Washington, DC: Brookings Institution Press, 2004); but see David R. Jones, "Do Major Policy Enactments Affect Public Evaluations of Congress? The Case of Health Care Reform," *Legislative Studies Quarterly* 38, no. 2 (2013): 185–204. For a theory of congressional parties that is based on this notion, see Cox and McCubbins, *Setting the Agenda.*

23. David R. Jones, "A More Responsible Two-Party System? Accountability for Majority and Minority Party Performance in a Polarized Congress," *Polity* 46, no. 3 (2014): 470–92.

24. Andrew Dugan, "Republican Party Favorability Sinks to Record Low," Gallup, October 9, 2013, http://www.gallup.com/poll/165317/republican-party-favorability -sinks-record-low.aspx.

25. Dan Balz and Scott Clement, "Poll: Major Damage to GOP after Shutdown and Broad Dissatisfaction with Government," *Washington Post*, October 22, 2013, https://www.washingtonpost.com/politics/poll-major-damage-to-gop-after -shutdown-and-broad-dissatisfaction-with-government/2013/10/21/dae5c062-3a84 -11e3-b7ba-503fb5822c3e_story.html.

26. Jonathan Weisman and Ashley Parker, "Republicans Back Down, Ending Crisis over Shutdown and Debt Limit," *New York Times*, October 17, 2013, http://www .nytimes.com/2013/10/17/us/congress-budget-debate.html.

27. Sahil Kapur, "Boehner's Allies Say Budget Deal with Obama Will Boost Republican 2016 Nominee," Bloomberg, October 27, 2015, https://www.bloomberg. com/politics/articles/2015-10-27/boehner-allies-say-budget-deal-with-obama-will -boost-republican-2016-nominee.

28. George C. Edwards III, William Mitchell, and Reed Welch, "Explaining Presidential Approval: The Significance of Issue Salience," *American Journal of Political Science* (1995): 108–34.

29. Jeremy W. Peters, "Cry of GOP in Campaign: All Is Dismal," *New York Times*, October 9, 2014, http://www.nytimes.com/2014/10/10/us/politics/republican-strat egy-midterm-elections.html.

30. Gillian K. SteelFisher, Robert J. Blendon, and Narayani Lasala-Blanco, "Ebola in the United States—Public Reactions and Implications," *New England Journal of Medicine* 373, no. 9 (2015): 789–91.

31. Lindsey Cormack, "The Ebola Outbreak Generated Greater Response from Republican Lawmakers," *Washington Post*, November 14, 2014, https://www.washing

tonpost.com/news/monkey-cage/wp/2014/11/14/the-ebola-outbreak-generated-greater-response-from-republican-lawmakers.

32. Andrew Dugan, "Democratic Party Favorable Rating Falls to Record Low," Gallup, November 12, 2014, http://www.gallup.com/poll/179345/democratic-party-favorable-rating-falls-record-low.aspx.

33. David R. Jones, "A More Responsible Two-Party System? Accountability for Majority and Minority Party Performance in a Polarized Congress," *Polity* 46, no. 3 (2014): 470–92.

34. Jones, "Party Brand Images."

35. Philip E. Converse, "The Nature of Belief Systems in Mass Publics," in David Apter, ed., *Ideology and Discontent* (New York: Free Press, 1964).

36. On this point, see Lee, *Beyond Ideology*.

37. This is similar to the theory of "issue ownership," which argues that the public trusts the Republican Party to handle certain issues, like national defense, and the Democratic Party to handle other issues, such as education policy, and therefore elections are largely about each party trying to force the conversation onto grounds that it already knows are more favorable to it; John R. Petrocik, "Issue Ownership in Presidential Elections, with a 1980 Case Study," *American Journal of Political Science* (1996): 825–50.

38. Eric Bradner, "GOP Stokes Fears over Ebola, ISIS," CNN, October 9, 2014, http://www.cnn.com/2014/10/09/politics/gop-stokes-border-fears-over-ebola-isis.

39. David Eldridge, "Democrats Blame Budget Battles for Fumbled Ebola Response," *Roll Call*, October 16, 2014, http://www.rollcall.com/news/home/democrats-blame-budget-battles-for-fumbled-ebola-response.

40. Josh Michaud, Jennifer Kates, Somalee Banerjee, Anne Jankiewicz, and David Rousseau, "The 2014 Ebola Outbreak," *JAMA* 312, no. 14 (2014): 1388.

41. Michael Grunwald, *The New New Deal: The Hidden Story of Change in the Obama Era* (New York: Simon and Schuster, 2012), 149.

42. Tim Groeling, *When Politicians Attack: Party Cohesion in the Media* (Cambridge: Cambridge University Press, 2010); Brandon Rottinghaus and Kent L. Tedin, "Presidential 'Going Bipartisan' and the Consequences for Institutional Approval," *American Behavioral Scientist* 56, no. 12 (2012): 1696–717.

43. House Speaker Weekly Briefing, September 11, 2014.

44. Presidential speech to the nation, September 10, 2014.

45. Ali Weinberg, "Some Lawmakers Call for Strengthening Obama's Hand against ISIS," ABC News, November 10, 2015, http://abcnews.go.com/ABCNews/lawmakers-call-strengthening-obamas-hand-isis/story?id=35106784.

46. Shibley Telhami, "Are Americans Ready to Go to War with ISIL?" Brookings Institution, January 8, 2016, https://www.brookings.edu/opinions/are-americans-ready-to-go-to-war-with-isil.

47. Steven Dennis, "Obama Touts Congressional Support for Syria Airstrikes," *Roll Call*, September 23, 2014, http://www.rollcall.com/news/home/obama-touts-congressional-support-for-syria-strikes.

48. Jim Acosta and Jeremy Diamond, "Obama ISIS Fight Request Sent to Congress," CNN, February 12, 2015, http://www.cnn.com/2015/02/11/politics/isis-aumf-white-house-congress.

49. Amber Phillips, "President Obama's Push for Military Authorization to Fight ISIS Won't Go Anywhere in Congress. Here's Why," *Washington Post*, December 7, 2015, https://www.washingtonpost.com/news/the-fix/wp/2015/12/07/3-reasons -congress-wont-authorize-obamas-use-of-force-against-the-islamic-state.

50. Linda Qiu, "Comparing the GOP Candidates' ISIS Strategies with Obama's," December 26, 2015, http://www.politifact.com/truth-o-meter/article/2015/dec/26/ comparing-gop-candidates-isis-strategies-obamas.

51. President-elect Trump's first press conference, January 11, 2017.

52. Regarding partisan competitiveness, see Frances E. Lee, *Insecure Majorities: Congress and the Perpetual Campaign* (Chicago: University of Chicago Press, 2016).

53. David R. Jones, "The Effect of Political Trust in National Elections under Unified and Divided Government" (paper presented at the annual meeting of the American Political Science Association, Philadelphia, PA, September 1–4, 2016); Lee, *Insecure Majorities*; Stephen P. Nicholson, Gary M. Segura, and Nathan D. Woods, "Presidential Approval and the Mixed Blessing of Divided Government," *Journal of Politics* 64, no. 3 (2002): 701–20; Thomas J. Rudolph, "Who's Responsible for the Economy? The Formation and Consequences of Responsibility Attributions," *American Journal of Political Science* 47, no. 4 (2003): 698–713.

54. Groeling, *When Politicians Attack.*

CHAPTER 4

Unilateral Presidential Authority

Uses and Abuses

James P. Pfiffner

The authority of the president in the constitutional order can be exercised in a number of ways, from the clearly legitimate, to the arguably unconstitutional. The framers of the Constitution rejected the British model of government by designing a separation of powers system, in which the three separate branches share governing powers. The range of presidential authority can be examined with the following distinctions in mind.

1. *Explicit constitutional authority*: Presidents can negotiate treaties, appoint judges and officers of the executive branch, veto bills, and conduct wars—all with some congressional participation. They can grant pardons, without any direct congressional check.
2. *Implied powers*: In order to carry out their executive duties, presidents can appoint White House staff, including "policy czars"; negotiate executive agreements;[1] recognize foreign countries; direct regulation and rulemaking by executive branch agencies; and create executive branch agencies and programs.[2] In carrying out these duties, they can use a number of unilateral policy actions, including executive orders, memoranda, "letters" establishing administration policy, proclamations, and national security directives.
3. *Asserted powers*: Presidential assertions of authority are often clearly legitimate, but they sometimes stretch executive prerogative, such as when they make executive agreements,[3] exercise executive privilege, write signing statements, or issue secret national security directives. These assertions of presidential prerogative can be used in legitimate ways, but they can also be used to get around congressional objections.

This chapter will first consider unilateral actions of presidential discretion in domestic policy, including executive orders, memoranda, agency rulemaking, policy guidance to agencies, and emergency declarations. It will then turn to assertions of presidential authority concerning national security, including the use of military force, coercive interrogation, indefinite detention of suspects, surveillance of Americans, signing statements, and targeted killing. The overall argument of the chapter is that executive discretion in executing the laws is necessary but that unchecked executive power is dangerous.

UNILATERAL POWER IN DOMESTIC POLICY

The Constitution prescribes a policy-making process that includes the introduction of bills in Congress, passage by both houses, a presidential signature or qualified veto, and possible review and interpretation by the judiciary. The president is to "take care that the Laws be faithfully executed," by directing the executive branch of the government. But in order to execute the law, the president must necessarily use discretion for several reasons: (1) Congress does not have the expertise (or time) to specify details of administrative practice in implementing the law; (2) laws are often vague in order to garner sufficient support in Congress; and (3) for each law, there is a myriad of specific circumstances that demand discretionary decisions by administrators who apply the law in specific cases.

In the early twenty-first century, with Congress polarized along partisan lines, presidents sometimes felt that they had to act alone in order to accomplish their policy priorities. For instance, in 2004 President Bush, in announcing several faith-based initiatives, declared that "Congress wouldn't act . . . I signed an executive order. That means I did it on my own."[4] In 2011, facing a Congress dominated by Republicans, President Obama said that if Congress would not act on important policy issues, such as immigration reform, he would use his executive powers to act alone. "We can't wait for an increasingly dysfunctional Congress to do its job." "Where they won't act, I will. . . . I've told my administration to keep looking every single day for actions we can take without Congress."[5] In 2014 he said, "I can use [this] pen to sign executive orders and take executive actions and administrative actions that move the ball forward."[6] Obama's remarks referred to his proposed immigration reforms, discussed below.

This section will examine the range of authorities and instruments that presidents can use in executing the law in domestic policy. Most presidential and other executive branch administrative directives are routine and uncontroversial. But some constitute policy making, and some may arguably be used to circumvent congressional intent.

Executive Orders and Proclamations

Perhaps the most visible formal administrative actions are executive orders, which are not mentioned in the Constitution but which are a legitimate way for a president to execute the laws. According to a 1957 report of the House Government Operations Committee, "Executive orders and proclamations are directives or actions by the President" based on law or the president's constitutional powers. "Executive orders are generally directed to, and govern actions by, Government officials and agencies," and they have the force of law.[7]

In contrast, proclamations "in most instances affect primarily the activities of private individuals."[8] Of the more than nine thousand presidential proclamations, most are symbolic or ceremonial, announcing, for example, National Mentoring Month. But they also establish public policy, as when President Ford granted pardons to Vietnam War draft evaders.[9] Proclamations are also used by presidents to set aside federal lands for preservation for historic purposes, pursuant to the Antiquities Act of 1906. Presidents have created more than 150 national monuments, such as FDR's setting aside the Jackson Hole, Wyoming, area in 1943 or President Obama's creation of the Bears Ears National Monument in 2016. In creating national monuments, presidents can act unilaterally and quickly; a number of proposals to limit presidential authority were considered by the 114th Congress, but none of them became law.[10] The 1957 House Report stated that "The difference between Executive orders and proclamations is more one of form than of substance."[11]

Executive orders that are firmly based in law or the president's constitutional authority have the force of law, as do proclamations and memoranda based on those grounds. Although most major governmental policies are accomplished through legislation, presidents have established important policies through issuing executive orders. For instance,

- FDR established the Executive Office of the President (1939)[12]
- FDR ordered the internment of Japanese Americans (1942)[13]
- Truman desegregated the military services (1948)[14]
- Truman ordered the seizure of steel mills to prevent strikes (1952)[15]
- Eisenhower enforced desegregation of Arkansas schools (1957)[16]
- Kennedy established the Peace Corps (1961)[17]
- LBJ ordered equal opportunity in housing (1965)[18]
- Reagan centralized regulatory review in the Office of Management and Budget (1981)[19]
- Bush established the Office of Homeland Security (2001)[20]
- Obama prohibited US intelligence agencies from using torture (2009)[21]

Executive orders can be symbolic, routine, or policy formulating. Symbolic orders are often ceremonial, such as creating new military medals. Routine orders merely specify how agencies are to execute the law, as is the president's constitutional duty. But when the president issues an executive order to depart in significant ways from previously established policy or to interpret the law in ways seemingly in conflict with congressional intentions or to accomplish policy purposes that could not make it through Congress, the president, in effect, exercises lawmaking authority.

Every president since George Washington has issued executive orders, but their systematic numbering did not begin until the Federal Register Act was passed in 1936. In addition, there were many previously unnumbered orders that have not been systematically accounted for; executive memoranda and "letters" have not been systematically numbered. The University of California, Santa Barbara, American Presidency Project has compiled the number of executive orders for all presidents and calculated the average number per year for each president.[22] Early presidents issued orders in the double digits, though Ulysses Grant issued more than 200, and Theodore Roosevelt, in accord with his "stewardship" approach to the presidency, issued more than 1,000, as did Woodrow Wilson. Franklin Roosevelt issued more executive orders than any other president, 3,721, which also made him the leader in average number of orders per year at 307.[23]

After World War II, the number of executive orders dropped sharply, and beginning with Eisenhower, the average number per year ranged from 33 (Obama) to 80 (Carter).[24] After the election of Ronald Reagan, the average number per year dropped from 68 between 1961 and 1980 to 43 per year from 1981 to 2012.[25] This decrease, however, did not signal less presidential administrative direction, because the number of policy-significant (as opposed to routine) orders tripled from the 1950s through the 1990s.[26] In rebutting accusations that he was using executive orders excessively, President Obama argued that he had issued only 20 executive orders in 2013, the fewest in more than a century; in the same year, however, he issued 41 memoranda to agencies.[27]

Memoranda

Although more recent presidents issued fewer formal executive orders than their immediate predecessors, that does not mean that they backed off using unilateral presidential directives to accomplish their priorities. Short of executive orders and proclamations, presidents can accomplish many of the same goals by issuing formal memoranda and directives to agencies (until 1978 they were called "presidential letters"). Presidential memoranda are basically instructions to an agency to take some administrative action. If the president determines that they have "general applicability and legal effect," they are published in the *Federal Register* (693 from 1946 to 2013), though many more memoranda are issued that are not cited in the *Federal Register*.[28]

If they are published and issued under the president's legal authority, memoranda have the same force of law as executive orders, and are enforceable in federal court.[29] The main difference between executive orders and other directives, such as memoranda, is that executive orders are (since 1935) numbered and must be published in the *Federal Register*, while only some memoranda are published in the *Federal Register*. The use of substantive policy memoranda (rather than routine or symbolic) has been increasing, and they have been used to accomplish significant policy changes.

Presidents may be tempted to use memoranda because they are less visible than executive orders, and they are not codified; thus they give presidents the opportunity to accomplish their policy goals below the radar, without public notice. On the other hand, when they want to take credit for their administrative determinations, they can publicly call attention to them to take credit for helping part of their constituencies.[30] President Obama issued memoranda to an unprecedented degree and (through 2014), Obama memoranda outnumbered executive orders.[31]

Agency Rules and Regulations

In order to implement laws, federal agencies and commissions have to issue regulations to specify how the law will be administered, and presidents can make policy in executive branch agencies through the administrative process. The process for this type of policy making is formalized through the Administrative Procedure Act (APA) of 1946.

Since these rules carry out the law, they have the force of law and are enforceable in court. In order to issue a regulation, agencies must comply with the Administrative Procedure Act, which requires that proposed regulations be justified and published in the *Federal Register*, which requires at least a thirty-day period during which the public can submit comments, for or against the proposed rule. Once the thirty days have passed and comments have been taken into consideration, the rule becomes finalized and has the force of law.

It is difficult to reverse a rule once it is finalized, because courts, under the Chevron doctrine, presume the legitimacy of a rule as long as it is "reasonable." If a president wants to reverse a rule, the agency must go through the APA procedure again and provide justification for the change. Of course, Congress can change the law in order to reverse a policy the agency is implementing, but the full legislative process is a cumbersome way to change a specific policy.

Congress also gave itself the authority to reverse individual rules or regulations within sixty days of their issuance when it passed the Congressional

Review Act in 1996. But the reversal requires a joint resolution of Congress, which can be vetoed by the president. This probably explains why only one of seventy-two thousand final rules issued since 1996 has been reversed, since a president would likely veto a reversal by Congress of a rule issued by an agency during his administration. A new president of a different party and a like-minded Congress, however, may choose to reverse rules issued during the final six months of an administration of the other political party.[32]

Proposed regulations have also been required to be submitted to the Office of Information and Regulatory Affairs (OIRA) in the Executive Office of the President, for cost-benefit analysis. This extra hurdle can be used by presidents to stop regulations that go against administration policy preferences.[33]

Reversing Unilateral Policy Making

Executive orders, proclamations, and memoranda may have the force of law, but they can be nullified by courts, Congress, or a future president. A succeeding president can easily revoke or replace previous unilateral actions, which commonly happens when a president of a different political party is elected.

Reversal of Executive Orders

As mentioned above, presidential authority to issue executive orders is subject to checks from the other branches. Since public law is more authoritative than presidential directives, unless the president bases his actions on clear constitutional grants of power, Congress can override them by "amending, nullifying, repealing, revoking, or terminating the authority on which it is founded."[34] For instance, after George H. W. Bush issued an executive order directing the Department of Health and Human Services to create a human fetal tissue bank for research, Congress passed a bill stating, "the provisions of Executive Order 12806 shall not have any legal effect."[35] Congress can also use its fiscal authority to deny funds to certain executive branch activities, as it did when it thwarted President Obama's 2009 executive order to close the US prison in Guantanamo.[36]

Executive orders can also flip back and forth when the presidency changes hands. For instance, in reaction to abuses of presidential power in the Nixon administration, President Carter issued Executive Order (EO) 12065 to require more open access to government policies and classification, replacing President Nixon's EO 11652. President Reagan reversed Carter's order with his own (EO 12356). President Clinton revoked Reagan's order with EO 12958. President George W. Bush then issued EO 13233 to assert more presidential control over the release of governmental records. After President Obama's first day in office, he revoked the Bush order and later replaced it with his own approach to classification (EO 13526).[37]

President Reagan, in order to curb federal regulations, issued Executive Orders 12291 and 12498, which required all proposed agency regulations to be submitted to the Office of Management and Budget (OMB) for cost-benefit analysis. Agencies could not issue the proposed regulations until the OMB allowed them to, and often the OMB stopped proposed regulations. President Clinton, however, reversed these orders as well as "all amendments" and "all guidelines issued under those orders" when he issued EO 12866.[38] When President Obama came to office, he reversed the Bush administration policies on harsh interrogation techniques by EO 13491.

Federal courts can also reverse executive orders. The quintessential example of this is the Supreme Court decision in *Youngstown Sheet & Tube v. Sawyer* (1952). President Truman had issued an executive order seizing the nation's steel mills because of a threatened strike by workers, which might have hindered US production capacity during the war in Korea. The court declared Truman's actions to be an unconstitutional exercise of presidential discretion, because the Constitution did not authorize such actions and Congress had rejected a provision in the Taft-Hartley Act that would have authorized such actions by the president. The court declared, "the founders of this nation entrusted the lawmaking power to the Congress alone in both good and bad times."[39] Notwithstanding the declaration of the court, presidents do exercise, in effect, lawmaking power when they issue executive orders that are not reversed in federal court or by Congress (subject to a presidential veto).[40]

Reversal of Memoranda

Presidential memoranda have also been reversed by presidents, for example, on the issue of abortion. President Reagan issued the "Mexico City Policy," which denied US government funding for nongovernmental organizations that provided "advice, counseling, or information regarding abortion, or lobbying a foreign government to legalize or make abortion available."[41] As soon as President Clinton was inaugurated, he reversed Reagan's policy with a memorandum to the secretary of health and human services with instructions to lift the "gag rule" established by the GHW Bush administration.[42] When George W. Bush became president, he issued a memorandum to reinstate the "Mexico City" policy of the Reagan administration.[43] On his third day in office, President Obama reversed Bush's reinstatement of Reagan's policy by memorandum.[44]

Another series of memorandum reversals by presidents concerned restrictions on foreign aid for nongovernmental organizations that allowed abortions. The restrictions were established by President Reagan, reversed by Bill Clinton, reinstated by George W. Bush, and reversed again by Obama in 2009.[45] Upon taking office, newly elected presidents can also delay the implementation of regulations. The incoming administrations of Presidents Clinton and George W. Bush issued memoranda instructing departments and agencies to extend for sixty days the implementation of regulations that were issued by the previous administration but had not yet gone into effect. Their purpose was to determine if the proposed regulations were inconsistent with the new administration's policy preferences and potentially to withdraw any that were.[46]

Reversal of Obama Immigration Policy Directives

In contrast to formal administrative rules and regulations, presidents can issue general directives or policy guidance to instruct agencies how to administer their programs (e.g., agency policy statements, interpretive guidance, press releases, etc.). These directives do not have the force of law and can be easily reversed by a new administration by issuing new policy guidance.[47] One example of policy guidance is President Obama's controversial policy guidance to the Department of Homeland Security concerning immigration policy, and its subsequent reversal by the judiciary.

In 2013 the Senate passed an immigration reform bill (the "Dream Act"); a majority in the House of Representatives favored the bill, but Speaker John Boehner refused to bring it to the floor for a vote because Democratic votes would have been necessary for it to pass. In response, President Obama decided to use administrative action to accomplish some of the goals of the Dream Act by initiating a program called Delayed Action for Childhood Arrivals (DACA).

On June 15, DHS Secretary Janet Napolitano issued a directive based on "prosecutorial discretion" to prioritize deportation of persons residing in the country illegally. Under the directive, deportation would be delayed for two-year periods for children who came to the United States before their sixteenth birthday, were in school or the military, and had not been convicted of a crime. The program would not be a path to citizenship or change immigrants' legal status, though they would be allowed to work and go to school without fear of deportation for the period in which they were covered by the policy. The policy covered between one and two million children.

In November 2014 President Obama decided to expand the DACA program to include the parents of children covered by DACA; the new directive was called Deferred Action for Parents of Americans (DAPA). This policy was directed by DHS Secretary Jeh Johnson to expand the DACA program to prioritize the deportation of criminals and grant deferred deportation status to the parents of US citizens or those with lawful permanent residency. This would have extended limited protection from immediate deportation to between four and five million people. The main legal argument of the Obama administration was that in enforcing the law, priorities had to be set, and DAPA was a legitimate exercise of prosecutorial discretion.

Texas and other states sued to block implementation of the programs, arguing that the policy directive had important substantive effects on US immigration policy as well as imposing costs on states and was thus an abuse of executive discretion. The fifth circuit court of appeals affirmed a lower court's injunction to stop implementation of the policy. It decided that President Obama exceeded his executive discretion in setting the policies in DAPA. When the Obama administration appealed, the Supreme Court voted 4 to 4, which had the effect of allowing the lower court decisions to stand.

DACA and DAPA were clear cases of a president trying to accomplish through administrative direction policies that Congress would not enact. Setting priorities for the enforcement of the law is a legitimate exercise of administrative discretion. In the case of DAPA, however, the policy implications of the administrative actions were significant, and Congress had previously rejected the policies. Thus the arguments that Obama had exceeded his executive discretion were reasonable.[48]

Emergency Powers

The Constitution did not grant any emergency authority to presidents, and the only authority to suspend the right of habeas corpus was placed in Article I. Nevertheless, in times of genuine national security or domestic emergencies, presidents are expected to take action. Many of these actions are pursuant to the president's authority to take care that the laws be faithfully executed. In addition, Congress has over the years provided the president with standby emergency authorities covering some aspects of unforeseen situations in which quick action must be taken in order to protect lives, property, or national security.

In the twentieth century presidents declared a large number of national emergencies, and in the 1970s Congress decided to examine their usage. It found that a number of national emergencies from previous decades were still in effect, despite the end of the emergencies they were declared to deal with. A Special Committee on National Emergencies found that a total of 470 delegations of emergency authority had been enacted, four of which were still in effect,[49] since there were no automatic provisions for their termination after the emergency had been dealt with. In response, Congress passed the National Emergencies Act in 1976.[50]

The act provided for the termination of national emergency delegations after two years, unless they were renewed by Congress. It also provided procedures by which presidents could declare national emergencies, including reporting requirements to Congress. Between the enactment of the law in 1976 and 2007, more than forty emergency powers were invoked by executive order, many of them concerning trade restrictions regarding national security.[51] Generally, over the past century, emergency powers of the president have come to be circumscribed more formally in public law. Most recent actions taken by presidents under the National Emergencies Act have been narrowly tailored.

In a genuine national emergency, such as the 9/11 attacks, the president would have great leeway in dealing with the emergency.[52] In fact, the proclamation of President Bush after the 9/11 attacks (Number 7463) was still in effect more than a decade after it was issued. President Obama continued to extend the emergency proclamation annually with notices published in the *Federal Register*.[53]

NATIONAL SECURITY POLICY

The framers of the Constitution, mindful of the abuses of European monarchs in the previous several centuries, designed a government that would keep executive powers in check, particularly in war making and national security. In a letter to Thomas Jefferson, James Madison observed: "The constitution supposes, what the History of all Govts demonstrates, that the Ex. is the branch of power most interested in war, & most prone to it. It has accordingly with studied care, vested the question of war in the Legisl."[54] John Jay expressed the framers suspicions of executives in "Federalist No. 4": "absolute monarchs will often make war when their nations are to get nothing by it, but for purposes and objects merely personal, such as a thirst for military glory, revenge for personal affronts, ambition, or private compacts to aggrandize or support their particular families or partisans." Madison, commenting on the dangers of executive overreach, observed, "It is in war, finally, that laurels are to be gathered; and it is the executive brow they are to encircle. The strongest passions and most dangerous weaknesses of the human breast; ambition, avarice, vanity, the honourable or venial love of fame, are all in conspiracy against the desire and duty of peace."[55]

Thus the Constitution in Article I, Section 8, gives most war powers to Congress, including the authority to "declare war," "make Rules concerning Captures on Land and Water," "raise and support Armies," "make Rules for the Government and Regulation of the land and naval forces," and "make all Laws which shall be necessary and proper for carrying into Execution the foregoing Powers, and all other Powers vested by this Constitution in the Government of the United States, or in any Department or Officer thereof." Presidents can unilaterally make executive agreements with other countries;

these have virtually the same effect as treaties, except that they do not have to be ratified by the Senate and are not the "supreme Law of the Land," as Article VI of the Constitution provides for treaties. Executive agreements made pursuant to a treaty or law are not constitutionally problematical. But executive agreements based on the sole authority of the president can be used to avoid congressional approval, such as President Obama's joint agreement (along with other nations) with Iran to put its military nuclear development on hold. Presidents have issued executive agreements at an increasing rate. Total executive agreements since 1789 were more than 18,000, but since 1939 more than 7,300 were made, in contrast to 1,100 treaties.[56]

The framers left to the executive only the "commander in chief" authority. According to Alexander Hamilton, in "Federalist No. 69," the commander in chief authority "would amount to nothing more than the supreme command and direction of the military and naval forces, as first General and admiral of the Confederacy; while that of the British king extends to the *declaring* of war and to the *raising* and *regulating* of fleets and armies—all which, by the Constitution under consideration, would appertain to the legislature" (emphasis in original). The general interpretation of the commander in chief clause in Article II is that once Congress has decided to go to war, the president has very broad leeway to decide how to deploy troops as well as make tactical and strategic decisions.

The reality of national security dynamics over US history, however, is that presidents in fact have gained much of the power of initiative in national security matters. The national security power of the president has continually increased since the mid-twentieth century, and the last time Congress declared war was in World War II. A turning point came in 1950, when North Korean troops invaded South Korea, and President Truman sent US troops to Korea without a congressional declaration. The Cold War with the Soviet Union came to dominate national security concerns in the 1960s, and the possibility of a nuclear strike meant that the president had to be able to strike back before there was time to consult with Congress.

In 1973, in response to the "imperial" presidencies of Presidents Johnson and Nixon, Congress asserted itself and tried to rein in the president's war-making powers by passing the War Powers Resolution (overriding President Nixon's veto), among other checks on executive power. This act called for presidential consultation with Congress and limited unilateral deployments of US forces to sixty days (with a possible thirty-day extension). Presidents, however, never recognized the constitutionality of the War Powers Resolution. Even after the end of the Cold War, Presidents George H. W. Bush and Bill Clinton asserted the authority to send US troops into battle without congressional approval—Bush in Kuwait (though he did receive congressional approval) and Clinton in the Balkans. But neither fundamentally challenged congressional constitutional powers in unusual ways.

In the twenty-first century, however, President George W. Bush began to assert executive power in unprecedented ways.[57] At the beginning of his administration, he and Vice President Cheney felt that previous presidents had let Congress impinge on constitutional executive prerogatives, and that presidential powers had to be reasserted. The attacks of 9/11 provided the opportunity for them to greatly enhance presidential power in matters concerning national security. Senator Obama criticized some of the unilateral actions of President Bush and reversed a few (e.g., interrogation policy), but in important areas he continued Bush's policies. This section will examine Presidents Bush and Obama's assertions of executive power in national security. President Obama's exercise of Article II constitutional authority did not approach the level of assertions by President Bush, but neither did he explicitly give up much of the claimed executive power.

The Use of Military Force

Over the history of the United States, aside from major wars, many presidents have taken military action without gaining the agreement of Congress. These have been primarily justified by the need to protect US lives or property. Most of these interventions have not amounted to wars, but some of them have involved significant engagements and may or may not have included congressional authorizations.

After 9/11 President Bush asked Congress for an authorization for use of military force (AUMF) to invade Afghanistan to defeat the Taliban government that had harbored the al Qaeda terrorists who attacked the United States. The enacted AUMF authorized President Bush to "use all necessary and appropriate force" against any group that "committed, or aided the terrorist attacks" on 9/11. In October 2002, Congress passed another AUMF to authorize the Bush administration to invade Iraq. Constitutionally, an AUMF fulfills the constitutional requirement that the president obtain the consent of Congress before going to war, and President Bush used these authorizations in his wars in Afghanistan and Iraq.

In 2014, after the Islamic State (ISIS or ISIL) committed many atrocities and occupied territory in Iraq, President Obama decided that the Islamic State was a threat to US security and sent several thousand US troops to aid Iraqi forces that were fighting ISIS. To justify his actions he cited the 2001 AUMF that authorized military action against al Qaeda, even though ISIS was renounced by al Qaeda and was not coordinating attacks with it. Critics argued that Obama was stretching the 2001 authorization so liberally that it could be used to justify virtually any military intervention justified as a confrontation with terrorism.[58]

In the spring of 2011, President Obama decided to deploy US air power in Libya. Rebels were fighting the military forces of Libyan dictator Muammar

Gaddafi. Gaddafi's troops threatened to slaughter thousands of civilians in Benghazi. This posed a serious humanitarian threat and President Obama decided to intervene, and so the United States cooperated with several other NATO countries to impose a no-fly zone over Libya and help defeat Gaddafi's troops.

The administration justified its actions primarily based on a United Nations Security Council resolution that was adopted on March 17, 2011, which authorized members to protect civilians and civilian-populated areas that were under threat of attack. But the UN resolutions can only authorize US actions internationally; they do not supersede the US Constitution with respect to the war power. The Constitution specifies that only Congress can declare war, with the recognition that the president can act unilaterally to repel sudden attacks. Obama did not seek congressional authorization for the use of force in Libya.

After US forces had been engaged in Libya for sixty days, the time limit set in the War Powers Act of 1973 expired, and the act required that the president obtain congressional approval or withdraw US forces. Rather than arguing that the War Powers Act was unconstitutional, the Obama administration asserted that US actions in Libya did not constitute the nature of "hostilities" envisioned by the War Powers Act, and thus the sixty-day clock was not triggered. Obama's decision to use military power in Libya was an assertion that military power could be used unilaterally in humanitarian interventions. Future presidents will be able to refer to this precedent when they decide to deploy military forces unilaterally.

Coercive Interrogation

Shortly after the 9/11 attacks, US forces in Afghanistan sent hundreds of suspected allies of al Qaeda to the US prison compound at Guantanamo Bay, Cuba, for interrogation, though only 5 percent of them were captured by US troops.[59] Memoranda from Defense Secretary Rumsfeld authorized a range of harsh techniques that could be used to extract intelligence from suspects. The CIA acted under separate authorization to use enhanced interrogation techniques (EITs) on high-value detainees at "black sites" in several countries.

In fall 2002 military leaders were under intense pressure from the White House to provide actionable intelligence on possible future terrorist attacks. High-level Bush administration officials as well as military and CIA lawyers traveled to Guantanamo to brief its commanders on the legal aspects of using harsh interrogation techniques. According to a Department of Defense report, twenty-four thousand interrogations took place at Guantanamo from 2002 to 2005.[60] In February 2002, President Bush declared that the Geneva Conventions did not apply to how the United States treated suspected al Qaeda prisoners.

In 2002 and 2003, Secretary of Defense Rumsfeld approved a range of harsh tactics that included to hooding, use of dogs, "prolonged solitary confinement" of detainees, keeping detainees "naked in totally empty concrete cells and in total darkness," "prolonged short shackling in stress positions," and "extreme temperatures." The use of these techniques by US military personnel at Guantanamo, Bagram Air Force Base in Afghanistan, and the Abu Ghraib prison in Iraq were documented in formal reports by the Department of Defense.[61] The use of coercive interrogation techniques by the CIA, including waterboarding, was documented in the report of the Senate Select Committee on Intelligence; the executive summary was released in December 2014.[62]

In his campaign for the presidency Barack Obama criticized the Bush administration for its interrogation policies and promised to close the prison at Guantanamo if he were elected. After he won, he moved to keep his promises in order to make a clear break with the policies of the Bush administration. Two days after his inauguration, on January 22, he mandated the closing of the Guantanamo Bay detention facility (EO 13492) "as soon as practicable, and no later than 1 year from the date of this order." The same day he issued Executive Order 13491, directing the CIA to adhere to the policies specified in the Army field manual on interrogation, all of which comply with the Geneva Conventions; no EITs could be used in interrogations.

In addition to the Geneva Conventions and the Convention Against Torture, the United States has several laws prohibiting torture; Congress passed the Detainee Treatment Act of 2005.[63] After the summary of the Senate Select Committee Report was released, Congress passed and President Obama signed the National Defense Authorization Act for Fiscal Year 2016, Section 1045 of which limited interrogation techniques to those specified in the Army Field Manual 2-22.3, which exclude torture.

Despite these laws, in his campaign for the presidency Donald Trump rejected legal prohibitions on torture and threatened to reintroduce the techniques of harsh interrogation: "Would I approve waterboarding? You bet your ass I would—in a heartbeat. . . . Believe me, it works. And you know what? If it doesn't work, they deserve it anyway, for what they're doing. It works."[64] He also threatened to "take out their families, when you get these terrorists."[65] The anti-torture laws might make it difficult for President Trump to reintroduce the use of torture for purposes of interrogation, but the Geneva Conventions and previous laws did not stop President Bush from authorizing their use between 2002 and 2008.

Indefinite Detention of Terrorist Suspects

During the Bush presidency, more than seven hundred prisoners were incarcerated at Guantanamo Bay, Cuba, many of whom had been subjected to coercive interrogation. By the time he left office there was bipartisan support for closing the prison camp, which had become an international symbol of US abuse of detainees. When Obama became president, about two hundred detainees were left.

Early in his administration Obama issued an executive order that the prison be closed, but Congress passed several measures making it difficult or impossible for Obama to follow through on his intention. Congress also made it exceedingly difficult for Obama to transfer detainees out of Guantanamo, either into the continental United States for trial or to other countries.

Obama had determined that most of the detainees could be set free without undue risk to the United States. Some of the remaining detainees could be tried for crimes, either by military courts or Article III courts. But others had to be held indefinitely without trial, since their prosecution was compromised by the use of evidence against them obtained by torture. At the end of his administration, Obama had been successful in resettling 179 detainees in other countries, though about 60 detainees remained in the prison.

Most problematic with respect to executive prerogative was Obama's determination that some Guantanamo prisoners would be held indefinitely without trial. Holding persons accused of crime indefinitely without prosecuting them for crimes runs up against the Fifth Amendment to the Constitution, which states that "No person" shall be "deprived of life, liberty, or property, without due process of law." During a war, it is legitimate to capture enemy soldiers and hold them for the duration of the conflict, but there is no obvious end of terrorist threats to the United States. Before he became president, Donald Trump said that he would "load [Guantanamo] up with some bad dudes."[66]

Domestic Surveillance of Americans

After abuses of domestic governmental surveillance by presidents of both parties were revealed by the Church Committee in 1975, Congress passed the Foreign Intelligence Surveillance Act (FISA) to ensure accountability and due process. Presidents had previously ordered domestic surveillance of American citizens based on their own interpretation of executive authority. The FISA, enacted in 1978, limited surveillance of domestic activities to cases in which there was evidence of foreign espionage. The act created the Foreign Intelligence Surveillance Court (FISC) to review surveillance programs, judge their legality, and issue warrants (orders) to surveil individuals in the United States believed to be connected to foreign powers.

A month after 9/11, in October 2001, President Bush secretly created the President's Surveillance Program (PSP) and authorized the National Security Agency (NSA) to monitor communications related to foreign intelligence that were coming into or going out of the United States. Under FISA, communications passing into or out of the United States required a FISC order. But President Bush issued the order based on his own interpretation of his constitutional authority as president. In 2005 the *New York Times* revealed that the National Security Agency had been collecting a broad range of communications of Americans without the required warrants by the FISC, raising the issue of the constitutional protections of the Fourth Amendment against unreasonable searches and seizures and the requirement for warrants based on probable cause.

The broader point here is that President Bush asserted the authority to ignore the law and created a program of domestic surveillance that was forbidden by FISA. When it was exposed, he argued that it was within his executive authority to do so. When that argument was not seen as compelling, he convinced Congress to grant the president authority, as interpreted by the FISC, to continue the surveillance he had initiated. President Bush established precedents for much broader surveillance of Americans without warrants than had existed before his presidency.[67]

When Barack Obama was a senator, he asserted that President Bush exceeded his legitimate executive authority when he ordered surveillance of Americans without warrants. Yet when he came into office, Obama continued these programs, the extent of which were secret from the public and unknown to many members of Congress. Thus, despite his previous skepticism about NSA surveillance of Americans, after becoming president, Obama came to be convinced that NSA's collection of bulk communications data on all Americans was both constitutionally acceptable and necessary for national security.

In June 2013, former NSA contractor Edward Snowden released secret NSA documents demonstrating that the NSA had been collecting in bulk the metadata on virtually all US telephone communications. The legal justification for the massive surveillance of millions of persons who were not suspected of crimes was based on an interpretation of the FISA that members of Congress did not foresee and did not think they had authorized in law. Thus Congress passed the USA Freedom Act in June 2015. The act prohibits the NSA from collecting bulk metadata of US phone calls but allows telecommunication companies to store the data in their servers. The NSA can have access to the data upon the presentation of a warrant from FISC for access to a specific person or entity suspected of foreign terrorist links.

President Bush's decisions about domestic surveillance of Americans became authorized in law and were accepted by a president of the opposite party as necessary. It was only the Snowden revelations that alerted Congress of the reinterpretation of the FISA and prompted it to change the law to reflect its original intentions. Americans concerned about civil liberties and privacy did not claim that the NSA's huge databases of domestic communications had been abused by the Bush or Obama administrations. But given precedents of abuse in American history, addressed by the Church Committee in 1975, the possibility of future abuses is troublesome.

Signing Statements

A signing statement is a declaration by the president when he signs a bill into law; these statements usually thank supporters of the bill and explain how the law will benefit the country. Occasionally, however, presidents use signing statements to declare that they do not feel bound by certain provisions of the law; these are termed constitutional signing statements. Constitutional signing statements had been used occasionally in the latter half of the twentieth century, but President George W. Bush used them to an unprecedented extent. He issued more than 1,000 constitutional challenges to provisions in more than 150 laws during his first six years in office. He used signing statements to assert the unilateral right of the executive to choose which provisions of laws to enforce and which to ignore. For instance, he used signing statements to indicate that he did not feel bound by all of the provisions of laws regarding reporting to Congress pursuant to the PATRIOT Act; the physical coercion of prisoners contrary to the Detainee Treatment Act of 2006; whistle-blower protections for the Department of Energy; the number of US troops in Colombia; the use of illegally gathered intelligence; and the publication of educational data gathered by the Department of Education.[68]

The implications of these sweeping claims to presidential authority call into question the very meaning of the rule of law. Despite the Constitution's granting lawmaking power to Congress, the use of signing statements to, in effect, nullify parts of the law provides the president with the ability to exercise an absolute veto or an item veto, which were rejected by the framers of the Constitution.[69] The "take care" clause of Article II thus can be effectively ignored.

Before he was president, Senator Obama denounced President Bush's use of signing statements and, as president, declared that "Constitutional signing statements should not be used to suggest that the President will disregard statutory requirements on the basis of policy disagreements." He promised to "act with caution and restraint, based only on interpretations of the Constitution that are well-founded."[70] Although President Obama did not use signing statements nearly as often as President Bush—issuing fewer than fifty objections to provisions in laws—he argued that they were occasionally necessary when there was a serious disagreement about the constitutional authority of the president and Congress.

Many presidents have issued signing statements, and some of them implied that they would not follow parts of the laws they were signing. In recent presidencies, these statements have been arguably unconstitutional. Nevertheless, occasionally Congress does pass laws that may impinge on presidential constitutional authority, so there is no clear remedy aside from self-restraint on the part of the president. President Bush expanded the scope of signing statements in ways that future presidents could easily abuse. President Obama's use of constitutional signing statements, despite his comparative restraint, leaves open the possibility that future presidents will again use signing statements to achieve a veto of parts of a law with no opportunity for congressional override.

Drones and Targeted Killing

In the 1970s, after several failed attempts to assassinate Fidel Castro, President Ford issued an executive order forbidding assassinations. But after 9/11 the Bush administration argued that killing selected individuals who were involved in terrorism was part of the war on terror and not covered by Ford's executive order.[71] Toward the end of his administration, President Bush began to use armed, unpiloted aerial vehicles, commonly known as drones, to kill terrorists in Pakistan. When Obama became president, he greatly expanded the use of drone attacks to kill militants in Pakistan and Iraq and extended their use to Yemen, among other nations.

Although President Bush authorized fewer than fifty drone strikes, the Obama administration made use of armed drones, outside of hot battlefields, a major tactic for the United States in carrying out its campaign against terrorists who were believed to threaten the United States. President Obama significantly increased the use of drone attacks to more than four hundred attacks in Pakistan and Yemen, killing between two thousand and four thousand militants and three hundred civilians when he was in office.[72]

President Obama justified the US drone policy in public talks and several released documents. In May 2013, he argued that the use of drones was part of a "just war," which is being "waged proportionally, in last resort, and in self-defense." The targets are "highly skilled al-Qaida commanders, trainers, bomb makers, and operatives," and "these strikes have saved lives." He argued it is a "legal" war against "an organization that right now would kill as many Americans as they could if we did not stop them first."[73]

He said that he would kill only those who presented an imminent threat to US personnel and whom it is infeasible to capture. The administration argued that there was an elaborate clearance process within the executive branch before a drone strike was authorized. But according to a white paper released by the Department of Justice, the definition of imminent threat was quite elastic.[74] The Obama administration even argued that a drone strike could be used to kill US citizens who were actively inciting war against the United States. This was the case when a US drone strike killed Anwar al-Aulaqi in 2011.

Despite the many advantages of drones, their use raises a number of concerns regarding their legality and strategic value. The guilt of the people targeted in US drone strikes was determined by intelligence that was not made public. Thus there is no external check on the accuracy of the intelligence or due process before executing the individuals. Killing US citizens by drones sets a dangerous precedent with respect to the constitutional rights of due process guaranteed in the Fifth Amendment. From a policy perspective, the killing of hundreds of suspected militants as well as innocent bystanders in Pakistan has led to charges that the United States is acting arbitrarily.

One of the most profound actions that governments can take is to take a person's life. Presidents Bush and Obama have established precedents for the extrajudicial killing of suspected terrorists without any congressional or due process check.

CONCLUSION

Presidential assertions of power are understandable; they want to fulfill campaign promises and achieve policy goals within a system that deliberately limits executive power. Divided government and polarization in Congress have often thwarted attempts to address important policy issues, making unilateral executive actions tempting. The framers of the Constitution understood the temptations to presidential aggrandizement and created a separation of powers system designed to limit executive power. The framers expected that Congress would act to protect its own constitutional power, but they did not foresee the creation of strong political parties and debilitating partisan polarization of politics. Because of partisan loyalty and political timidity, Congress has often abdicated its rightful constitutional authority and thus has aided and abetted presidential assertions of power.

Presidential candidates encourage high expectations of policy success by blaming the other party's presidents for problems they could not prevent and promise to fix those problems if they are elected. But once in office, presidents have to deal with the high expectations they raised during their campaigns, and this encourages them to seek as much political and constitutional leverage as they can through unilateral actions. Precedents set by Presidents Bush and Obama have created more leeway for subsequent presidents to assert the same powers, and if history is any guide, they will stretch precedents to suit their own purposes.

The nation's chief executive wields much more power than the framers of the Constitution anticipated, though in 1789 Thomas Jefferson had some intimation of the future of the office: "The TYRANNY of the legislature is really the danger most to be feared, and will continue to be so for many years to come. The tyranny of the executive power will come in its turn, but at a more distant period."[75] That "more distant period" arrived 150 years after his prediction—in the latter half of the twentieth century. Insofar as there is any threat of one branch dominating governance in the twenty-first century, it will be the executive branch.

NOTES

The author would like to thank John Woolley, as well as the editors of this volume, for comments on an earlier draft of this chapter.

1. Executive agreements pursuant to a statute or to implement a ratified treaty are implied by the "take care" clause in Article II. See Michael John Garcia, "International Law and Agreements: Their Effect upon U.S. Law" (Washington, DC: Congressional Research Service, 2015), 5–6.

2. Presidents have authority over rulemaking in executive branch agencies (such as the Food and Drug Administration, the Federal Trade Commission, and the Occupational Safety and Health Administration), but they cannot directly control rulemaking by independent regulatory boards and commissions (such as the Federal Communications Commission, the Federal Energy Regulatory Commission, and the Federal Reserve Board).

3. "Sole" executive agreements, not pursuant to a treaty or a law, are often made by presidents. When they are made pursuant to the president's constitutional authority, such as recognizing the government of a foreign country, they are presumably legally binding. But if the president's authority is ambiguous, courts may not enforce them. See Garcia, "International Law and Agreements," 5–6.

4. "President's Remarks at Faith-Based and Community Initiatives Conference," White House (March 3, 2004), referring to Executive Orders 13199 and 13279.

5. "Remarks by the President on the Economy and Housing," White House Press Secretary (October 24, 2011).

6. "Remarks by the President Before Cabinet Meeting" (January 14, 2014), White House Press Office.

7. Vanessa K. Burrows, "Executive Orders: Issuance and Revocation" (Washington, DC: Congressional Research Service, March 25, 2010), 1.

8. Quotes are from Burrows, "Executive Orders," 1.

9. Proclamation 4313. See Phillip Cooper, *By Order of the President*, 2nd ed. (Lawrence: University Press of Kansas, 2014), 174.

10. Carol Hardy Vincent, "National Monuments and the Antiquities Act" (Washington, DC: Congressional Research Service, 2016), ii.

11. Quoted in Burrows, "Executive Orders," 1.

12. Executive Order (EO) 8248.

13. EO 9066.

14. EO 9981.

15. EO 10340.

16. EO 10730.

17. EO 10924.

18. EO 11063.

19. EO 12291.

20. EO 13328.

21. EO 13491.

22. Many executive orders before the Federal Register Act of 1936 were not numbered, and so the numbers reflect the best estimates of scholars.

23. University of California, Santa Barbara, American Presidency Project, "Executive Orders," http://www.presidency.ucsb.edu/data/orders.php.

24. Ibid.

25. John T. Woolley and Gerhard Peters, "Do Presidential 'Memo Orders' Substitute for Executive Orders? New Data," *Presidential Studies Quarterly* (Forthcoming, June 2017).

26. Andrew Rudalevige, "The Presidency and Unilateral Power: A Taxonomy," in Michael Nelson, ed., *The Presidency and the Political System*, 10th ed. (Washington, DC: CQ Press, 2013), 484. See also William G. Howell, *Power without Persuasion* (Princeton, NJ: Princeton University Press, 2003); and Kenneth Mayer, *With the Stroke of a Pen: Executive Orders and Presidential Power* (Princeton, NJ: Princeton University Press, 2001).

27. Andrew Rudalevige, "The Letter of the Law: Administrative Discretion and Obama's Domestic Unilateralism," *The Forum* 12, no. 1 (2014): 35.

28. Kenneth S. Lowande, "After the Orders: Presidential Memoranda and Unilateral Action," *Presidential Studies Quarterly* (December 2014): 733.

29. Randolph D. Moss, "Legal Effectiveness of a Presidential Directive, as Compared to an Executive Order," Memorandum Opinion for the Counsel to the President, Office of Legal Counsel, Department of Justice (January 29, 2000); John Contrubis, "Executive Orders and Proclamations" (Washington, DC: Congressional Research Service, 1999), 20.

30. John T. Woolley and Gerhard Peters, "Presidential Choice of Forum for Issuing Orders: Theoretical Issues and New Data," manuscript of November 14, 2016, 3.

31. Lowande, "After the Orders," 731.

32. For details, see Maeve Carey et al., "Memorandum: Obama Administration Ruled Potentially Eligible to Be Overturned under the Congressional Review Act in the 115th Congress" (Washington, DC: Congressional Research Service, November 17, 2016); Christopher Davis and Richard Beth, "Agency Final Rules Submitted After May 30, 2016" (Washington, DC: Congressional Research Service, November 9, 2016).

33. In 2016, Executive Orders 12866 and 13563 governed this process. See the Office of Management and Budget website: https://www.whitehouse.gov/omb/oira, accessed December 28, 2016.

34. Contrubis, "Executive Orders and Proclamations," 15.

35. Burrows, "Executive Orders," 5.

36. EO 13492.

37. For a full analysis of these reversals, see Phillip J. Cooper, *By Order of the President*, 2nd ed. (Lawrence: University Press of Kansas, 2014), 31–33.

38. EO 12866, quoted in Contrubis, "Executive Orders and Proclamations," 19.

39. 343 US 579 (1952), 586–89.

40. Contrubis, "Executive Orders and Proclamations," 15.

41. *Weekly Compilation of Presidential Documents* 29 (1993): 88. See Cooper, *By Order of the President*, 117.

42. *Weekly Compilation of Presidential Documents* 29 (1993): 88. See Cooper, *By Order of the President*, 117.

43. *Weekly Compilation of Presidential Documents* 37 (2001): 216. See Cooper, *By Order of the President*, 119.

44. Cooper, *By Order of the President*, 119.

45. Lowande, "After the Orders," 724.

46. See Memorandum to Senator Tom Coburn, "PPACA Provisions and Potential Use of Executive Orders" (Washington, DC: Congressional Research Service, November 14, 2011), 6.

47. Todd Garvey, "General Policy Statements: Legal Overview" (Washington, DC: Congressional Research Service, April 14, 2016), ii.

48. Other examples of using administrative guidance were Obama's instructions to the Justice Department not to pursue prosecution in states that legalized the use of marijuana and the Department of Education's guidance on the treatment of civil rights for transgender people. CRS Legal Sidebar, "With the Stroke of a Pen: What Executive Branch Actions Can President-elect Trump 'Undo' on Day One?" (Washington, DC: Congressional Research Service, November 22, 2016), 1.

49. Much of this section is based on Harold Relyea, "National Emergency Powers" (Washington, DC: Congressional Research Service, 2007).

50. The law abolished many of the provisions of the presidential-declared emergencies still in effect. Relyea, "National Emergency Powers," 10.

51. For a list of all these executive orders, see Relyea, "National Emergency Powers," 13–16.

52. Such as President Bush's Proclamation 7463 of September 14, 2011 (3 CFR2001) as cited in Relyea, "National Emergency Powers," 15.

53. Cooper, *By Order of the President*, 191.

54. Letter of April 2, 1798. *The Writings of James Madison*, ed. Gaillard Hunt, 9 vols (New York: G.P. Putnam's Sons, 1900–1910). Found at http://press-pubs.uchicago.edu/founders/documents/a1 -8-11s8.html.

55. James Madison, 1793. *The Writings of James Madison*, vol. 6, p. 174, quoted by Louis Fisher in "Exercising Congress's Constitutional Power to End a War," Statement before Congress (January 30, 2007), Law Library of Congress, 4.

56. Garcia, "International Law and Agreements," 5–6.

57. See James P. Pfiffner, *Power Play: The Bush Presidency and the Constitution* (Washington, DC: Brookings, 2008).

58. Shoon K. Murray, "Stretching the 2001 AUMF: A History of Two Presidencies," *Presidential Studies Quarterly* 45, no. 1 (March 2015).

59. Joseph Felter and Jarret Brachman, *An Assessment of 516 Combatant Status Review Tribunal (CSRT) Unclassified Summaries* (New York: West Point, Combating Terrorism Center, July 25, 2007).

60. Church Report, Albert T. Church, Naval Inspector General and Vice Admiral, "Executive Summary" (unclassified summary of longer report completed February 2005), http://www.defenselink.mil/news/Mar2005/d20050310exe.pdf.

61. For details and documentation, see James P. Pfiffner, *Torture as Public Policy* (Boulder, CO: Paradigm Publishers, 2010), chapter 3.

62. Senate Select Committee on Intelligence, Findings and Conclusions, Executive Summary, declassified December 3, 2014.

63. For details of the legal aspects of US torture, see Pfiffner, *Torture as Public Policy*, chapter 5.

64. Jenna Johnson, "Donald Trump on Waterboarding," *Washington Post*, November 23, 2015.

65. CNN/Politics, http://www.cnn.com/2015/12/02/politics/donald-trump-terrorists-families.

66. Missy Ryan and Julie Tate, "With Final Detainee Transfer, Obama's Guantanamo Policy Takes Its Last Breath," *Washington Post*, December 28, 2016.

67. For details and documentation, see James P. Pfiffner, "Presidents Bush, Obama and the Surveillance of Americans," in Michael Genovese, ed., *The Quest for Leadership: Essays in Honor of Thomas E. Cronin* (Amherst, NY: Cambria Press, 2015), 131–48.

68. For details, see James P. Pfiffner, "Presidential Signing Statements and Their Implications for Public Administration," *Public Administration Review* 69, no. 2 (March/April 2009): 249–55.

69. A veto negates the whole law unless overturned by a two-thirds majority in both houses of Congress. Signing statements usually object to specific provisions in the law, which amounts to an item veto. An item veto allows an executive to veto individual parts of a law and let the rest of the law take effect. A number of states allow an item veto in their constitutions, but the president has no authority for an item veto.

70. Barack Obama, "Memorandum on Presidential Signing Statements" (March 9, 2009), https://www.whitehouse.gov/the-press-office/memorandum-presidential-signing-statements.

71. Murray, "Stretching the 2001 AUMF," 287.

72. John P. Abizaid and Rosa Brooks, *Recommendations and Report of the Task Force on US Drone Policy* (Washington, DC: Stimson Center, June 2014): 19, 28.

73. Abizaid and Brooks, *Recommendations and Report of the Task Force on US Drone Policy*, 19.

74. Department of Justice White Paper, "Lawfulness of a Lethal Operation Directed Against a U.S. Citizen Who Is a Senior Operational Leader of Al-Qa'ida or an Associated Force" (Draft, November 8, 2011).

75. Arthur Schlesinger Jr., *The Imperial Presidency* (Boston: Houghton Mifflin, 1973), 377.

CHAPTER 5

Congress, the President, and the Politics of Federal Regulation

Claudia Hartley Thurber

President Obama had stunning legislative success in his first two years in office, with the passage of 334 laws, including the historic stimulus package, health-care reforms, and financial reform legislation.[1] All embodied the broad outline of what they were intended to accomplish.[2] During Obama's subsequent years in office, the Democrats, a bare majority party or a minority party in the Senate, were too few to overcome filibusters, and the solidly Republican-controlled House of Representatives, fraught with dissension, could not seem to overcome its ideological recalcitrance and legislate.

With a deadlocked, do-nothing Congress, the president focused on federal regulations, executive orders, and presidential memoranda to further advance and implement his policies. The Patient Protection and Affordable Care Act (the Affordable Care Act or Obamacare) and Dodd-Frank Wall Street Reform and Consumer Protection Act (Dodd-Frank) mandated extensive rulemaking. Federal government departments, agencies, and independent regulatory agencies promulgated regulations pursuant to these new enabling statutes. In addition, major legislation from as far in the past as the 1970s also required rulemaking. For example, in just two areas of the environment, the Clean Air Act of 1970 and the Clean Water Act of 1972 have provisions that require rulemaking. The Occupational Safety and Health Administration (OSHA) and the Mine Safety and Health Administration (MSHA) also promulgated significant rules under Obama to protect workers in general industry, construction, maritime work, and mining. Under the Food Safety Modernization Act, the Food and Drug Administration (FDA) addressed food safety from produce to animal feed to human food, with the goal of preventing unsafe food from reaching the market. The Department of Agriculture (USDA) made progress on further implementation of the Healthy, Hunger-Free Kids Act of 2010.

How many of these regulations will survive or be altered by President Donald J. Trump remains to be seen, but he campaigned on an antiregulatory platform, and his early picks to head departments and agencies suggest he will decimate, to the extent he can, President Obama's regulatory legacy and institute radical changes in regulatory policy, which he may well accomplish with majorities in the Senate and House of Representatives of members of his own party.

The executive branch, the president's administrative tool, but also answerable to the Congress and the courts, is an important component in the rivalry for political power in American democracy. Congress passes broad legislation. The administrative agencies, usually through notice and comment rulemaking, interpret the laws and define their terms; promulgate the specific rules that explain how an affected individual, organization, or business can meet the requirements of the law; and set the deadlines for compliance. There are many reasons why the Congress passes laws that lack specificity, but probably the main one is the authors' need to get support for passage from their colleagues who hold different views. The more specific the law, the more difficult it is to build a majority vote in Congress. Regulatory policy and action in the form of rules and guidance documents have far-reaching effects on individuals, corporations, and organizations, and on state, local, and tribal governments. As the Congress and the president compete for power, the federal executive branch enhances the president's power to implement his policies through rulemakings that hone the requirements in the congressional statutes. Laws are rarely self-executing. Through regulatory policy, the president can set his political goals by prioritizing what issues will be addressed in his administration, and determine how best to make the rules cost effective, faithful to their underlying legislation, and fair.

Federal rules and regulations affect everyone as they conduct their affairs, be they personal, social, or work related. Federal rulemaking is initiated and completed by the federal agencies pursuant to their statutory authority; the Administrative Procedure Act of 1946 (APA);[3] a myriad of legislation that has been enacted over the last half century and made applicable to the federal rulemaking process; and court decisions on rules that have become further requirements, precedents, and directions affecting not only the subject rulemaking, but also subsequent rulemakings. The rules, based upon congressional statutes that are known as enabling statutes, are legislative in nature, as they affect prospective behavior.

Rulemaking occurs throughout the executive branch of government, but certain departments and agencies promulgate a greater number of significant rules. They include the Departments of Treasury, Agriculture, Labor, Health and Human Services, Homeland Security, Housing and Urban Development, Transportation, Energy, Education, and Veterans Affairs, as well as agencies such as the Environmental Protection Agency (EPA) and

FDA. Independent federal agencies that engage in rulemaking include the Commodities Futures Trade Commission (CFTC), Consumer Product Safety Commission (CPSC), Federal Elections Commission, National Labor Relations Board (NLRB), Social Security Administration, Federal Communications Commission, and Securities and Exchange Commission (SEC). Independent federal agencies can be just as powerful and usually make their rules in the same way as other agencies, but they often have fewer procedural requirements. The major difference lies in the structure of independent agencies, which typically are headed by a commission or board whose members are appointed by a president, but in many cases have to be nonpartisan (meaning balanced by party) and serve staggered terms (meaning they hold their position for more than one presidency). Finally, a sitting president cannot easily fire board and commission members, whereas he can fire the political appointees in the executive agencies at will.

We are all affected by rules governing the quality of the air we breathe, the food we eat and the water we drink, the clothes we wear (and the fabric from which they are made), the car we drive, the marshland next to our house, the conditions under which we work, the access we enjoy to health care, the information to which we are entitled in our financial dealings, the security of our investments, and the scheduling and safety of the airplane in which we travel, to name just a few areas. No one can escape the reach of federal rules, from the day we are born in a hospital, through our education and employment years, to our sunset years in assisted living or nursing homes; but then few of us would want to return to the days when unsafe conditions abounded in nearly all areas of life.

COSTS OF FEDERAL REGULATION

The costs of federal regulations are high, but the benefits are even higher. Major rules, as defined in Executive Order (EO) 12866 as Significant Regulatory Actions, typically result in a rule that may:

- Have an annual effect on the economy of $100 million or more or adversely affect in a material way the economy, a sector of the economy, productivity, competition, jobs, the environment, public health or safety, or state, local, or tribal governments or communities;
- Create a serious inconsistency or otherwise interfere with an action taken or planned by another agency;
- Materially alter the budgetary impact of entitlements, grants, user fees, or loan programs or the rights and obligations of recipients thereof; or
- Raise novel legal or policy issues arising out of legal mandates, the president's priorities, or the principles set forth in EO 12866.[4]

Table 5.1. Estimates of Total Annual Benefits and Costs of Major Federal Rules by Agency, October 1, 2004–September 30, 2014

Agency	Number of Rules	Benefits (in billions of 2010 dollars)	Costs (in billions of 2010 dollars)
Department of Agriculture	4	1.0–1.4	1.0–1.4
Department of Energy	20	16.4–29.0	6.3–9.0
Department of Health and Human Services	16	17.7–35.9	1.2–4.9
Department of Homeland Security	2	0–0.6	0.1–0.3
Department of Housing and Urban Development	1	2.8	1.1
Department of Justice	4	2.1–4.8	1.0–1.3
Department of Labor	8	8.9–25.8	2.7–6.2
Department of Transportation (DOT)	28	18.7–32.9	8.5–16.3
Environmental Protection Agency (EPA)	32	160.2–787.7	37.6–45.4
Joint DOT and EPA	3	33.0–59.9	8.9–16.9
Total	120	260.9–981.0	68.4–102.9

Source: US Office of Management and Budget, *2015 Report to Congress on the Benefits and Costs of Federal Regulations and Unfunded Mandates on State, Local, and Tribal Entities* (March 10, 2016).

Rulemaking can move at a glacial pace, with a particular rule taking more than a decade to promulgate and defend from legal challenges, meaning a regulation frequently spans several presidential terms. Of the 38,457 final rules published in the *Federal Register* from fiscal year (FY) 2005 through FY 2014, the Office of Management and Budget (OMB) reviewed 2,851 and considered 549 to be major rules. OMB included 120 final rules in its ten-year analysis. Table 5.1 shows that costs for the 120 major rules promulgated from 2004 to 2014 by the federal rulemaking agencies were between 68.4 and 102.9 billion (2010) dollars, while their benefits ranged from 260.9 to 981.0 billion (2010) dollars.[5]

Often, particular agencies or offices within a department or agency are responsible for the majority of rules or most significant rules. Table 5.2 shows the agencies and offices that promulgated the most or most significant rules.[6]

Independent regulatory agencies also issued major rules, and OMB reported the major rules issued from October 1, 2013, to September 30, 2014.[7] Of the seventeen rules issued by nine agencies, most dealt with regulating the financial sector. The Office of the Comptroller of the Currency, Federal Deposit Insurance Corporation (FDIC), and Federal Reserve System promulgated four rules on how much capital banks must hold and on increasing the stringency of the prudential standards for large bank holdings.

Table 5.2.   Estimates of Annual Benefits and Costs of Major Federal Rules: Selected Program Offices and Agencies, October 1, 2004–September 30, 2014

Agency	Number of Rules	Benefits (in billions of 2010 dollars)	Costs (in billions of 2010 dollars)
Department of Agriculture			
Animal and Plant Health Inspection Service	3	1.0–1.4	0.9–1.1
Department of Energy			
Energy Efficiency and Renewable Energy	20	16.4–29.0	6.3–9.0
Department of Health and Human Services			
Food and Drug Administration	5	0.4–14.0	0.2–0.5
Center for Medicare and Medicaid Services	10	17.2–21.7	0.9–4.2
Department of Labor			
Occupational Safety and Health Administration	5	1.1–3.8	0.7–0.8
Employee Benefits Security Administration	3	7.9–22.2	2.1–5.4
Department of Transportation			
National Highway Traffic Safety Administration	12	15.8–27.4	6.6–13.0
Federal Aviation Administration	6	0.4–1.6	0.5–1.1
Federal Motor Carriers Safety Administration	4	0.9–2.2	0.3
Federal Railroad Administration	3	1.1–1.2	0.7–1.7
Environmental Protection Agency			
Office of Air	22	157.4–777.9	36.6–44.1
Office of Solid Waste and Emergency Response	4	0–0.3	−0.3 – −0.4
Office of Water	4	1.1–4.0	0.6–0.7
Department of Transportation/ Environmental Protection Agency			
National Highway Traffic Safety Administration/Office of Air	3	33.0–60.0	8.9–16.9

Source: US Office of Management and Budget, *2015 Report to Congress on the Benefits and Costs of Federal Regulations and Unfunded Mandates on State, Local, and Tribal Entities* (March 10, 2016).

The CFTC and SEC issued two major rules on information sharing between regulated entities and consumers and investors. The SEC issued a rule to reduce the risk effects in money markets. Because the agencies issuing these rules are independent, they are by law not subject to the rulemaking requirements of EOs 12286 or 13563 to submit cost and benefit data to OMB. However, the Small Business Regulatory Enforcement Act requires the

Government Accountability Office to report on all major rules, so though cost-benefit numbers do not always meet the standard of the executive orders, information is collected and reported.

These data set forth the rulemaking entities, costs, and benefits, where available, as well as trends for the period, but their accuracy in showing the implementation through rulemaking of a president's policies generally increases in the later years of an administration. Because a major rule can take years, even occasionally decades, to promulgate, a sitting president may have to spend the early years of his administration dismantling to the extent possible his predecessor's regulatory initiatives, a task that succeeds in proportion to the stage of the rulemaking. Final rules promulgated and effective usually require a new rulemaking to withdraw, whereas rules in earlier stages such as preproposal and proposed can be terminated by policy direction from the president or, in the case of proposed rules, by notice of withdrawal. However, termination of a predecessor's rulemaking means there will be less time and fewer resources spent on promulgating one's own rules. Moreover, the slow pace of rulemaking means that final rules implementing a president's policy may not show up in OMB's analysis during his presidency. Still other rules are "court ordered" and may not have been issued based on the policy of the administration at the time. These often include deadlines and cannot be ignored.

LEGAL REQUIREMENTS

The legal basis for rulemaking is the APA. The APA requires agencies to publish a notice of proposed rulemaking, provide an opportunity for public participation, and publish the final rule with its explanation.[8] These basic requirements still provide a "floor" for agency actions, but agency rulemaking requirements have been greatly expanded over the years by enabling statutes, court decisions, specific legislation, executive orders, and agency practice.

In cases where a person or group of persons is dissatisfied with a rule that has been promulgated, several appeals processes are available. The first is an appeal to the agency, which is usually a letter pointing out where the writer believes the agency misinterpreted the evidence or failed to follow prescribed procedures. If the petitioner has convinced the agency that it has made a mistake, the agency will likely publish a technical amendment for a small change or engage in further rulemaking in order to address an error. If satisfaction is not forthcoming from an appeal to the agency, the APA provides for judicial review.[9] Courts have defined the rights of persons aggrieved by agency action that was based on the administrative record. Judges must consider relevant factors for errors of judgment and whether the rule is based on the administrative record. The standard for judicial review is "arbitrary and capricious," which will be found if the agency failed to follow requirements in statutes (the APA, the agency's enabling statute, the Paperwork Reduction Act, the National Environmental Policy Act, and others); failed to consider important aspects of the issues; made decisions counter to the evidence; or made decisions that did not plausibly represent just a difference of views or particular agency expertise. "Arbitrary and capricious" is a low standard; other statutes are stricter, requiring the rule to be based on "substantial evidence in the record as a whole," and through statutes and court decisions more requirements, such as that the rule be technologically and economically feasible, have been added over time.

Court challenges to the promulgation of a rule made by persons or groups that are affected by it are set forth in statutes, including the APA and the agency's enabling statute, but generally challenges to the rule must take place within the first fifty-nine days of the promulgation. Where there are multiple parties challenging the rule, the actions are combined and heard in one court. For example, in a challenge to OSHA's 2015 respirable crystalline silica standard, the American Foundry Society, the National Association of Manufacturers, industry trade groups, and a union coalition of the United Auto Workers, United Steelworkers, AFL-CIO and North American Building Trades Unions, among others, sued the US Department of Labor. The suits were consolidated and scheduled to be heard in the United States Court of Appeals for the DC Circuit.[10] In OSHA's other recent major rule, concerning the exposure of workers to hexavalent chromium, Public Citizen; the United Steel, Paper and Forestry, Rubber, Manufacturing, Energy, Allied Industrial, and Service Workers International Union; and the Edison Electric Institute were joined by several industry associations, as interveners, in suing the agency. In that case, the Third Circuit Court of Appeals upheld all of the rule's provisions, save the exposure determination provisions, which were remanded to OSHA for further rulemaking.[11]

Major rules often have many diverse litigants, usually one side characterized as wanting the rule vacated for agency failure to meet its legal obligations, particularly as to risks and costs, and the other side wanting the rule sent back to the agency for more work because they allege the agency did not follow its statutory mandates in promulgating a rule that was insufficiently protective. Courts can uphold the agency action, uphold parts of the rule and remand the rule for further agency consideration, or vacate the entire rule. Finally, judicial appeal can also occur when an agency action is enforced against a person or entity. In this process, the appellant usually must present the case to an administrative law judge and a review commission prior to the federal courts.

Since 1996, there has been another way to vacate an agency rule, and that is by a finding of disapproval by both houses of Congress under the Congressional Review Act (CRA).[12] Nearly all major rules, well over 72,000 since 1996, are submitted to Congress for review, but only one rule, OSHA's Ergonomics Rule, has been disapproved. A CRA disapproval is a serious act as, by law, the department or agency is prevented from ever promulgating a rule that is substantially similar to the rule that was disapproved, which likely means there can be no further regulation on the disapproved subject. Rarely, the Senate and the House of Representatives will come together to make a joint resolution of disapproval under the CRA. President Obama vetoed five resolutions involving very significant rules, including a Department of Labor rule on fiduciary duty and conflicts of interest in investment advice;[13] an NLRB rule on representation procedures;[14] and EPA's rules defining waters, addressing greenhouse gases, and providing guidance for carbon pollution from electric utility generating units.[15] The vetoes were not overturned, as a two-thirds vote is needed to override a veto, which generally requires a Senate and House with a super-majority of the same party.

While these results suggest the CRA has not been effective, it is equally possible that the agencies have been writing their rules to avoid the application of the CRA. If this is true, and the mere existence of the CRA has a chilling effect on rulemaking, rules may well be promulgated to avoid the congressional notice and ire that the Ergonomics Rule received, making outright disapproval under the act unnecessary. However, in early 2017, President Trump signed thirteen bills approved by the Republican-led Congress pursuant to the CRA that erased rules on the environment, labor, financial protections, Internet privacy, abortion, education, and gun rights.

THE REGULATORY PROCESS

The regulatory process begins with a catalyst, which could be a specific requirement in a new law or an action pursuant to an enabling statute that is the result of a petition, a catastrophe, or a policy decision to address an issue. The agency generally collects information on such issues as costs and benefits, necessity, risks, affected persons or groups, and the quality of available data. If the rule will have a significant economic impact on a substantial number of small entities, the Small Business Regulatory Enforcement Act (SBREFA), a part of the Regulatory Flexibility Act, requires specific economic analyses. Moreover, the EPA and OSHA are required to set up SBREFA panels made up of affected small-business representatives, and write a report of the comments and proceedings that must be signed by the Small Business Administration, OMB's Office of Information and Regulatory Affairs (OIRA), and EPA or OSHA. Finally, EPA or OSHA must address the issues raised during the SBREFA process in the preamble to the proposed rule.

The draft proposed rule, which will become the notice of proposed rulemaking (NPRM), is reviewed by OIRA for compliance with EO 12866,[16] which has been supplemented and reaffirmed by the more detailed instructions on general principles, public participation, integration and innovation, flexible approaches, science, and retrospective analyses of existing rules in EO 13563.[17] In addition, OIRA reviews the draft for compliance with its guidelines on data quality and peer review, other laws such as the PRA and NEPA, and the president's priorities. OIRA also sends the draft to other federal entities that may have an interest in its contents for their comments. Following OMB approval, the NPRM is published in the *Federal Register*, public comment periods are set, and a public hearing is scheduled, if a request has been made or is anticipated. Along with research acquired by the agency, the comments, hearing testimony, and exhibits become part of the administrative record upon which the rule will be based. Following the close of the comment periods, the agency, using the entire record, drafts the final rule, which then goes through all the administrative approval processes and is published in the *Federal Register* and submitted to Congress for review under the CRA.

PRESIDENT OBAMA'S ACCOMPLISHMENTS

The EPA has the distinction of promulgating the most rules with the highest costs, so it is not surprising that EPA generates controversy for its past, current, and future rulemakings, and is a prime target for President Trump's deregulation efforts. During President Obama's first term, the EPA's finding that greenhouse gases pose a threat to public health and the environment allowed the agency to move forward with proposed standards on National Emissions Standards for Hazardous Air Pollutants (NESHAP) for energy producers, industrial boilers and process heaters, commercial and industrial solid-waste incinerations, cooling water intake structures, and disposal of coal combustion residuals from electric utilities. A short list of EPA's final regulations in President Obama's first term includes rules that exempt previously covered compounds and equipment from spill prevention; emission standards that add and revise limit for portland cement, for mercury, total hydrocarbons, particulate matter, and hydrochloric acid; air quality standards for sulfur dioxide, primarily for power plants; NESHAPs for internal combustion engines; a source rule for boilers and process heaters; and the first federal air standards regulating gas wells that use hydraulic fracturing technology.[18]

President Obama signaled in his 2013 second inaugural address that he would respond to the threat of climate change, as failure to do so would betray children and future generations. He added that though some can deny science, no one can "avoid the devastating impact of raging fires, and crippling drought, and more powerful storms."[19] His response came via the EPA using existing statutes and regulations, not congressional initiatives.

During Obama's last year in office, the EPA, pursuant to the Clean Air Act, promulgated final rules updating its standards for municipal landfill air pollution and creating new standards for oil and natural gas air pollution involving methane, smog-forming volatile organic compounds, and toxic air pollutants.[20] EPA also again finalized its Mercury and Air Toxics Standards for Power Plants, after the Supreme Court had found EPA error in the agency's finding that it did not need to consider costs in its "appropriate and necessary" requirement.[21] In response to the court finding, EPA reopened its rulemaking record and proposed a supplemental finding that a consideration of cost does not alter the EPA's previous determination that it is appropriate and necessary to regulate air toxic emissions from coal- and oil-fired electricity-generating units. EPA also finalized under President Obama a Clean Power Plan, intended to cut harmful pollution from the power sector by 32 percent below 2005 levels and cut smog- and soot-forming emissions threatening public health by 20 percent.[22] This Clean Power Plan, one of the EPA's most controversial rules, was stayed by the Supreme Court on February 9, 2016, pending judicial review by the US Court of Appeals for the District of Columbia Circuit, which heard arguments *en banc* on September 27, 2016. Other rules completed late in the Obama administration included, among others, formaldehyde standards for composite wood;[23] a national pollutant discharge system for municipal storm sewers permit remand rule;[24] and second-phase greenhouse gas emissions and fuel efficiency standards for medium- and heavy-duty engines and vehicles.[25]

Financial reform regulation has been mainly pursuant to the Dodd-Frank Act, which has required extensive rulemaking. As of midsummer 2016, of the 390 rulemakings required under that law, 274 were finalized and 36 proposed, leaving only 80 that remained to be proposed. The fact that the statute places regulation-writing authority in several entities, including the Federal Reserve System and its new Consumer Financial Protection Bureau (CFPB), the SEC and its new Office of Credit Ratings, the Treasury Department and its new Federal Insurance Office, and the FDIC, has not resulted in a speedier, more efficient process.

The Dodd-Frank legislation covers consumer protection by creating the CFPB, an independent watchdog whose job it is to ensure clear, accurate information for consumers on mortgages, credit cards, loans, and other financial products, and to protect consumers from hidden fees, abusive terms, and deceptive practices. The Financial Stability Oversight Council watches over banks and other financial firms such as hedge funds, looking to identify systemic risks from large companies, products, and activities. No longer can these financial institutions look forward to bailouts, as the council can require greater reserves to preclude the "too big to fail" debacle of AIG. A continuing source of controversy and potential litigation is the "Volcker Rule" prohibiting banks from owning and investing in hedge funds for themselves. Risky derivatives (credit swaps) are to be regulated by the SEC or the Commodity Futures Trading Commission in a separate exchange to encourage transparency and prevent crises. The new Federal Insurance Office is charged with identifying insurance companies whose practices and failures create extreme risk and studying the insurance industry with the goal of making affordable insurance available to minorities. Finally, Dodd-Frank encourages reporting of security violations with financial rewards.

Several agencies have proposed important rules pursuant to Dodd-Frank. The SEC proposed a standard that would direct the national securities exchanges and national securities associations to prohibit the listing of any security of an issuer that is not in compliance with Dodd-Frank requirements for disclosure of the issuer's policy on incentive-based compensation and recovery of incentive-based compensation that is received in excess of what would have been received under an accounting restatement.[26] In addition, five agencies and the SEC jointly prepared a rule to implement Section 956 of the Dodd-Frank Act, which requires that the agencies jointly issue regulations or guidelines (1) prohibiting incentive-based payment arrangements that the agencies determine encourage inappropriate risks by certain financial institutions or that could lead to material financial loss; and (2) requiring those financial institutions to disclose information concerning incentive-based compensation arrangements to the appropriate federal regulator.[27] This rule, which remained in the preproposal stage at the time of this writing, is likely an easy target for the incoming Trump administration. The CFPB also promulgated important final rules in the last four months of the Obama administration, including final rules on real estate settlement procedures, mortgage lending, disclosure of race and ethnicity, electronic fund transfers, fair credit reporting, higher priced home appraisals, and adjustments to certain exemptions.[28]

Regulations and guidelines issued pursuant to the Affordable Care Act were extensive, too, but most of this major guidance and rulemaking had been completed by the middle of President Obama's second term. Although several agencies were responsible for promulgating relevant rules, the Department of Health and Human Services (HHS) had the primary responsibility for this set of rules. One important rule recently promulgated by HHS involves nondiscrimination in health programs and activities.[29]

The USDA also issued rules in the last months of President Obama's term, including a rule addressing distribution and control of donated foods, which revises and clarifies requirements to ensure that USDA-donated foods are distributed, stored, and managed in the safest, most efficient, and cost-effective manner, and reduces administrative and reporting requirements.[30] The USDA also issued its final Supplemental Nutrition Assistance Program (SNAP) Promotion rule, which places new limitations on the use of SNAP program funds for promotion, outreach, or recruitment activities associated with the SNAP program.[31]

The Department of Transportation (DOT) under President Obama promulgated final rules addressing high-hazard flammable trains, braking and standards for new and existing tank cars, classifications of unrefined petroleum-based products, and rail routing through risk assessment and information documents.[32] In late 2016, the DOT also finalized its interim final rule on traveling with electronic cigarettes by prohibiting passengers and crew from carrying battery-powered portable electronic smoking devices in checked baggage or charging devices or batteries on board.[33] The DOT extended the e-cigarettes smoking ban to include all charter (i.e., non-scheduled) flights where a flight attendant is a required crew member.[34] The National Highway Traffic Safety Administration promulgated a final rule on rear visibility that requires all vehicles over ten thousand pounds manufactured after May 1, 2018, to have rear visibility technology that expands the field of view to enable the driver to avoid deaths and injuries from back-over accidents.[35] Another rule issued late in the Obama administration deals with mishandled baggage, particularly wheelchairs and scooters.[36]

The Department of Labor's primary rulemaking agencies are OSHA and MSHA, but a 2016 rule from the department's Wage and Hour Division also has far-reaching consequences. The rule extends overtime pay protection to over four million workers.[37] On November 22, 2016, the US District Court, Eastern District of Texas granted an injunction enjoining the department from enforcing the overtime rule. The Department of Justice is appealing the injunction to the US Court of Appeals for the Fifth Circuit.

OSHA is continuing to address such risks to workers as occupational exposures to infectious diseases, noise in construction, and combustible dust, and is exploring rulemakings to prevent workplace violence in health care, occupational exposures to 1-Bromopropane, and back-over injuries and fatalities.[38] Consistent with EO 13563 on Improving Regulatory Review, OSHA is reviewing its standards for bloodborne pathogens and process safety management, among other issues, and working to determine how best to remove obsolete permissible exposure limits for chemical standards. Very significant final rules issued late in the Obama administration address the hazards of silica dust, walking-working surfaces, and beryllium, all of which have a long history of agency consideration.[39] The silica standard covers occupational exposure in general industry and the maritime industry, and in a separate standard, construction work. It protects 2.3 million workers from silicosis and lung disease, among other health problems. The "Walking-Working Surfaces" rule, better known as "Slips, Trips, and Falls," updates older general industry standards on falls, which are among the leading causes of serious work-related injuries and deaths, and establishes requirements for personal fall protection systems. The rule is estimated to prevent 29 fatalities and 5,842 lost-workday injuries every year. OSHA's new beryllium rule reduces employee exposures by 10 times in certain general industry operations, such as foundry and smelting, where adverse health effects include cancer and chronic beryllium disease. This rule is estimated to save 96 lives per year.

MSHA finalized a rule under President Obama addressing proximity detection systems for continuous mining machines in underground coal mines, which requires underground coal mine operators to equip continuous mining machines with proximity detection systems that will reduce the potential for pinning, crushing, or striking accidents in underground coal mines. In 2014, MSHA also promulgated a standard that addresses the hazards of lung disease by providing for full-shift sampling by personal dust monitors; redefining the term "normal production shift"; and adding reexamination and decertification requirements for persons certified to sample for dust and maintain and calibrate sampling devices.[40] The rule provides for single-shift compliance sampling by MSHA inspectors; establishes sampling requirements for mine operators' use of the Continuous Personal Dust Monitor; requires operator corrective action on a single, full-shift operator sample; changes the averaging method to determine compliance on operator samples; and expands requirements for medical surveillance of coal miners. Ongoing areas of regulation include civilian penalty adjustments, the examination of working places in metal and nonmetal mines, exposure to diesel exhaust, and detection systems for mobile machines in coal mines.[41]

The Department of Energy (DOE) also engaged in extensive rulemaking under Obama. In 2012, the Energy Efficiency Program for Consumer Products and Commercial Equipment set efficiency standards for residential clothes washers, fluorescent lamp ballasts, and residential dishwashers. In the last two years of President Obama's administration, the DOE promulgated standards for residential air conditioners and heat pumps, new commercial and residential buildings, residential dishwashers and refrigeration products, and nuclear power activities.[42] Work continues on other efficiency standards, such as residential conventional cooking products, tests for manufactured housing, and chronic beryllium disease prevention.[43] Pursuant to EO 13563, some existing regulations being reviewed include standards for battery chargers and external power supplies, standards for distribution transformers, and alternate efficiency determination methods and rating methods for consumer products and commercial and industrial equipment.

The list of departments and agencies and some of their most recent rules is long, but represents only a small part of federal government rulemaking over a presidential term. Not all rules are equal; some affect many people and others directly affect fewer people. It is important to remember that a department or agency can only promulgate rules that naturally fall within their enabling statutes and that the law does not demand that all wrongs be righted at the same time. Each chief administrator will set his or her priorities, subject to legislative or court action.

ADMINISTRATION BY EXECUTIVE ORDERS AND EXECUTIVE MEMORANDA

Everything a president does as president is a presidential action. Some of these actions carry the force of law and some represent merely the president's wishes. Executive orders, though they apply only to the federal government, can effectively implement a president's policies or repeal the policies of a president's predecessor, and can become voluntary standards of conduct for others outside the federal government. As former OIRA Administrator Cass Sunstein has written:

> Executive actions are nothing new, and presidents, both Republican and Democratic, have properly undertaken a large number of them. They are an established part of our constitutional system—and are typically legitimate because Congress itself has previously authorized them.[44]

Sometimes, as in the case of President Obama's response to the Russian government's hacking operations to influence the US elections, an executive order and a presidential memorandum are issued.

Executive orders give presidents additional power in their competition with Congress over policy making. President Obama had signed 266 executive orders by December 27, 2016, directing his administrative agencies on domestic and international topics large and small. Some of the most important dealt with ethics in the executive branch, Guantanamo detainees, economic recovery, the placement of sanctions on officials of other countries, and protection of the Arctic and Bering Seas.[45] He also used the executive order format (and a memorandum to the Speaker of the House and the president of the Senate) to revoke some of President George W. Bush's executive orders that were not in line with his own;[46] set forth his regulatory policies;[47] order regulatory agencies to comply with past executive orders;[48] promote international cooperation;[49] and identify and reduce regulatory burdens.[50]

Presidential memoranda, which were used extensively by President Obama to address such topics as gun safety, immigration, foreign relations, and the order of succession within government agencies, also further the president's policy goals.[51] Depending on their wording, they can also carry the force of law, but if so, they are subject to legislation and the courts. On

January 16, 2013, frustrated with the lack of congressional action following the massacre at Sandy Hook, President Obama issued three presidential memoranda dealing with tracing of firearms, public health research on gun violence, and the availability of national criminal records.[52] Other memoranda issued late in Obama's presidency addressed cancer, vetoes of legislation on conflicts of interest and sponsorship of terrorism, the normalization of relations with Cuba, legal transparency concerning the use of military force, and the withdrawal of parts of the Arctic Shelf and areas off the Atlantic Coast from mineral leasing.[53] President Obama also issued a memorandum responding to malicious cybersecurity actions by the Russians aimed at influencing the US election.[54]

Both executive orders and presidential memoranda can be used by the president to address issues quickly and exert maximum control over his or her administration, thus giving the president much power. A new president can nullify all of his or her predecessor's orders and memoranda with a single executive order. However, because of the breadth of issues covered by executive orders and presidential memoranda, it is unlikely all would fall at the stroke of a pen by any new president. Nevertheless, new presidents usually nullify some previous executive orders and presidential memoranda in one way or another.

PRESIDENT DONALD J. TRUMP

President-elect Donald J. Trump campaigned against regulations, criticizing many of those in effect and criticizing the fact that like every president before him, President Obama would be promulgating a flurry of "midnight regulations" at the end of his presidency. Bold campaign promises and statements can be hard to keep, and may be especially difficult for a president who has had no experience governing, though Trump, as a businessman and citizen, has been on the receiving end of many regulations. So what precisely is a "midnight regulation" and what tools does the new president have to get rid of or at least minimize the effects of his predecessor's regulations?

A "midnight regulation" is not a precise term, but generally refers to regulations promulgated in the last year, but particularly the last months, of a presidency. Since a sixty-day waiting period is required for a rule to become effective, a new president can, by administrative action, withdraw a rule prior to its effective date. With respect to the transition from Obama to Trump, this means that rules promulgated prior to November 21, 2016, would have completed their sixty-day waiting period by the time Trump took office. Given the many rules issued by Obama during his final months in office, there were many new regulations that the incoming president had the potential to withdraw. What else can be done by a new president depends on the stage of the regulation—that is, whether it is in the proposal stage, final, effective, or under a court challenge.

For the first two to three months of a president's term, the rules in the prefinal stage are usually put on hold so that the new president can evaluate them and see if they meet with the president's policy objectives. The exception to this is when a court has ordered the agency to promulgate a rule within that time period. The new president can then withdraw the prefinal rules, direct the agency to consider different factors, or slow down the development of the rule. Withdrawing the rule would probably require a *Federal Register* notice with reasons for the withdrawal, but the other two actions would be well within the president's prerogative as the chief administrator, with notice to the public given in the agency's semiannual regulatory agenda and annual plan. President Trump's policy objectives, judging from his speeches, are at odds with his predecessor's, so it is likely the new president will take advantage of the time to carefully review and evaluate the regulations in the pipeline.

For regulations recently promulgated (final rules), the new president has several options. If the rule is within the period of review allowed Congress under the Congressional Review Act—in this case, generally final rules submitted to Congress on or after June 13, 2016—committees in both houses could make a finding of disapproval and the president could sign the resulting legislation, rendering the regulation and anything the agency might later promulgate that is substantially similar void. While Congress has reviewed many rules since the act was passed in 1996, and the Senate or House have made findings of disapproval, the only successful CRA disapproval, of OSHA's Ergonomics Standard, prevented the agency from later rulemaking (though OSHA did subsequently issue some guidance on several areas of work related to the rule). At the time President Bush signed the legislation, which was completed within his first two months in office, the Senate and the House had Republican majorities. That configuration exists for President Trump, who moved quickly to make extensive use of the CRA at the outset of his term in office.

If the rule is under a court challenge, President Trump will likely ask for a delay and, after reviewing the arguments, ask to amend the government's position to bring it in line with his policy goals. Major rules, especially those that are controversial, nearly always end up in court, and some that raise particularly important issues wend their way to the Supreme Court. As to the decisions rendered by the courts, they can include stays, approval of the rule, approval of parts of the rule, remand of the rule or parts of the rule to the agency for further consideration, or disapproval of the entire rule.

Administratively, President Trump can withdraw rules that have not become effective, extend a rule's effective dates, make technical changes in the rules, or withdraw rules, even when they are effective, but that would generally require the development of formal reasons through extensive rulemaking. As noted above, rulemaking is costly, using agency time and resources, and these limited resources cannot be fully used to support and develop a new president's agenda unless the agenda is to simply get rid of as much of his predecessor's rules as possible. Rulemaking is a slow process, with some rulemaking efforts spanning several administrations, which means the policies of several administrations are often seen in the final rule. Moreover, the affected parties have invested their time and resources in the process and in many instances have begun to comply with what they believe will be required of them. Finally, as many issues cross state lines, most affected parties would rather be responsible for one regulation, however imperfect, than fifty state regulations, each reflecting its own particular situation as to the regulation. In short, there are reasons for President Trump to have a careful approach in dealing with Obama's policies. But predicting what President Trump will do with the many regulations, executive orders, and presidential memoranda of his predecessor is particularly difficult, since his pronouncements have lacked specificity and he has no governing experience that can be looked to in order to guide an analysis leading to a prediction.

NOTES

1. An earlier assessment of regulatory policy in the latter part of the George W. Bush presidency and the first two years of President Obama's administration appeared in Claudia Hartley Thurber, "The Politics of Regulation in the Obama Administration," in James A. Thurber, ed., *Obama in Office* (Boulder, CO: Paradigm Publishers, 2011), 199–210; and Claudia Hartley Thurber, "The Politics of Federal Regulation: Congress Acts, the President Hones His Policies by Regulation," in James A. Thurber, ed., *Rivals for Power: Presidential-Congressional Relations*, 5th ed. (Lanham, MD: Rowman & Littlefield, 2013), 201–17.

2. Thurber, ed., *Obama in Office*. Major new laws included the American Recovery and Reinvestment Act of 2009, Pub. L. 111-5; Patient Protection and Affordable Care Act, Pub. L. 111-148; and Dodd-Frank Wall Street Reform and Consumer Protection Act, Pub. L. 111-203.

3. Administrative Procedure Act, 5 U.S.C. 553.

4. William J. Clinton, 1993 Regulatory Planning and Review, Executive Order 12866, *Federal Register*, vol. 58, p. 51735, October 4, 1993.

5. US Office of Management and Budget, *2015 Report to Congress on Benefits and Costs of Federal Regulations and Unfunded Mandates*, 9–10.

6. Ibid., 11–12.

7. Ibid., 31–37.

8. APA 5 U.S.C. §§ 551–559; rulemaking is specific to code § 553.

9. 5 U.S.C. §§ 701–706.

10. *North America's Building Trades Unions v. Occupational Safety and Health Administration, U.S. Department of Labor,* USCA Case #16-1105.

11. *Public Citizen and United Steelworkers v. OSHA, 2009,* 557 F.3rd 165 (3rd Cir. Court of Appeals).

12. 5 U.S.C. §§ 801–808.

13. H.J.Res. 88, 114th Cong., Department of Labor: Definition of the Term Fiduciary; Conflict of Interest Rule—Retirement Investment Advice.

14. S.J.Res. 8, 114th Cong., National Labor Relations Board, Representation-Case Procedures.

15. S.J.Res. 22, 23, and 24, 114th Cong., EPA Clean Water Rule: Definition of Waters of the United States; Standards of Performance for Greenhouse Gas Emissions from New, Modified, and Reconstructed Stationary Sources: Electric Utility Generating Units; and Carbon Pollution Emission Guidelines for Existing Stationary Sources: Electric Utility Generating Units.

16. William J. Clinton, 1993, Regulatory Planning and Review, Executive Order 12866, *Federal Register,* vol. 58, p. 51735, October 4, 1993.

17. Barack Obama, Improving Regulation and Regulatory Review, Executive Order 13562, *Federal Register,* vol. 76, pp. 3821–23, January 18, 2011.

18. Unified Agenda and Regulatory Plan, 2012 Agency Statements of Regulatory Policy, Environmental Protection Agency, http://www.reginfo.gov/public.

19. President Barack Obama's inaugural speech, January 21, 2013.

20. Standards of Performance for Municipal Solid Waste Landfills, *Federal Register,* vol. 81, p. 59332, August 29, 2016; Municipal, July 14, 2016; May 12, 2016, amended June 3, 2016; Oil and Natural Gas Sector: Emission Standards for New, Reconstructed, and Modified Sources, *Federal Register,* vol. 81, p. 35824, June 3, 2016.

21. Michigan v. EPA, 135 S. Ct. 2699 (2015).

22. Carbon Pollution Emission Guidelines for Existing Stationary Sources: Electric Utility Generating Units, *Federal Register,* vol. 80, p. 64661, October 23, 2015.

23. Formaldehyde Standards for Composite Wood Products, *Federal Register,* vol. 81, p. 89674, December 12, 2016.

24. National Pollutant Discharge Elimination System: Municipal Separate Storm Sewer System, *Federal Register,* vol. 81, p. 89320, December 9, 2016.

25. Greenhouse Gas Emissions and Fuel Efficiency Standards: Medium- and Heavy-Duty Engines and Vehicles; Phase 2, *Federal Register,* vol. 81, p. 73478, October 25, 2016, effective December 27, 2016.

26. Listing Standards for Recovery of Erroneously Awarded Compensation was proposed pursuant to Section 954 of the Dodd-Frank Wall Street Reform and Consumer Protection Act of 2010.

27. As of January 13, 2017, five of the six agencies that will be proposing these important standards have agreed on the draft; only the SEC has yet to agree. The draft can be found at the agency websites: https://www.ncua.gov/About/Documents/Agenda%20Items/AG20160421Item2b.pdf; http://www.occ.gov/news-issuances/news-releases/2016/nr-occ-2016-49a.pdf; https://www.fdic.gov/news/board/2016/2016-04-26_notice_dis_a_fr.pdf; https://www.fhfa.gov/SupervisionRegulation/Rules/RuleDocuments/Incentive-Based%20Compensation%20NPR_4-26-16.pdf; http://www.federalreserve.gov/newsevents/press/bcreg/bcreg20160502a2.pdf.

28. The full titles of these final rules are Amendments to the 2013 Mortgage Rules under the Real Estate Settlement Procedures Act and the Truth in Lending Act; Status of New Uniform Residential Loan Application and Collection of Expanded Home Mortgage Disclosure Act Information about Ethnicity and Race in 2017; Prepaid Accounts under the Electronic Fund Transfer Act and the Truth in Lending Act; Electronic Fund Transfers (Regulation E); Amendments, Fair Credit Reporting Act Disclosures, Truth in Lending (Regulation Z); Threshold Adjustments, Appraisals for Higher-Priced Mortgage Loans Exemption Threshold Adjustments, Consumer Leasing (Regulation M); Annual Threshold Adjustments, Home Mortgage Disclosure (Regulation C); Adjustment to Asset-Size Exemption Threshold, and Truth in Lending Act (Regulation Z); and Adjustment to Asset-Size Exemption Threshold.

29. Nondiscrimination in Health Programs and Activities, *Federal Register*, vol. 81, p. 31375, May 18, 2016, effective July 18, 2016.

30. Requirements for the Distribution and Control of Donated Foods & TEFAP: Implementation of the Agricultural Act of 2014, *Federal Register*, vol. 81, p. 23086, April 19, 2016.

31. Supplemental Nutrition Assistance Program Promotion, *Federal Register*, vol. 81, p. 92550, December 20, 2016.

32. Hazardous Materials: FAST Act Requirements for Flammable Liquids and Rail Tank Cars, *Federal Register*, vol. 81, p. 53935, August 15, 2016; Enhanced Tank Car Standards and Operational Controls for High-Hazard Flammable Trains, *Federal Register*, vol. 80, p. 26643, May 8, 2015.

33. Hazardous Materials: Carriage of Battery-Powered Electronic Smoking Devices in Passenger Baggage, *Federal Register*, vol. 81, p. 31529, May 19, 2016.

34. Use of Electronic Cigarettes on Aircraft, *Federal Register*, vol. 81, p. 11415, March 4, 2016.

35. Federal Motor Vehicle Safety Standards; Rear Visibility, *Federal Register*, vol. 79, p. 19177, April 4, 2014.

36. Reporting of Data for Mishandled Baggage and Wheelchairs and Scooters Transported in Aircraft Cargo Compartments, *Federal Register*, vol. 81, p. 76300, November 2, 2016.

37. Overtime, Defining the Exemptions for Executive, Administrative, Professional, Outside Sales and Computer Employees under the Fair Labor Standards Act, *Federal Register*, vol. 81, p. 32391, May 23, 2016.

38. See Current Regulatory Plan and the Unified Agenda of Regulatory and Deregulatory Actions, Fall 2016, regulations.gov.

39. Occupational Exposure to Respirable Crystalline Silica, *Federal Register*, vol. 81, p. 16285; Walking-Working Surfaces and Personal Protective Equipment (Fall Protection Systems), *Federal Register*, vol. 81, p. 82494, November 18, 2016; Occupational Exposure to Beryllium, *Federal Register*, vol. 82, p. 2470, January 9, 2017.

40. Lowering Miners' Exposure to Respirable Coal Mine Dust, Including Continuous Personal Dust Monitors, *Federal Register*, vol. 79, p. 24813, May 1, 2014.

41. See Current Regulatory Plan and the Unified Agenda of Regulatory and Deregulatory Actions, Fall 2016, regulations.gov.

42. Procedural Rules for DOE Nuclear Activities, *Federal Register*, vol. 81, p. 94910, December 27, 2016; Procedures for Determining Eligibility for Access to Classified Matter or Special Nuclear Material, *Federal Register*, vol. 81, p. 71331, October 17, 2016.

43. See Current Regulatory Plan and the Unified Agenda of Regulatory and De-regulatory Actions, Fall 2016, regulations.gov.

44. Cass R. Sunstein, "When Presidents Wait and Act on Their Own," *Bloomberg. com*, February 27, 2013.

45. Ethics Commitments by Executive Personnel, Executive Order 13490; Review and Disposition of Individuals Detained at the Guantanamo Bay Naval Base and Close of Detention Facilities, Executive Order 13492; Establishing the President's Economic Recovery Advisory Board, Executive Order 13501; Blocking Property of Certain Persons Contributing to the Situation in Ukraine, the South Sudan, and Central African Republic, Executive Orders 13660, 13661, 13662, 13685, 13664, and 13667; Enhancing Coordination of National Efforts in the Arctic, Executive Order 13689; and Bering Sea Climate Resilience, Executive Order 13754.

46. Revocation of Certain Executive Orders Concerning Regulatory Planning and Review, Executive Order 13497, *Federal Register*, vol. 74, p. 6113, February 4, 2009.

47. Improving Regulation and Regulatory Review, Executive Order 13563, *Federal Register*, vol. 76, p. 3821, January 18, 2011.

48. Regulation and Independent Regulatory Agencies, Executive Order 13579, *Federal Register*, vol. 76, p. 41587, July 11, 2011.

49. Promoting International Regulatory Cooperation, Executive Order 13609, *Federal Register*, vol. 77, p. 26413, May 1, 2012.

50. Identifying and Reducing Regulatory Burdens, Executive Order 13610, *Federal Register*, vol. 77, p. 28469, May 10, 2012.

51. See, for instance, Providing an Order of Succession within the National Endowment for the Arts, issued December 23, 2016.

52. Tracing of Firearms in Connection with Criminal Investigations; Engaging in Public Health Research on the Causes and Prevention of Gun Violence; and Improving the Availability of Relevant Executive Branch Records to the National Instant Criminal Background Check System, issued January 16, 2013.

53. Cancer Moonshot Task Force, January 28, 2016; Veto of HJ Resolution to nullify the Department of Labor's conflict of interest rule, June 6, 2016; Veto Message from the President concerning S 2040, the Justice Against Sponsors of Terrorism Act, September 23, 2016; Presidential Policy Directive concerning US-Cuba Normalization, October 14, 2016; Steps for Increasing Legal and Policy Transparency Concerning the United States Use of Military Force and Related National Security Operations, December 5, 2016; Withdrawal of Certain Portions of the United States Arctic Outer Continental Shelf from Mineral Leasing, December 20, 2016; and Withdrawal of Certain Areas off the Atlantic Coast on the Outer Continental Shelf from Mineral Leasing, December 20, 2016.

54. Taking Additional Steps to Address the National Emergency with Respect to Significant Malicious Cyber-Enabled Activities, December 29, 2016.

CHAPTER 6

Congressional Investigations

An Important Check on Presidential Power

Douglas L. Kriner

The great historian Arthur Schlesinger Jr. is perhaps best remembered for his 1973 jeremiad, *The Imperial Presidency*.[1] Scholars had long observed that presidential power had expanded considerably beyond the Article II confines placed upon it by the framers. Indeed, writing even before the dramatic growth of presidential power following World War II, Edward Corwin noted that presidential history is "largely the history of aggrandizement."[2] However, Schlesinger argued that the Johnson and Nixon administrations had pushed presidential power to new heights by advancing claims of extraordinary unilateral presidential authority to act without the consent of, and even absent any check from, Congress. Recalling Madison's prescient warning that war is "the true nurse of executive aggrandizement,"[3] the immediate impetus for the imperial presidency was the war in Vietnam. So great were the war powers claimed by both presidents, that Schlesinger judged the 1970s American president "the most absolute monarch in the world" on questions of war and peace. Moreover, having articulated these inherent powers in the foreign policy realm, it was all but inevitable that similar claims would spill over into the domestic sphere.[4] However, less than a year after Schlesinger's tome was published, Nixon had resigned, and the imperial presidency had been replaced by an (albeit short-lived) era of "congressional resurgence."[5]

The stunning reversal put into sharp relief an oft-overlooked, but powerful instrument for battling against presidential overreach: the congressional investigation. Indeed, writing only two years after *The Imperial Presidency*, Schlesinger extolled investigations as perhaps the key weapon in Congress's arsenal when endeavoring to check presidential aggrandizement. In this assessment, Schlesinger echoed Harry Truman, who rose to national prominence not for his prowess as a legislator, but as a tenacious investigator. In his farewell address to the Senate, Truman opined: "In my opinion, the power of investigation is one of the most important powers of Congress. The manner in which the power is exercised will largely determine the position and prestige of the Congress in the future." In light of recent events, Schlesinger concluded that Truman could have gone even further. Indeed, "the manner in which Congress exercises the investigative power," Schlesinger argued, "will largely determine in years to come whether the problem posed in the *51st Federalist* can be satisfactorily answered—whether the constitutional order will in the end oblige the American government to control itself."[6]

Since Schlesinger wrote, Congress has undergone significant institutional changes, many of which, such as the rise of rampant obstructionism in the Senate, have weakened the institution and its ability to keep pace with an ascendant executive.[7] However, Congress has continued to employ the investigative arm of its committees to shine a public light on alleged abuse and misconduct in the executive branch, at times with great effect. Little more than two years after winning one of the greatest electoral landslides in American history, the Iran-Contra hearings brought the Reagan administration to the brink of political disaster. Revelations of clandestine meetings with foreign governments, friend and foe, high-stakes arms deals, and shredded documents gripped the public and brought back the Watergate-era mantra, "what did the president know, and when did he know it?" While Reagan would avoid impeachment, many administration officials were not so lucky, and the lengthy investigation proved a significant political handicap for much of the president's last two years in office. Similarly, despite producing the longest peacetime economic expansion in American history, the Clinton years are perhaps best remembered for an almost endless string of inquests into allegations of misconduct—even an inquiry into the potentially improper use of the White House Christmas card list—that culminated in proceedings to impeach the president for personal misconduct and an alleged cover-up of these indiscretions. Finally, while many of the Republican-led inquests during the Obama presidency proved to have more bark than bite, the years-long inquiry into the administration's response to the terror attacks on the American consulate in Benghazi claimed one high-profile casualty: then–secretary of state and 2016 Democratic presidential nominee Hillary Clinton. Secretary Clinton's use of a private e-mail server, which dominated the campaign, including its final weeks when the FBI reopened its investigation into the case, was uncovered incidentally pursuant to the protracted and wide-ranging inquest.

Despite having produced some of the most dramatic moments in American political history, political science has largely overlooked investigations as a nonlegislative, but nonetheless potent, congressional check on presidential overreach.[8] In an oft-overlooked chapter of his seminal book *Divided We Govern*, David Mayhew argued that "beyond making laws,

Congress probably does nothing more consequential than investigate alleged misbehavior in the executive branch."[9] However, until recently only a few isolated studies endeavored to explore investigative politics systematically.[10] Moreover, these studies have focused almost exclusively on the factors that drive variation in Congress's exercise of its investigative power, rather than providing a systematic assessment of investigations as a potential source of congressional leverage vis-à-vis the executive.[11]

Drawing on the insights of Truman, Schlesinger, and Mayhew to take seriously investigations as a valuable tool with which Congress can constrain an ascendant executive offers an important corrective to the dominant scholarly paradigm, which emphasizes only the institutional barriers that often all but preclude legislative redress. Separation of powers scholarship has focused intently on the relative institutional capacities of the president and Congress and found the legislature to be decisively lacking. For all the reasons identified by Alexander Hamilton, presidents have the important advantage of initiative. Perhaps most important, since the dawn of the Republic presidents have articulated and exercised the power to effect significant changes in policy unilaterally. Exploiting the unity and energy of the executive, presidents change policy with the stroke of a pen and challenge other institutional actors to act to restore the status quo.[12]

Congress, by contrast, is at a distinct disadvantage when trying to use its most direct constitutional check on presidential overreach: the power to enact new legislation compelling the administration to change course. The legislature's institutional shortcomings are legion. First, Congress is beset by collective action problems. Whereas presidents have strong incentives to bolster the power of their institution, individual members of Congress, each a political entrepreneur in his or her own right, have scant incentives to defend legislative prerogatives, particularly when this larger institutional goal conflicts with their immediate political interests.[13] Second, the legislative process is riddled with transaction costs; the necessity of cobbling together coalitions across multiple committees and two chambers means that even majority support for a legislative effort to rein in presidential overreach is no guarantee of legislative success. Finally, even if presidential opponents succeed in rallying the requisite majorities in both the House and Senate to check the president, the Senate filibuster and the presidential veto ensure that such efforts will only rarely become law. In the contemporary era of intense partisan polarization, these supermajoritarian barriers are almost insurmountable.[14]

Investigations are a crucial component of contemporary checks and balances precisely because they avoid many of the most severe limitations that all but preclude legislative redress. Most significantly, veto threats are irrelevant. Rather than requiring supermajority support, investigations can be commenced with only the swing of a chairman's gavel. Moreover, a series of rules changes in the mid-twentieth century bolstering committees' autonomous investigative power have greatly reduced transaction costs. Finally, individual entrepreneurs within Congress are often willing to pay the costs of launching and sustaining an investigation of the executive branch to reap the individual political benefits that the resulting publicity and national exposure affords. In this way, investigations can serve as a "common carrier" for the goals of ambitious individual members and for all legislators' shared stake in congressional power.[15]

Critically in an era of intense partisan polarization and seeming institutional dysfunction, Congress can therefore investigate when it cannot legislate. However, in stark contrast to legislation, investigations cannot, on their own, compel presidential compliance and mandate changes in public policy. Rather, investigations can only influence interbranch politics indirectly. By shining a light on alleged wrongdoing and focusing public scrutiny on executive misconduct, investigators can bring popular pressure to bear on the White House in ways that materially affect politics and policy. As such, investigations afford an admittedly imperfect and conditional check on presidential overreach. However, they do provide the president's opponents with a tool that is available when other constitutional mechanisms such as the power of the purse or the power to enact new legislation are not.

The following section describes three pathways through which investigations can produce significant changes in policy outcomes. The chapter then concludes with a pair of case studies illustrating investigative politics. The Church Committee case shows how an investigation can produce immediate policy change, both by spurring new legislation and prompting preemptive presidential concessions. The Benghazi inquest illustrates the changing nature of investigative politics in the intensely polarized contemporary era. Despite the time and resources dedicated to the inquest over multiple years, the investigation accomplished little in the way of immediate policy change. However, its broader impacts were considerable through the great political damage it inflicted both on the Obama administration and the electoral prospects of its would-be Democratic successor.

THREE PATHWAYS OF INFLUENCE

Over the past century, congressional investigators have held more than ten thousand days of hearings into alleged misconduct by actors within the executive branch.[16] Substantively, this impressive range of investigations spans the gamut from the most sensational probes that rattled the very foundation of multiple administrations—such as the McCarthy hearings, Watergate, Iran-Contra, and Whitewater/Lewinsky—to the more targeted investigations that focused on alleged misconduct in specific policy areas—such as maladministration of the Superfund toxic waste cleanup program during the early Reagan administration. That members of Congress would devote so much time and energy to investigations is unsurprising. Investigative hearings are a tailor-made venue for position-taking. Many investigations have been incredibly successful at garnering significant media attention as captured by the term Mayhew coined to describe significant investigations, "publicity probes." Moreover, when Congress investigates, it can impose significant political costs on the president. Perhaps most important, congressional investigations erode public support for the president, a critically important resource in dealing with Congress and an oft-employed metric for assessing presidential political capital.[17] But are most investigations mere political theater? Or do investigations routinely produce significant changes in policy outcomes?

Although investigations, in and of themselves, cannot compel policy changes, there are three pathways through which they can spur significant change. The first two are direct pathways through which investigations may prompt policy change in the substantive area targeted by the investigation. The final pathway is more indirect and suggests that investigations can have broad consequences for policy making in areas unconnected to the inquest itself because they shape presidents' calculation of the costs they stand to incur should they push policy too far from congressional preferences.

Spurring Legislation

North Dakota Senator Gerald Nye earned a reputation as one of the early twentieth century's most tireless investigators for his roles in both the Teapot Dome investigation and as the chair of an eponymous committee investigating the alleged role played by the munitions industries in precipitating American involvement in World War I. Nye argued that investigations yield great benefit by serving as an impetus to new legislation. "Out of practically every investigation there comes legislation improving the security of the Government and the people against selfishness and greed."[18] Clearly, Nye exaggerated the efficacy of investigations in routinely producing legislative remedies to alleged misconduct. However, investigations may under some conditions help overcome the barriers to effective legislative response to abuses of power in the executive branch.

By linking the personal political ambitions of an investigative entrepreneur with the collective institutional interests of Congress as a whole, investigations can help overcome the collective action dilemma that often thwarts legislative efforts to check presidential overreach. Spearheading an investigation can greatly increase a legislator's public profile; following up an inquest with successful legislation can further cement a legislative entrepreneur's legacy or burnish his or her prospects for career advancement.

Mayhew argued that members often shy away from investing too much effort in legislating because of the difficulty of successfully claiming credit for anything other than parochial provisions.[19] However, it is significantly easier for investigators to claim credit for legislation that is a direct product of high-profile hearings. As a result, investigative leaders may be willing to expend the time and political capital needed to overcome the transaction costs and build the requisite coalitions to move bills through the legislative process.

Aside from the fundamental collective action dilemma, the legislative process itself is an arduous one, replete with veto points. In most cases, legislation curbing presidential power, limiting executive discretion more broadly, or even simply adjusting policy so that it better reflects congressional rather than presidential preferences is unlikely to overcome these hurdles. However, investigations have the potential to significantly increase the prospects of legislation overcoming these veto points by building and sustaining public demand for remedial action. When investigations succeed in generating significant media attention and in provoking popular calls for action, more members may perceive their own electoral interests as being best served by supporting legislative efforts at reform. This is critically important to building support for legislation among the president's copartisans, for whom institutional and partisan incentives are in conflict. Public pressure is essential to encouraging such members to determine that their personal political interests are best served by breaking with their party leader and responding to demands for change.

Finally, investigations can also influence presidents' calculations when deciding whether or not to veto legislation that successfully passes both chambers. Even when presidents are confident that their veto will be sustained, they also surely consider the political costs they risk should they veto legislation that is demanded by the public. By raising the salience of an issue and turning public opinion against the president's positions, investigations can make vetoes costlier than they otherwise would have been. As a result, investigations may enable legislation to pass that would never have become law in their absence.

Prompting Preemptive Presidential Action

However, investigations need not result in new legislation to produce significant changes in public policy. Rather, investigations may also prompt presidents themselves to make unilateral policy concessions. Investigations increase the possibility of such concessions for two reasons. First, because investigations increase the prospects for legislative action to curb executive overreach, presidents may act unilaterally to move the status quo away from their own ideal point and closer to that of their opponents in Congress in the hopes of sapping support for an even more dramatic legislative shift. The unilateral politics literature has shown how presidents, when major legislation is imminent, can act unilaterally and make policy concessions to peel off support in Congress for more extreme action.[20] By raising the prospects for legislative success, investigations can also increase the incentives for presidents to preemptively make unilateral policy concessions.

Second, presidents may feel pressure to act even when a legislative response from Capitol Hill is not imminent. Investigations of misconduct or abuse of power, either explicitly or implicitly, cast the administration in a bad light. Lengthy investigations can seriously erode public support for the president and diminish the administration's stock of political capital. As a result, presidents may judge that their political interests are best served by making policy concessions or changing course in the hope of forestalling additional hearings and minimizing the political fallout from the inquest. Presidents may make concessions to avoid these political costs, even when the prospects for legislative redress are remote at best. If investigators can arouse and sustain media and public scrutiny, the political costs of staying the course and resisting any concessions may be considerable.

Anticipated Reactions

There is a third, more indirect pathway through which investigations in one policy area may affect politics and policy much more broadly. Investigations may not simply affect presidential calculations in the policy venue of the investigation itself. Rather, they may also affect presidential behavior more broadly in policy areas unrelated to that immediately under investigation. One of the main mechanisms through which investigations impose political costs is by eroding popular support for the president. Presidents damaged by recent investigations with a lower reserve of political capital may adopt a more modest and restrained approach to a range of issues than a president who has not been politically damaged by a costly investigation. Prominent investigations also inform presidents' calculations about the likelihood of congressional pushback and the political costs they stand to incur should their future actions provoke Congress's ire should they reach too far. A costly investigation in one policy area reminds the president of the political costs he risks should his actions provoke new committee probes in another policy realm.

This indirect dynamic is consistent with Neustadt's advice to presidents about the critical importance of making careful choices with an eye toward defending future power prospects. For example, one of Neustadt's "cases of command" examined the political fallout of Truman's firing of General Douglas MacArthur for insubordination during the Korean War.[21] Truman's decision was plainly justified by the facts, and MacArthur bowed to the president's order and ceded his command. However, MacArthur's firing triggered a lengthy, public, and politically disastrous congressional inquest into the administration's decision and alleged overall mismanagement of the war. While the investigation produced little in the way of concrete efforts to change the administration's prosecution of the conflict, its broader political costs to Truman's professional reputation and his ability to gain traction for other policy priorities were considerable.

Similarly, the immediate legislative legacy of the Iran-Contra investigation was modest—three laws that closed legislative loopholes exploited by Reagan to pursue the Contra aid program.[22] However, the wider impact of Iran-Contra stretched far beyond these narrow efforts to enact legislation circumscribing the president's freedom of action in foreign policy. The investigation significantly weakened Reagan's political position and contributed to a series of important defeats. Most immediately, as the hearings unfolded Reagan lost two key veto battles over the Clean Water Act and a highway reauthorization bill, and the Senate rejected one of Reagan's Supreme Court nominees and forced another to withdraw.[23] Absent the political fallout caused by Iran-Contra, Reagan may well have prevailed in some or even all of these cases, with considerable consequences for public policy.

By weakening the president's political position and shaping anticipatory calculations of congressional pushback should the administration go too far, investigations focused on one narrow policy area can have more widespread ramifications for politics and policy and serve as a broader check on presidential power.

DIRECT INFLUENCE: THE CHURCH COMMITTEE

While 1974 may be best remembered for the culmination of the Watergate scandal and the resignation of President Richard Nixon, it also produced several sensational leaks concerning abuse within the intelligence community that would trigger one of the major investigations of the post-Watergate era.[24] On September 8, 1974, papers across the country revealed that the Nixon administration had authorized more than $8 million for CIA covert activities to destabilize and overthrow the Chilean regime of Salvador Allende.[25] The details were leaked to the press by Massachusetts Democrat Michael Harrington. Harrington had learned of the CIA's Chilean machinations earlier that year during secret executive session testimony of CIA Director William Colby before the House Armed Services Committee. Harrington leaked the testimony to the press in the hopes of building public pressure for a more thorough investigation into the CIA's activities.[26]

The clamor for an investigation only grew when in December of that year the *New York Times* published a column by Seymour Hersh unveiling a laundry list of abuses committed by the CIA, including many instances of the agency turning its clandestine powers against domestic enemies of the Nixon administration.[27] Hersh obtained many of his materials from a report—referred to within the agency as the "family jewels"—commissioned by CIA Director James Schlesinger in the hopes of wiping the slate clean after Watergate.

Seeking to avoid a politically damaging congressional investigation, on January 5, 1975, President Ford announced the creation of a blue ribbon commission chaired by Vice President Rockefeller to determine "whether the CIA has exceeded its statutory authority," and if so to propose recommendations for reform. As CIA Director William Colby remembered, the administration hoped that the commission would "still the outcry and thus prevent a full investigation of intelligence from getting started."[28]

However, Ford's gambit failed and on January 27, 1975, the Senate voted 82–4 to create a Select Committee to Study Government Operations with Respect to Intelligence Activities. Idaho Democrat Frank Church, who would announce his own bid for the Democratic presidential nomination in August, was tapped to head the bipartisan panel that would henceforth be widely known as the Church Committee.[29]

The early months of the Church Committee were spent in a protracted dance with the executive branch over access to administration and intelligence officials and, more importantly, to reams of sensitive documents. By the fall of 1975 the committee was ready to take its case to the public in televised hearings. The undertaking was always politically risky. From the very outset CIA officials had warned that the investigation jeopardized national security and even put American lives in danger.[30] President Ford upped the ante on August 19 when he declared in a nationally televised address: "Intelligence in today's world is absolutely essential to our national security—even our survival. It may be even more important in peace than in war. Any reckless Congressional action to cripple the effectiveness of our intelligence services in legitimate operations would be catastrophic."[31]

Nevertheless, the investigators persevered and the public hearings commenced with an inquiry that cut straight to the heart of accountability within the CIA: the agency's failure to comply with a 1970 presidential order to cease production of and destroy existing stockpiles of biological weapons. These initial hearings presented to the public a scene seemingly ripped from a James Bond movie. The committee revealed that the CIA had maintained a secret store of deadly poisons, enough to kill the entire population of a small city. For dramatic effect, at the hearing Senator Church held aloft an actual dart gun designed to deliver an almost imperceptibly small poisoned dart into an unsuspecting target from more than three hundred feet away. The carefully planned visual procured the desired effect from the media. The front page of the *Chicago Tribune* blared, "CIA bares poison arsenal," and right under the headline was a large picture of the bespectacled Senator Barry Goldwater aiming the dart gun itself and staring down its telescopic sight.[32]

While critics charged that Church was "dazzled by the klieg lights" and more interested in playing to the cameras than conducting a reasoned and fair investigation, the chairman did take the opportunity to remind the media of the larger issue: how the CIA command and control structure had permitted this stockpile to persist (apparently it was the product of actions taken by a midlevel official with little oversight from the top) despite the president's order to eliminate it. "The real question here," Church reminded reporters, "is how presidential orders can be disobeyed on a matter of such importance."[33]

As the fall progressed, the Church Committee turned its attention increasingly to allegations of abuses of power in domestic spying and surveillance. They investigated the "Huston Plan," named after a Nixon aide who sought to enlist the FBI, CIA, and National Security Agency (NSA) in an elaborate effort to intensify surveillance on domestic dissenters. They probed Operation CHAOS, a clandestine CIA operation that spied on student protesters. Inquiries into mail-opening programs revealed an operation that had been conducted on a much larger scale than previously suspected.

The Church Committee clashed most publicly and vehemently with the Ford administration when it finally set its sights on the activities of the NSA in late October 1975. Ford insisted that any disclosure of the ultrasecretive NSA's activities, past or present, could harm national security. However, Church pushed on, arguing that the investigation was essential to examine activities of "questionable propriety and legality," and to ensure that the NSA never again violated the "inalienable rights guaranteed Americans by the Constitution."[34]

By late November 1975, after considerable debate and unease in the Senate, the Church Committee finally released its interim report on the CIA's assassination programs. The report, which gripped and divided the nation, traced the evolution of various plots to assassinate Cuba's Fidel Castro and Congo's Patrice Lumumba. Poisoned cigars, exploding seashells, and even Mafia hits were among the plans considered by the CIA—and revealed by the Church Committee. The report also uncovered mountains of evidence that various officials from across the executive branch had discussed diverse plots against a number of other leaders, including our supposed ally Ngo Dinh Diem of South Vietnam, Rafael Trujillo of the Dominican Republic, and René Schneider of Chile.[35] Some in the press hailed the committee for uncovering the intelligence community's dark past in the hopes of preventing future abuses. The *Los Angeles Times* acknowledged the costs of the exposure, but argued that "such embarrassment is often the price paid for maintaining an open society, the cost exacted so that the American people can know of the activities of their government, and so that abuses of power, where they exist, can be exposed and corrected."[36] Conservative commentator James Kilpatrick, however, charged that the committee's inconclusive report came at too dear a price: "The committee report provides a rich meal for America's detractors to feed on. . . . The committee feels the assassination allegations should be told because democracy depends upon a well-informed electorate, but do the people have to know *everything*?"[37]

Public opinion reflected these divergent points of view. By the end of 1975, just under 40 percent of Americans held a positive view of the committee; 40 percent held a negative assessment of it; and the remainder were unsure. However, the committee's revelations had undeniably tarnished the image of the CIA. In a December 1975 survey, less than a third of Americans held a positive view of the CIA, versus 49 percent who saw it in a negative light. When queried about specific abuses, public sentiment was even more one-sided. For example, 61 percent agreed that the CIA and FBI's spying on prominent Americans entailed a violation of basic rights. Finally, on the question of which party would do a better job at controlling the CIA, Democrats enjoyed an almost two-to-one advantage.[38]

By January 1976, the Church Committee had largely wrapped up its formal public hearings and begun to focus on producing its final report and recommendations for legislative reforms. The committee was well aware that some measure of cooperation with the White House was essential; as Senator Miller reminded the group, "we've all got to keep the threat of a presidential veto in mind when we're spending all these long hours drafting reform legislation."[39] Despite efforts at accommodation, it was plain to all that many members of the Church Committee wished to see more far-reaching reform than the Ford administration would support. In his January 19 State of the Union address, President Ford leveled a public blow against the committee, implicitly calling its public airing of the intelligence agencies' dirty laundry a "crippling of our foreign intelligence services [which] increases the danger of American involvement in direct armed conflict."[40] Such charges gained even greater resonance following the December 23 murder of the CIA station chief in Athens, Greece, a tragedy that critics laid at the Church Committee's feet.[41] Rather than entrusting the task of reforming the intelligence agencies to a dangerous congressional committee, Ford announced his intention to do so unilaterally.

On February 17, 1976, in what the press accurately dubbed "a pre-emptive end-run on the Congress," President Ford announced executive order 11905 during a prime-time press conference. The executive order reorganized the intelligence community along the lines suggested by the Rockefeller Commission in mid-1975; it also included new measures to prevent future leaks and banned any employee of the United States from engaging or conspiring to engage in political assassination. Many Republicans hailed the measures, with Church Committee Vice Chairman John Tower praising them as "positive and carefully planned." Most Democrats and many liberal pundits, such as Anthony Lewis, derided the reforms as little more than "a blueprint for more secrecy, greater executive power, and less congressional oversight."[42] The White House plainly hoped that making even these modest concessions would sap the political drive for more dramatic changes. Church, however, remained resolute, declaring, "I think the president reaches beyond his power. . . . You cannot change law by executive order."

Church, who hoped that success would boost his political fortunes and prospects for higher office, was instrumental in overcoming the transaction costs and other barriers to legislative action that would place greater constraints on the intelligence agencies and the executive branch. Having invested so much in the investigation and staked his national political reputation on its success, Church had an incentive to see the investigation produce concrete changes in law that would both bolster Congress's institutional position against the executive, and serve his own political interests. Church was thus incentivized to subsidize the costs of collective action by doing much of the legislative groundwork and public advocacy needed to make legislation possible.

Most directly, the Church Committee led to the enactment of S Res 400, creating the Senate Select Intelligence Committee to bolster legislative oversight. More than twenty years after Senator Mike Mansfield's initial proposal for such a committee, Church and colleagues were able to marshal the public uproar generated by the investigation to make Mansfield's vision a reality.[43] In addition to providing more vigorous oversight of intelligence activities, the select committee was specifically given sole jurisdiction over all intelligence authorization requests, and it required the administration to submit all major intelligence activities, including covert operations, to the committee for its review (though efforts to grant it veto power were defeated).[44]

The Church Committee also set the stage for the passage two years later of another major piece of legislation during the Carter administration: the Foreign Intelligence and Surveillance Act of 1978 (FISA). Both contemporary journalistic sources and subsequent analysts make clear that FISA was a direct response to the Church Committee investigations and its revelations. For example, in 1978 the *Washington Post* reported, "The Senate intelligence reform bill, on which hearings have now begun, was an outgrowth of the detailed investigation into intelligence abuses by the Church Committee."[45] Similarly, a Congressional Research Service report prepared in the midst of a new intelligence gathering scandal during the mid-2000s echoed this assessment: "The Foreign Intelligence Surveillance Act of 1978, P.L. 95-511, 92 Stat. 1783 (October 25, 1978), 50 U.S.C. §§ 1801 et seq. (hereinafter

FISA), was enacted in response both to the Committee to Study Government Operations with Respect to Intelligence Activities (otherwise known as the Church Committee) revelations regarding past abuses of electronic surveillance for national security purposes and to the somewhat uncertain state of the law on the subject."[46]

FISA was an attempt to resolve the murkiness regarding the legality of electronic surveillance. In its final report, the Church Committee had reviewed the intelligence agencies' long history of wiretapping and bugging American citizens without a warrant. The report argued the dangers to privacy and abuse of power were even greater in the electronic age:

> The inherently intrusive nature of electronic surveillance, moreover, has enabled the Government to generate vast amounts of information—unrelated to any legitimate government interest—about the personal and political lives of American citizens. The collection of this type of information has, in turn, raised the danger of its use for partisan political and other improper ends by senior administration officials.[47]

FISA banned warrantless electronic eavesdropping on communications involving American citizens, and created the Foreign Intelligence Surveillance Court to review and approve executive branch requests for surveillance using different standards of evidence than those required in a civilian court. The law was hailed for restoring the balance between the exigencies of national security and cherished civil liberties, and it governed American intelligence gathering policies for almost twenty-five years, until the Bush administration's authorization of warrantless wiretaps in contravention to the FISA statute prompted a major interbranch clash over the scope of presidential unilateral power.[48]

Thus, the Church Committee investigation illustrates both direct pathways of investigative influence on policy. The dramatic revelations of executive misconduct uncovered by the committee captured the public eye and built support for significant changes to rein in future abuses. Against this backdrop, President Ford tried to preempt support for more robust reforms by making policy concessions to congressional critics via executive order. However, investigators judged that the administration had not gone far enough, and Church and others skillfully leveraged the political pressure generated by the investigation to build support for a series of legislative initiatives bolstering congressional power and placing checks on the autonomy of the intelligence agencies.

INDIRECT INFLUENCE: THE BENGHAZI INVESTIGATION

In sharp contrast to the Church Committee, the Benghazi investigation produced little in the way of concrete legislation or preemptive presidential policy changes. However, the nearly four-year-long investigation nonetheless had considerable influence on politics and policy through indirect means.

On September 11, 2012, protesters, enraged by Egyptian media coverage and denunciations of an amateur video insulting the prophet Muhammad, scaled the walls of the American embassy in Cairo, tore down the American flag, and replaced it with the black banner of militant Islam.[49] That same evening, heavily armed militants stormed the American consulate in Benghazi, Libya. An extended firefight reduced the compound to a smoldering ruin and left four Americans, including the ambassador to Libya, Christopher Stevens, dead.[50] Almost immediately, the Republican presidential candidate Mitt Romney publicly condemned the administration for its failed policy response to the Arab Spring.

To answer critics' charges, on September 16 the administration dispatched UN Ambassador Susan Rice to the Sunday morning talk shows. Rice asserted that the best intelligence suggested that the attack on the consulate was an impromptu response to the events in Cairo. "Our current best assessment," Rice said, "based on the information that we have at present, is that, in fact, what this began as, it was a spontaneous—not a premeditated—response to what had transpired in Cairo."[51]

Congressional Republicans were divided over how to respond to the attack. Several prominent Republicans, including Kentucky senator Rand Paul, called for Congress to cut off aid to Islamic countries. However, others, including John McCain and Lindsey Graham, were adamant that aid should continue.[52] While Republicans could not agree on a policy response, all could agree that the tragedy afforded an opportunity to attack the White House. As a result, with fewer than four weeks remaining before Election Day, the House Oversight and Government Reform Committee, led by Chairman Darrell Issa (R-CA), launched the first investigative hearings into the Benghazi attack.

Issa and committee Republicans launched a two-pronged assault on the administration and its role in the disaster. Perhaps the paramount focus of the preelection phase of the investigation was on the public response of the White House to the tragedy, particularly Susan Rice's public claim that the attack was not organized terrorism, but rather a spontaneous response to the controversial Internet video offensive to Islam that had also triggered the Cairo protests. The administration consciously chose to deceive the American people, Republicans alleged, in a desperate effort to shield the larger failure of their policies in the Middle East and the resurgence of al Qaeda. On CBS News, *Face the Nation*, Senator Lindsey Graham (R-SC) charged:

> They're trying to sell a narrative, quite frankly, that the Mid East, the wars are receding and al Qaeda has been dismantled, and to admit that our embassy was attacked by al Qaeda operatives and Libya leading from behind didn't work I think undercuts that narrative. They never believed that media would

investigate. Congress was out of session, and this caught up with them. I think they've been misleading us, but it finally caught up with them.[53]

The investigation also examined alleged failures by the State Department to provide adequate security for the consulate. Toward this end, Chairman Issa produced witnesses who testified that the State Department had explicitly rejected requests for additional security at the consulate.[54] However, committee Democrats fought back effectively against these charges by arguing that congressional Republicans had led the charge to cut the appropriation for diplomatic security. Indeed, Vice President Biden used this counterattack with considerable effect in his televised debate with Congressman Paul Ryan, arguing that blaming the administration for security lapses was hypocritical: "This lecture on embassy security—the congressman here cut embassy security in his budget by $300 million below what we asked for, number one. So much for the embassy security piece."[55]

The investigation failed to pay immediate political dividends, and President Obama was comfortably reelected when voters headed to the polls on November 6. Undeterred, less than two weeks after the election, three different committees held hearings on Benghazi with a primary focus on the truthfulness of White House statements about what had precipitated the attack. The star witness in this second round of hearings was then-Director of the Central Intelligence Agency and hero of the Iraq War, General David Petraeus. Petraeus informed lawmakers that the CIA had quickly determined the gunmen who attacked the consulate were extremists linked to al Qaeda. However, to avoid tipping off the terrorists by making the information public, the talking points provided to the administration that were the basis of Ambassador Rice's controversial statements suggested that the attack was likely a response to the anti-Islam video that had also triggered the protests in Cairo.[56] Democrats claimed that Petraeus's testimony exculpated the president.[57] Congressional Republicans and conservative media were unconvinced—with some even alleging that the White House had blackmailed Petraeus with the Paula Broadwell affair to coerce his exonerating testimony.[58] However, with the election over, Republican investigators quickly shifted the brunt of their fire away from Susan Rice and President Obama to a new target: the secretary of state and presumptive 2016 Democratic front-runner, Hillary Clinton.

Three factors complicated the Republican investigators' efforts to blame the State Department and inflict political damage on Secretary Clinton. First, during recent budget showdowns, Republicans had led the charge for budget cuts—including substantial cuts to the diplomatic security budget. The 2012 fiscal year budget included only $2.1 billion to secure more than 275 diplomatic posts.[59] Indeed, the only legislative shift produced by the Benghazi investigation was to increase funding for diplomatic security in future fiscal years—a policy initially supported by the Democrats.[60] Second, before investigators could ramp up their attacks on security lapses, the blue ribbon commission created by the administration to analyze the security failure released its report, and the State Department endorsed and agreed to implement its recommendations. Finally, and most problematically, in November 2012 media reports leaked to the public a surprising revelation. The American consulate in Libya was more than a diplomatic post. It was also a screen for a clandestine CIA presence in Benghazi. Indeed, of the thirty Americans evacuated from Benghazi, only seven worked for State; almost all of the others were clandestine CIA personnel. As the *Wall Street Journal* reported:

> The CIA's secret role helps explain why security appeared inadequate at the U.S. diplomatic facility. State Department officials believed that responsibility was set to be shouldered in part by CIA personnel in the city through a series of secret agreements that even some officials in Washington didn't know about.[61]

Revelations about the CIA's secret mission and role in providing security for the diplomatic mission could rationally have tempered the investigative furor on Capitol Hill. Probing further into security arrangements almost certainly risked sensitive revelations of clandestine intelligence activities in Libya. However, congressional Republicans pushed on, largely undeterred. Senator Lindsey Graham accused the State Department of hiding behind the CIA and endeavoring to pass the buck: "Obviously somebody in the State Department [is] trying to say, when it comes to security, it was their job, not ours." "Well here's what somebody needs to ask," Graham continued. "If that were so, why did the people on the ground not know that?"

On January 23, 2013, investigators trained their fire directly at Secretary Clinton when she appeared before both the Senate Foreign Relations and House Foreign Affairs Committees. Clinton praised the department's response to the attacks, noting that the Pickering and Mullen Accountability Review Board had also commended the department for "timely and exceptional coordination," and speedy decision making. Clinton also emphasized the progress already made in implementing the twenty-nine recommendations made by the board. Committee Republicans strained mightily to focus the hearing on the State Department's refusal to grant requests for additional security in the summer of 2012 and to tie Secretary Clinton personally to those decisions. Secretary Clinton denied that she ever saw the requests, and she referred her inquisitors to the Accountability Review Board, which noted that such requests do not ordinarily reach the secretary of state.[62]

Somewhat surprisingly, amid the charges and Clinton parries, any discussion or even acknowledgment of the CIA's role in providing security at the compound was all but absent. Indeed, the only oblique reference to the CIA at all occurred when Senator Paul asked Secretary Clinton whether the administration was facilitating the transfer of arms from Libya to Turkey via the annex. Following protocol, Clinton replied curtly, "You will have to direct that question to the agency that ran the annex," without ever mentioning the CIA by name.[63]

Democrats in both chambers largely rallied to Clinton's defense and accused their colleagues on the other side of the aisle of playing politics with national security. Senator Dianne Feinstein argued that instead of conducting a serious investigation into security failures and how best to correct them, Republicans had hijacked the hearings in the hopes of politically damaging Clinton. "My concern is when Hillary Clinton's name is mentioned 32 times in a hearing, then the point of the hearing is to discredit the Secretary of State, who has very high popularity and may well be a candidate for president," Feinstein argued.[64]

Yet Clinton's testimony did not conclude the investigation into Benghazi. In April 2013, Issa's House committee, which began the investigative spate, issued its preliminary report on the attacks, including a strong indictment of Secretary Clinton and allegations that she lied to the committee and had personally approved reductions in security at the consulate.[65] Chairman Issa reiterated the claims in public on Fox News: "The secretary of state was just wrong. She said she did not participate in this, and yet only a few months before the attack, she outright denied security in her signature in a cable in April, 2012."[66]

Congressional investigators were buoyed by strong public support for continued investigations. A May 2013 poll revealed 69 percent of Americans agreeing that the Benghazi attack involved serious questions that still needed to be investigated further; a majority, 52 percent, strongly agreed with this statement, versus only 21 percent who disagreed.[67] House Republicans held additional hearings on Benghazi in September 2013 and in April 2014.

Then on May 8, 2014, almost twenty full months after the attack, House Republicans ensured that the investigation would continue through the midterm elections and well into the 2016 presidential election cycle by creating a new Select Committee on the Events Surrounding the 2012 Terrorist Attack in Benghazi. The decision to continue the investigation can only be explained as a political calculation that keeping Benghazi in the public eye could redound to the Republicans' electoral advantage by weakening both Obama, and even more important, Hillary Clinton.

In March 2015, investigators uncovered their greatest and most damaging revelation—and it had virtually nothing to do with the events in Benghazi. In response to the Benghazi committee's requests for all of the secretary's e-mails, on March 3 a Clinton spokesman revealed that Clinton had used a private e-mail server during her tenure at the State Department in addition to the official departmental e-mail system. The next day, Chairman Trey Gowdy issued Clinton a subpoena for all e-mails sent through this private server. This triggered eighteen months of frenetic investigation and speculation into whether Clinton had ever knowingly or unknowingly sent classified material through her private server.

The political damage inflicted on Clinton was undeniable. Indeed, House Majority Leader Kevin McCarthy openly boasted about it on Fox News:

> Everybody thought Hillary Clinton was unbeatable, right? But we put together a Benghazi special committee. A select committee. What are her numbers today? Her numbers are dropping. Why? Because she's untrustable. But no one would have known that any of that had happened had we not fought to make that happen.[68]

The political damage would increase exponentially when the FBI launched its own inquiry into Clinton's e-mails. After tension-filled months, Director Comey announced on July 5, 2016, that his investigation had concluded that, while Clinton was extremely negligent in her handling of classified material over e-mail, no charges should be filed. The matter seemed resolved. But then, less than two weeks before the election, Comey sent shock waves through the political system by reopening the case in response to the discovery of new e-mails pursuant to an unrelated investigation of former congressman Anthony Weiner, the estranged spouse of Clinton aide Huma Abedin. Less than forty-eight hours before the election, Comey quietly announced that the new FBI review had not changed his initial determination. However, by then the damage was done.

The polling evidence is unequivocal. A majority of Americans believed that Clinton had broken the law; 40 percent believed she had intentionally done so; and another 39 percent agreed that she had shown poor judgment.[69] Almost one in three Americans replied that the FBI's eleventh-hour decision to reopen the e-mail case made them less likely to vote for Clinton.[70] And Benghazi itself continued to undercut Clinton's campaign message of superior experience and judgment. In August 2016, almost four years after the attack, a majority of Americans said they were bothered "a lot" by Clinton's handling of the attack, versus only 23 percent who said they were not bothered at all by her performance in the crisis.[71]

Despite its extraordinary length, the Benghazi investigation had little direct influence on American policy in the Middle East. Congress did not pass any legislation mandating a change in Obama's conduct of foreign policy in the region. Similarly, the only preemptive action taken by the administration was a series of modest reforms to diplomatic security procedures advocated by the State Department's own Accountability Review Board. However, effecting change in foreign policy was not the Republican investigators' primary objective: politically weakening the Obama administration and Hillary Clinton's presidential prospects was. In this, the investigation succeeded tremendously. Given the razor-thin margin between Clinton and Trump in the 2016 election (Clinton, of course, won the popular vote by more than 2 percent), the consequences for policy are perhaps difficult to overstate. The Republicans' best hope to overturn many of Obama's crowning achievements, from the Affordable Care Act to his unilateral moves in immigration and environmental policy, was to first win back the Senate (which they did in 2014) and then the White House. A protracted and wide-ranging investigation into anything politically damaging that was even tenuously linked to Benghazi was an important part of this broader strategy.

CONCLUSION

The conventional wisdom correctly notes that in interbranch power struggles, Congress operates at a distinct disadvantage. Despite enjoying a much broader array of formal constitutional powers, the legislature is hamstrung by steep institutional barriers to their successful use. As a result, the pendulum of power in Washington has plainly swung from the first branch of government to the second.

Nonetheless, investigations offer Congress an informal, but important, check on presidential overreach. Congress can investigate when it cannot legislate. Investigations routinely attract significant media attention and focus public scrutiny on alleged executive misconduct. This, in turn, enables investigators to impose significant political costs on the administration, costs that can influence both legislative and presidential behavior.

Polarization has changed many facets of congressional politics, and investigative politics is no exception. Perhaps most important, polarization has made investigations in the contemporary polity almost exclusively a feature of divided government.[72] For example, when Hillary Clinton appeared poised to win the 2016 presidential race, Washington was abuzz with speculation that Jason Chaffetz and his House Oversight and Government Reform Committee would engage in endless investigations of alleged Clinton scandals. However, after Trump's surprise win, Chaffetz's investigative zeal all but disappeared, despite the enormous fodder of material provided by potential conflicts of interest with Trump's businesses, the Trump campaign's ties to Russia and charges of Russian interference in the election, and allegations of sexual assault, among others.[73] In the contemporary polarized era, partisan incentives almost completely overwhelm institutional ones.

Second, polarization has decreased the importance of the first two pathways of investigative influence and increased congressional reliance on the third. Throughout American history, many investigations, like the Church

Committee, produced either new legislation or preemptive presidential policy concessions. In a recent study of the policy consequences of Mayhew's list of major investigations, Kriner and Schickler found that between 1947 and 2002, a full 80 percent of major congressional probes influenced policy through one or both of these pathways.[74] However, rising partisanship and polarization have weakened these pathways by making the passage of legislation combating presidential overreach even less likely than it was in the past. Presidents may still make concessions in an effort to sap the strength of an investigation and avoid incurring greater political costs. However, presidents are much less likely to do so because they fear that legislation reining them in is imminent.

Instead, most investigations in the contemporary polity focus on the third, more indirect pathway of influence—ratcheting up the political costs on the administration. Investigations have always been political. Even the very first congressional investigation, into the War Department and its responsibility for an Indian massacre in 1791, was exploited by Jeffersonians to launch a partisan attack against leading Federalists, particularly Secretary of War Henry Knox and Alexander Hamilton. Congressional probes designed to score political points are nothing new. However, in the transformed political environment, recent investigations have tended to focus almost exclusively on politically damaging the White House as a long-term strategy for political gain and policy change.

Despite these important changes, investigations remain an important tool of interbranch conflict. When institutional barriers all but preclude other responses to presidential overreach, Congress can investigate. And when it does so, in certain conditions Congress can materially affect interbranch politics and policy outcomes.

NOTES

The argument of this chapter concerning the importance of congressional investigations as a check on presidential power and the pathways through which investigations can produce concrete changes in policy outcomes is abstracted from Douglas Kriner and Eric Schickler, *Investigating the President: Congressional Checks on Presidential Power* (Princeton, NJ: Princeton University Press, 2016). I would also like to thank Cory Willingham for valuable research assistance.

1. Arthur Schlesinger Jr., *The Imperial Presidency* (Boston: Houghton Mifflin Company, 1973).

2. Edward Corwin, *The President: Office and Powers* (London: H. Milford, Oxford University Press, 1941), 310.

3. James Madison, *The Writings of James Madison: 1790–1802*, ed. Gaillard Hunt (New York: G.P. Putnam's Sons, 1906 [1794]), 174.

4. Schlesinger, *The Imperial Presidency*, ix.

5. James Sundquist, *The Decline and Resurgence of Congress* (Washington, DC: Brookings Institution Press, 1981).

6. Arthur Schlesinger Jr. and Roger Burns, *Congress Investigates: A Documented History, 1792, 1974* (New York: Chelsea House Publishers, 1975), xxvi.

7. Thomas Mann and Norman Ornstein, *The Broken Branch: How Congress Is Failing America and How to Get It Back on Track* (New York: Oxford University Press, 2006).

8. Legal scholars have traced the evolution of the investigative power, which is mentioned nowhere in the Constitution, over time. See, for example, Nelson McGeary, *The Developments of Congressional Investigative Power* (New York: Columbia University Press, 1940); Peter Shane, "Legal Disagreement and Negotiation in a Government of Laws: The Case of Executive Privilege Claims Against Congress," *Minnesota Law Review* 71 (1987): 461–542; John Grabow, *Congressional Investigations: Law and Practice* (Clifton, NJ: Prentice Hall Law and Business, 1988). Historians have tended to focus intensely either on the causes and consequences of individual investigations, or the general arc of investigative practice over time. However, little scholarship in this vein endeavors to assess systematically the power of the investigative tool as a check on presidential overreach. See, for example, August Raymond Ogden, *The Dies Committee: A Study of the Special House Committee for the Investigation of Un-American Activities, 1938–1944* (Washington, DC: Catholic University of America Press, 1945); Donald Riddle, *The Truman Committee: A Study in Congressional Responsibility* (New Brunswick, NJ: Rutgers University Press, 1964); Arthur Schlesinger Jr. and Roger Burns, *Congress Investigates: A Documented History, 1792, 1974* (New York: Chelsea House Publishers, 1975); Telford Taylor, *Grand Inquest: The Story of Congressional Investigations* (New York: Simon and Schuster, 1955); James Hamilton, *The Power to Probe: A Study of Congressional Investigations* (New York: Vintage Books, 1976).

9. David Mayhew, *Divided We Govern: Party Control, Lawmaking, and Investigations, 1946–1990* (New Haven, CT: Yale University Press, 1991), 8.

10. Douglas Kriner and Liam Schwartz, "Divided Government and Congressional Investigations," *Legislative Studies Quarterly* 33 (2008): 295–321; David Parker and Matthew Dull, "Divided We Quarrel: The Politics of Congressional Investigations, 1947–2004," *Legislative Studies Quarterly* 34 (2009): 319–45; David Parker and Matthew Dull, "Rooting Out Waste, Fraud and Abuse: The Politics of House Committee Investigations, 1847 to 2004," *Political Research Quarterly* 66 (2012): 630–44.

11. For an important exception, see Paul Light, *Government by Investigation: Congress, Presidents, and the Search for Answers, 1945–2012* (Washington, DC: Brookings Institution Press, 2014). However, Light's focus is broader and includes many congressional investigations, such as the 2005 investigation into steroid use in Major League Baseball, that do not focus on alleged misconduct by some actor within the executive branch.

12. William Howell, *Power Without Persuasion: The Politics of Direct Presidential Action* (Princeton, NJ: Princeton University Press, 2003).

13. Terry Moe, "The Presidency and the Bureaucracy: The Presidential Advantage," in *The Presidency and the Political System*, ed. Michael Nelson (Washington, DC: Congressional Quarterly Press, 1994), 451.

14. Keith Krehbiel, *Pivotal Politics: A Theory of U.S. Lawmaking* (Chicago: University of Chicago Press, 1998).

15. Eric Schickler, "Entrepreneurial Defenses of Congressional Power," in *Formative Acts: Reckoning with Agency in American Politics*, ed. Stephen Skowronek and Matthew Glassman (Philadelphia: University of Pennsylvania Press, 2007).

16. For a detailed overview of investigative activity from 1898 through 2014, see Kriner and Schickler, *Investigating the President*, 35–40.

17. For the influence of investigations on presidential approval, see Douglas Kriner and Eric Schickler, "Investigating the President: Committee Probes and Presidential Approval, 1953–2006," *Journal of Politics* 76 (2014): 521–34. For the importance of presidential approval in shaping legislative success, see Brandice Canes-Wrone and Scott De Marchi, "Presidential Approval and Legislative Success," *Journal of Politics* 64 (2002): 491–509; Matthew Beckmann, *Pushing the Agenda: Presidential Leadership in US Lawmaking, 1953–2004* (New York: Cambridge University Press, 2010), 141–42.

18. Quoted in McGeary, *The Developments of Congressional Investigative Power*, 7.

19. David Mayhew, *Congress: The Electoral Connection* (New Haven, CT: Yale University Press, 1974).

20. Howell, *Power Without Persuasion*, 2003.

21. Richard Neustadt, *Presidential Power and the Modern Presidents* (New York: The Free Press, 1990 [1960]).

22. "Limited Legal Legacy Left by Iran-Contra," *CQ Almanac*, 1989, 541–43.

23. "Special Report: The Iran-Contra Affair," *CQ Almanac*, 1987, 61–76.

24. The National Security Act of 1947 created the CIA, but the scope of its intelligence-gathering authority was shrouded in ambiguity. See, for example, Patrick McGarvey, *CIA: The Myth and the Madness* (Baltimore, MD: Penguin, 1972).

25. Seymour Hersh, "C.I.A. Chief Tells House of $8 Million Campaign Against Allende in '70–73," *New York Times*, September 8, 1974, 1; Laurence Stern, "CIA Role in Chile Revealed: Anti-Allende Funding Put at $11 Million," *Washington Post*, September 8, 1974, A1.

26. L. Britt Snyder, *The Agency and the Hill: CIA's Relationship with Congress, 1947–2004* (Washington, DC: Center for the Study of Intelligence, 2008).

27. Seymour Hersh, "Huge C.I.A. Operation Reported in U.S. Against Antiwar Forces, Other Dissidents in Nixon Years," *New York Times*, December 22, 1974, 1.

28. William Colby and Peter Forbath, *Honorable Men: My Life in the CIA* (New York: Simon and Schuster, 1978), 398.

29. The House formed its own investigative panels, the first chaired by Lucien Nedzi (D-MI) and the second by Otis Pike (D-NY). The latter operated in parallel with the Church Committee. However, the Pike Committee failed to achieve the level of consensus in the House that the Church Committee succeeded in marshaling in the Senate; indeed, the Pike Committee's final report was never officially published because of heightened opposition. As a result, this case study focuses on the Church Committee, while acknowledging that both investigations played an important role in precipitating the major policy changes in intelligence that occurred throughout the late 1970s.

30. Robert Jackson, "CIA Critics Hinder Work, Colby Warns," *Los Angeles Times*, February 21, 1975, A1.

31. Gerald R. Ford, "Address in Minneapolis Before the Annual Convention of the American Legion," August 19, 1975. Online by Gerhard Peters and John T. Woolley, The American Presidency Project, http://www.presidency.ucsb.edu/ws/?pid=5174.

32. Harry Kelly, "CIA Bares Poison Arsenal: Dart Gun Can Kill Without Any Clues," *Chicago Tribune*, September 17, 1975, 1.

33. Johnson, *A Season of Inquiry*, 74.

34. *Congressional Quarterly Almanac*, 1975, 395.

35. George Lardner, "Senators Issue Report on CIA's Death Plots," *Boston Globe*, November 21, 1975, 1; Jim Squires, "Senate CIA Report: They Didn't Fix the Blame," *Chicago Tribune*, November 23, 1975, A1.

36. "Assassination and Foreign Policy," *Los Angeles Times*, November 23, 1975, 12.

37. James Kilpatrick, "Reflections on the CIA Report," *Los Angeles Times*, November 28, 1975, A7.

38. Just under a third, 32 percent, said Democrats; only 17 percent answered Republicans; 33 percent said it did not matter, while 18 percent were not sure. Survey conducted by Louis Harris & Associates, December 20–30, 1975, and based on 1,394 telephone interviews. Sample: National adult. [USHARRIS.012276.R02]. Retrieved October 17, 2014, from the iPOLL Databank, The Roper Center for Public Opinion Research, University of Connecticut, http://www.ropercenter.uconn .edu/data_access/ipoll/ipoll.html.

39. Johnson, *A Season of Inquiry*, 164.

40. Gerald R. Ford, "Address Before a Joint Session of the Congress Reporting on the State of the Union," January 19, 1976. Online by Gerhard Peters and John T. Woolley, The American Presidency Project, http://www.presidency.ucsb.edu/ws/?pid=5677.

41. For example, *Washington Star* columnist Charles Bartlett wrote, "the assassination of the CIA Station Chief, Richard Welch, in Athens is a direct consequence of the stagey hearings of the Church Committee . . . the Committee's prolonged focus on CIA activities in Greece left agents there exposed to random vengeance." Church flatly rejected the logic and fired back at similar charges from the White House, "Utterly untrue. And unworthy of a spokesman of the president even to permit such an innuendo." Quoted in Johnson, *A Season of Inquiry*, 161, 170.

42. Johnson, *A Season of Inquiry*, 193, 195.

43. The House followed suit a year later and in 1977 created its own Permanent Select Committee on Intelligence.

44. For an overview, see William Newby Raiford, "To Create a Senate Select Committee on Intelligence: A Legislative History of Senate Resolution 400," *CRS Report*, August 12, 1976. Since enactment of Hughes-Ryan in December 1974, the CIA had been required to submit briefings on covert operations to Congress; however, most such briefings were limited in scope. S Res 400, however, directed all intelligence agencies, not just the CIA, to report on sensitive operations to the newly created Select Intelligence Committee. Because they were established by simple resolution, these requirements were not initially legally binding; however, they were later codified by the 1980 Oversight Act.

45. David Wise, "Intelligence Reforms: Less Than Half a Loaf," *Washington Post*, April 23, 1978, D3.

46. Elizabeth Bazan, "The Foreign Intelligence Surveillance Act: An Overview of Selected Issues," *CRS Report*, July 7, 2008, 1. Another report noted, "The legislative history of FISA reflects serious concerns about the past NSA abuses reflected in the Church Committee reports." Elizabeth Bazan and Jennifer Elsea, "Presidential

Authority to Conduct Warrantless Electronic Surveillance to Gather Foreign Intelligence Information," *CRS Report,* January 5, 2006, 22.

47. Quoted in Bazan and Elsea, "Presidential Authority to Conduct Warrantless Electronic Surveillance to Gather Foreign Intelligence Information."

48. Ira Shapiro, "The Foreign Intelligence Surveillance Act: Legislative Balancing of National Security and the Fourth Amendment," *Harvard Journal on Legislation* 15 (1977–78): 119–204. Congress amended FISA after 9/11 to "modernize" the legislation. However, President Bush's unilateral authorization of the NSA program went even further. See Elizabeth Bazan, "The Foreign Intelligence Surveillance Act: An Overview of the Statutory Framework and Recent Judicial Decisions," *CRS Report,* March 31, 2003, RL 30465.

49. "Mysterious Anti-Muslim Movie Prompts Protest in Egypt," Associated Press, September 11, 2012, http://www.nytimes.com/2012/09/12/world/middleeast/movie -stirs-protest-at-us-embassy-in-cairo.html.

50. David Kirkpatrick and Steven Lee Myers, "Libya Attack Brings Challenges to the U.S.," *New York Times,* September 13, 2012, A1.

51. Jake Tapper, "Ambassador Susan Rice: Libya Attack Not Premeditated," ABC News, September 16, 2012, http://abcnews.go.com/blogs/politics/2012/09/ambas sador-susan-rice-libya-attack-not-premeditated.

52. Emily Cadei, "Fractured Reactions: Responses to Libya Attacks Reveal GOP Divide," *CQ Weekly* (September 17, 2012): 1858, http://library.cqpress.com.ezproxy .bu.edu/cqweekly/weeklyreport112-000004152983.

53. Transcript, *Face the Nation,* October 14, 2012, http://www.cbsnews.com/news/ face-the-nation-transcripts-october-14-2012-sen-graham-rep-issa-rep-cummings/2.

54. "The Security Failures of Benghazi," Hearing before the Committee on Oversight and Government Reform, House of Representatives, October 10, 2012, 112-193, p. 106.

55. http://www.debates.org/index.php?page=october-11-2012-the-biden-rom ney-vice-presidential-debate.

56. Jonathan Landay, "Petraeus: CIA Secrets Cut from Public Account After US Consulate Attack," McClatchy Tribune News Service, November 16, 2012.

57. Eric Schmitt, "Petraeus Says U.S. Tried to Avoid Tipping Off Terrorists After Libya Attack," *New York Times,* November 17, 2012, 10.

58. "Was Petraeus Blackmailed into Echoing Benghazi Lie?" *Investor's Business Daily,* November 19, 2012, A17.

59. Jonathan Broder, "Getting the Diplomatic Security You Pay For," *CQ Weekly* (October 15, 2012): 2050–51.

60. Susan Epstein, "Diplomatic and Embassy Security Funding Before and After the Benghazi Attacks," *CRS Report,* September 14, 2014.

61. Adam Entous, Siobhan Gorman, and Margaret Coker, "CIA Takes Heat for Role in Libya," *Wall Street Journal,* November 2, 2012, A1. See also Max Fisher, "WSJ: State Dept. and CIA had Secret, Botched Deal for Benghazi Security," *Washington Post,* November 2, 2012.

62. "Benghazi: The Attacks and the Lessons Learned," Hearing before the Committee on Foreign Relations, United States Senate, January 23, 2013, S Hrg. 113-184, p. 15.

63. Ibid., 42–43.

64. "On Benghazi Probe, GOP's Issa Says 'Hillary Clinton's Not a Target,'" NBC News, May 12, 2013, http://firstread.nbcnews.com/_news/2013/05/12/18209616 -on-benghazi-probe-gops-issa-says-hillary-clintons-not-a-target?lite.

65. Interim Progress Report for the Members of the House Republican Conference on the Events Surrounding the September 11, 2012, Terrorist Attacks in Benghazi, Libya, April 23, 2013, http://thehill.com/images/stories/blogs/globalaffairs/ benghazi.pdf.

66. Kevin Cirilli, "Darrell Issa: Hillary Clinton 'Wrong' on Benghazi," *Politico*, http://www.politico.com/story/2013/04/darrell-issa-hillary-clinton-benghazi-90560 .html#.

67. Survey Conducted by Gallup Organization, May 14–15, 2013, and based on 1,022 telephone interviews. Sample: National adult. Interviews were conducted with respondents on landline telephones and cellular phones. [USGALLUP.13MAY14.R03] A year later, support for continued investigations was just as strong, if not stronger: Conducted by Gallup Organization, June 9–10, 2014, and based on 1,012 telephone interviews. Sample: National adult. Interviews were conducted with respondents on landline telephones and cellular phones. The sample includes 50 percent landline and 50 percent cell phone respondents. [USGALLUP.061314.R01C]

68. Transcript, *Hannity*, September 29, 2015, http://www.foxnews.com/tran script/2015/09/29/rubio-cruz-talk-foreign-policy-govt-shutdown-mccarthy-on-how -differs-from.

69. CBS News Poll, October 2016 [survey question]. USCBS.101816.R56. CBS News [producer]. Cornell University, Ithaca, NY: Roper Center for Public Opinion Research, iPOLL [distributor], accessed January 2, 2017.

70. CBS News/*New York Times* Poll, October 2016 [survey question]. US-CBSNYT.110316.R56. CBS News/*New York Times* [producer]. Cornell University, Ithaca, NY: Roper Center for Public Opinion Research, iPOLL [distributor], accessed January 2, 2017.

71. Bloomberg Poll, August 2016 [survey question]. USSELZER.081016.R24C. Selzer & Co. [producer]. Cornell University, Ithaca, NY: Roper Center for Public Opinion Research, iPOLL [distributor], accessed January 2, 2017.

72. Kriner and Schickler, *Investigating the President*, 47–52.

73. Stephanie Akin, "Questions Loom for House's Top Investigator," *Roll Call*, December 14, 2016, http://www.rollcall.com/news/questions-loom-congresss-top -inquisitor.

74. Kriner and Schickler, *Investigating the President*, 160–70.

CHAPTER 7

White House–Congressional Relations in a Polarized Age

Gary Andres and Patrick Griffin

Partisan polarization paints a broad backdrop for the twenty-first-century Congress. Its bold brushstrokes now cover nearly every corner of the legislative canvas with bright lines of division, impacting roll-call votes, party-leadership tactics, committee legislative products, and political fundraising, to name a few.

Today's conventional wisdom asserts that polarization has reemerged over the past two decades after a hundred-year hiatus. Some also maintain that because the parties are so closely divided in Congress, power could change hands in any election, so unlike the decades of the past, there is no incentive to do anything with the opposition that might make them look effective.[1] Congressional parties in the US House and Senate have once again sorted into two homogeneous, ideological, warring camps. Democrats are now consistently more liberal and Republicans more uniformly conservative than at any time since Speaker Thomas Brackett Reed ruled a unified majority with military discipline in the late nineteenth century and the rank and file closely followed their leaders like a well-organized militia. In the last twenty years, these volunteer armies of partisans have regrouped and now regularly engage figuratively in hand-to-hand combat, much like they did in the late-nineteenth- and early-twentieth-century Congress.

Political scientists have offered compelling explanations for the return of polarization and the impact of closely divided parties in Congress, and the implications of these changes for legislative operations.[2] We do not intend to reiterate or review all the fine scholarly and popular descriptions about the causes and consequences of these hostilities in this chapter, but there's no way to understand the modern Congress—and how the president relates to this institution—without a big hat tip to the power of partisan polarization.

But a broader aperture is needed to fully understand the landscape of today's partisanship in Washington. Based on reading scholarly literature on the topic, one might assume that polarization is principally a congressional phenomenon. Our experience suggests otherwise. Partisanship's tentacles ensnare a lot more than just the daily workings around the Capitol. It now grabs most aspects of the Washington establishment—including interest groups and the media. Relations along both ends of Pennsylvania Avenue are also regularly impacted by strong partisan tides. Presidents and entire administrations get covered in its wash. Presidents who are skillful in using the tools made available to them through interest groups, lobbyists, the media, and technology can successfully leverage their agendas in this hyperpartisan world. In other words, these myriad forces of polarization—and how they are managed—must be factored in when considering a president's success in Washington. Moreover, these same factors must be considered in trying to better understand White House–congressional relations in a partisan age.

But because most scholarly research on partisanship is focused only on Congress, the full extent of our growing polarized politics on relations between presidents and lawmakers—and other aspects of the Washington establishment—is not well understood.

In this chapter we analyze another major spoke in the wheel of twenty-first-century partisan politics: the implications of polarization on White House–congressional relations and how presidents attempt to manage legislative affairs in this hyperpartisan age.

We propose a framework for understanding how presidents operate in today's hyperpartisan Washington culture. It begins by considering the president's institutional constraints and advantages. We next evaluate his political goals. Finally, we assess how political skills factor into this equation.

But there is another part of the calculation that also deserves consideration. The relationship between the president and Congress doesn't just take place between two governmental actors. Other forces, such as a faster and fragmented media—driven by new technological developments—and an explosion of interest groups also shape White House–congressional relations. These nongovernmental players and new technology also impact the tactics, strategies, and outcomes of legislative and regulatory battles between the branches. We argue that understanding White House–congressional relations in today's more partisan environment requires unpacking all of these factors.

POLARIZATION AND THE MODERN PRESIDENCY

Viewing polarization only through the prism of Capitol Hill misses a major changed dynamic in the American political system. Presidents are not immune from the spread of partisan polarization that has swept over

American politics during the past two decades. As a result, White House–congressional relations are regularly impacted by the partisan waves crashing across both ends of Pennsylvania Avenue.

As Congress has become more sorted into two warring camps, the White House has responded to this spreading partisan brushfire in two ways. First, it has supported its own side more aggressively. In other words, presidents have tried more deliberately and systematically to make their own congressional team look good. Second, they have more aggressively and methodically tried to make their opposition look bad.

This one-two punch of supporting "your own team" while scoring points at the expense of the other puts the president in a unique situation. Instead of trying to find common ground with both parties in Congress, presidents have become vocal cheerleaders for their side, taking positions that bolster their own party while becoming the "critic-in-chief" of the opposition.

Over the past two decades—in both Republican and Democratic White Houses—presidents have routinely singled out their own party for praise and the other for scorn. President Clinton regularly castigated Speaker Newt Gingrich and the Republican Congress for what he called extreme positions on taxes and spending. Presidents George W. Bush and Barack Obama did the same with the opposition party in Congress. At this writing in the first year of the Trump administration it is a bit early to determine clear patterns. On certain policies, like energy, environment, and the repeal of the Affordable Care Act, the new president is following clear patterns of siding with his partisans on the Hill. However, on other issues, like drug pricing, trade, and immigration, he is following a more populist, rather than partisan, path.

Of course, skirmishes between presidents and Congress have occurred since the earliest days of the republic. But with the growth of polarization and modern communications and the emergence of partisan-based interest groups (like Heritage Action on the right and the Center for American Progress on the left), and President Trump's use of social media, the frequency of these assaults is growing. The tenor of modern presidential-congressional relations feels qualitatively more partisan. Gestures like George H. W. Bush telling Congress he was reaching out his hand in bipartisan cooperation have been replaced by Barack Obama telling the House Republican majority leader, "elections matter and I won." Today there are simply more opportunities for congressional leaders to joust with the president and vice versa in a news cycle that is expanded and includes many more outlets, from blogs to cable outlets, to Internet news sites, to social media like Twitter, as well as some of the more partisan-based interest groups mentioned above.

The number of bipartisan congressional leadership meetings at the White House has also decreased in the past twenty years as polarization has grown. Being in the same room together is increasingly awkward in an environment laced with hostile comments in the media with one team attacking the other like a long-running major league rivalry. President George H. W. Bush met with Republicans and Democratic leaders at the White House about twice a month. These meetings decreased in frequency under Presidents Clinton and George W. Bush. Under President Obama they were even rarer, the political equivalent of a lunar eclipse.

With a major budget crisis looming, President Obama concluded in September 2011, based on his assessment of the behavior of the other side, that a major budget deal with congressional Republicans was not possible. This led him to a strategy of attacking and blaming the Republicans for their failure to cooperate in the run-up to his 2012 reelection campaign. At the same time, Republicans anticipated no political consequences in resisting a deal with the president or even resisting cooperation with the equally recalcitrant congressional Democrats. As a result, the possibility of a major budget deal to address the deficit—the so-called grand bargain—devolved into finger pointing and mistrust; it was a missed opportunity for bipartisan cooperation. But it was also a recent example of how polarization has impacted White House relations with Congress.

Not only did the two sides fail to reach agreement, but both sides savaged the other in ways and using communications mediums that literally did not exist twenty years ago. Outside groups, using sophisticated, targeted communications tools, reached out to respective core supporters on both sides to make their case, citing why either the president or congressional Republicans were wrong to walk away from a deal.

In the end, the entire episode transformed from a bipartisan opportunity for success to a partisan food fight with each side blaming the other for negotiating in bad faith. The Democratic team on the Hill supported President Obama while Republicans said he'd lost his political courage. In the end, both sides used the failure as a political weapon against their opponents in the 2012 election—guaranteeing the partisan vitriol would continue and impact presidential-congressional relations even into the next session of Congress after Obama won his reelection and the Republicans retained their House majority.

MANAGING RELATIONS WITH CONGRESS IN A POLARIZED WORLD

For the president, managing relations with Congress in this hyperpartisan environment is impacted by several factors. Like a promising rookie, every new president's achievements are based on a complicated mix of skill, circumstances, training, and even luck. Polarization only augments the level of difficulty. But we have identified three key variables that impact success:

- The president's institutional constraints and advantages
- The president's political goals
- The president's political and legislative skills

These three factors are distinct, but interrelated. For example, one institutional constraint (whether the president faces divided or unified party government) can impact political goals and can also sometimes magnify legislative success or shortcomings. A president facing a determined and hostile congressional majority of the other party might both limit his political goals and also appear less effective in accomplishing his legislative ends—think George W. Bush, Lyndon Johnson, and Donald Trump in their first terms with unified party control in Congress compared to George H. W. Bush (1989–1993), Bill Clinton after the 1994 election, or Barack Obama after 2010.

The president's institutional constraints and advantages, and his political goals and skills, are also impacted by modern communications technology and the dramatic growth of interest-group formation, organization, and mobilization over the past twenty years. We integrate the impact of these two important changes later in this chapter.

The President's Institutional Constraints and Advantages

Institutional constraints are the key starting point in understanding presidential-congressional relations. And the impact of these constraints has become even more important in today's hyperpartisan age.

The major variable here is party control—unified versus divided government. When the same party controls both Congress and the White House, the possibility for smooth relations between the branches, although not without challenges, improves considerably. Alternatively, divided government can produce gridlock and increased acrimony between the majority party in Congress and the president.

Party control can also impact the appearance of a president's legislative skills. Unified party control can make the White House look extremely competent and effective in enacting a legislative agenda, particularly if they have large enough majorities not to be constrained by rules of procedure or expected defections.

Alternatively, mixed-party government can make a White House look feckless in terms of legislative success. Lyndon Johnson, for example, looked like a master of the legislative process while enjoying large majorities of his party in both the House and Senate from 1964 to 1968. Gerald Ford—who also came from a congressional leadership background—appeared powerless and even incompetent in terms of getting Congress to pass his agenda while facing massive opposing majorities.

Of course, there are exceptions to this rule. Divided government doesn't always guarantee discord. President George H. W. Bush in 1990 and President Bill Clinton in 1996–1997 both negotiated major budget agreements with the opposing party majority. Nor does unified party control always result in smooth sailing. President Clinton could not move comprehensive health insurance reform through a Democratically controlled House and Senate in 1993 and 1994, and George W. Bush failed to enact Social Security reform in the beginning of his second term in 2005 despite controlling majorities in both the House and the Senate. But as a general matter, presidents normally get along better with Congress and find it easier moving their agenda forward when their own party also controls both houses of the legislature.

Partisan polarization has only amplified this reality. President Obama's White House in 2009 and 2010 worked very closely and cooperatively with the Democratic majorities in Congress, as did the Republican majority in Congress with President George W. Bush from 2001 to 2006. President Trump worked closely with Republicans in the House and the Senate early in his administration in an effort to repeal and replace the Affordable Care Act. Contrast this to the early 1960s—during a less polarized period—when the House majority, led by Speaker Rayburn, kept many of their own president's agenda bottled up and the "conservative coalition" (southern Democrats joining with Republicans) in the House often passed measures over the White House's objections.[3]

Unified party control also affects more than the lawmaking process. Many observers believe legislative oversight of the executive branch was more benign when Republicans controlled the Congress from 2001 to 2006 and President George H. W. Bush was in the White House. Legislative oversight became more intense after the Democrats became the congressional majority during the last two years of the Bush administration (2007–2008). But after President Obama was elected in 2008 and the Democrats enjoyed unified party control, legislative oversight waned again. After divided government returned following the 2010 election, legislative oversight grew intense again. During this iteration, congressional Republicans focused intensely on the actions of the Obama administration with investigations on matters like the "Fast and Furious" program where guns fell into the hands of drug gangs and Mexico, or the bankruptcy of Solyndra, a solar energy company that received loan guarantees from the Obama administration's Department of Energy based more on ideology and political connections than a sound business plan, at least according to Republicans in charge of the investigation.

President Trump took office with unified party control of the Congress, giving him and the Republicans in the Congress a substantial advantage in promoting and passing their agenda. This assumes that there is agreement between him and the congressional Republican leaders as to what those policy priorities will be. Adoption of their agenda in the House of Representatives should be relatively easy since they have the majority necessary to assert their will.

However, the Senate provides a different and not inconsequential challenge. The Republican leadership will need to hold together all members of their caucus plus at least six Democrats to secure the supermajorities necessary to pass many of their legislative initiatives done outside the context of special budget rules, like reconciliation. This is a result of the current filibuster rules that require sixty votes to terminate debate on legislative matters. Caucus unity in both chambers should not be taken for granted.

The President's Political Goals

Deciphering the president's political goals is another key factor in gaining a better understanding of White House–congressional relations in a partisan age. Sometimes the president may decide it is in his interest to work with Congress and develop joint accomplishments with lawmakers. Other times, a more overt partisan political approach might better fit the president's objectives.

In a more polarized Washington, political goals can be complex, nuanced, and dynamic. Still, understanding these goals can shed great light on White House–congressional relations, and why certain outcomes occur—or not.

President Clinton began his term in 1993 with majorities in both the House and the Senate. He also assembled a very ambitious domestic legislative agenda. His strategic goal was to be very prescriptive in the content of the legislation, move quickly and very aggressively. Another key element of the strategy was to write the legislation so that it would primarily pass with the support of only Democrats. While he did not initiate this strategy and occasionally resisted this approach, the Democratic leaders in the Congress prevailed on him that this was the most effective way to proceed. This approach did produce a number of positive legislative results; however, it failed most notably in his health-care reform initiative. More significantly, it allowed his entire presidency as well as the Democratic Congress to be susceptible to the charge of overreaching their mandate. This allegation along with others resulted in a Republican sweep in the midterm elections, forcing a total revamping of President Clinton's legislative strategy for dealing with the new Republican Congress beginning in January 1995.

President Clinton's strategy for the new Congress took a while to emerge. The new Republican leaders were proceeding on what they were characterizing as a mandate built upon the Contract with America, a brainchild of the new Speaker of the House, Newt Gingrich. As the initial strategy emerged from the White House, it began to shape up as a strategy of fierce confrontation with the new Republican House.

President Clinton would admit to making some mistakes in his first two years. Ironically, he felt the new leadership of the House was itself now overreaching, taking the country on a road to disaster. Congressional Democrats were in total support of Clinton's strategy of confrontation with the Republican House and amplified it at every opportunity. This battle was primarily fought in the context of competing comprehensive budget proposals from both sides. After months of haggling and government shutdowns, at about a year out from Clinton's reelection, there was a felt consensus that the aligned Democratic strategy prevailed.

Clinton could have remained in sync with the congressional Democrats as they desperately wanted him to do, and he could have done nothing to rehabilitate the Republicans before the upcoming election by working with them constructively. As history shows, the president pivoted again with a new set of strategic objectives for working with the same new Congress, which entailed looking for common ground rather than conflict. The Republican leadership also dramatically pivoted and saw it in their self-interest to find legislative areas of cooperation, and did. Together, they laid the groundwork for a ten-year deficit-reduction package that passed right after the election, tax cuts for small business, and an incremental but significant piece of health-care legislation for children, among others.

This latest strategic shift left the president's Democratic congressional colleagues in the cold as the 1996 election approached. It had the impression and reality of making them marginal players and replaceable. As a result, the president won reelection and the Republicans kept and expanded their majorities. This strategy appeared to produce the desired result of the electoral moment. However, the relationship between the president and the Republican Congress shifted dramatically shortly after the election to accusations of massive fundraising irregularities and hostile impeachment proceedings. In anticipating the troubled waters ahead, one might have concluded a Democratically aligned strategy may have been a better investment than triangulation in light of the challenges that lay ahead for Clinton's presidency. Nevertheless, President Clinton pursued a strategic electoral option that left the Democrats to vie for themselves—an approach they did not reciprocate in the scandal-ridden years of his second term.

Conversely, as noted above, by the summer of 2011, President Obama decided his political goal of getting reelected the following year was better served by running against Congress, particularly the Republican-controlled House. Could President Obama have "pulled a Clinton" and triangulated against his party and the Republican House in 2012? Maybe. We believe at least two factors suggested otherwise. The first was that it appeared the Senate Republican leader saw little political upside in leading his members in a strategy of large-scale compromise with President Obama. The other was likely the Democratic leader, Harry Reid, being very cognizant of Clinton triangulating in the past and determined to prevent this from happening with Obama. Our point is that in a more polarized Washington, choosing a strategy of running against the other party seems like the more reflexive and obvious choice, especially considering the ample evidence that there is little or no downside in not cooperating with the other side.

To date President Trump appears to be taking a two-track approach. On one hand he is suggesting a major change in how business will be done in DC—for instance, in calling for "draining the swamp," selecting "outsider" personnel to advise him and run his government, and imposing a five-year ban on lobbying for members of his administration. He is also taking an unconventional "populist" approach on some traditionally Republican issues like trade, drug pricing, and enhanced competition in defense spending, where he might enjoy the active support of some Democrats. At the same time he is working with a Republican Congress to largely implement a conventional conservative policy agenda in areas like tax reform, energy, and environment policies.

The President's Political and Legislative Skills

Assessing the president's political and legislative skills is another key to understanding White House–congressional relations in a more partisan age. Some of these skills are well known and have been key indicators of success for many years—during both hyperpartisan and less polarized eras. Others, however, are more critical in today's fragmented media environment and technologically advanced era. Let's start with some traditional political and legislative skills that help the president at almost any time.

The first is fundraising. The president's role as party builder is often exemplified by the president's ability to raise money for congressional challenger candidates and incumbents. Barack Obama, by some accounts, raised about $1 billion for his campaign, the Democratic National Committee, and candidates in 2012.[4] He was a fundraising juggernaut. By actively campaigning for candidates like this, presidents both build goodwill and potentially their numbers in the House and Senate.

Personal relationships with lawmakers are another key political and legislative skill. This is an intangible yet valuable asset that can help win support on close key votes to promote the White House agenda. President George H. W. Bush, as a former House member, had many strong relationships with lawmakers on both sides of the aisle that he drew upon frequently to help his relations with Congress. These friendships were formed over a long career in Washington. Presidents Clinton and George W. Bush, as former governors, were less well known in the corridors of the House and the Senate prior to arriving on the scene. Barack Obama only served a short tenure in the Senate before he won election in 2008. Clinton and Bush worked to compensate for their lack of Washington experience to develop these relationships. Critics say Obama remained aloof.

Process knowledge is yet another tool to help presidents succeed and manage relations with Congress. It's true we normally think of the president of the United States being above the mundane nuances of legislative procedure. But when it comes to moving the White House's agenda, some procedural knowledge can go a long way. Lyndon Johnson certainly used his background as Senate majority leader to influence the levers of power to get Congress to consider his agenda. Listening to his process discussions with legislative leaders as revealed on the Johnson tapes underscores how he used process knowledge to help advance his White House's interests.[5]

More recently, President Obama was able to enlist Vice President Joe Biden—a former senator with deep knowledge of the legislative process—to help advance the White House agenda on a host of negotiations with lawmakers. Working with Senate Republican Leader Mitch McConnell (R-KY) in January 2013, Biden used his process knowledge to help shepherd an agreement to allow taxes to increase on wealthier Americans, a victory that allowed Obama to say he fulfilled a major campaign promise.

President Trump, with admittedly little knowledge of how Washington works, used his selection of Vice President Mike Pence to fill this gap in the same way the selections of Joe Biden and Dick Cheney did for Presidents Obama and Bush. Vice President Pence comes with the institutional knowledge of both policy and process. In this regard he is likely to be a major asset to President Trump in building relationships as well as forming legislative strategy. At the same time, President Trump doesn't appear averse to reaching out to members and having his own personal conversations. If this continues, it could significantly affect his overall legislative success, especially if he included select Democrats.

One more traditional source of legislative and political skill is policy expertise. With the full force of the executive branch and its experts behind him, a president—either personally or through his staff—is in a strong position with respect to programmatic and budget information compared to the Congress. When the White House learns how to harness this advantage, it can usually gain a tactical edge over the legislative branch.

Indeed, one of the reasons why Congress passed the 1974 Budget Impoundment and Control Act was that the legislative branch felt at a disadvantage in terms of information and analysis. The Nixon administration consistently outmaneuvered Congress when it came to government-spending strategy. This new law, among other things, created the Congressional Budget Office to help lawmakers compete with the president's Office of Management and Budget in terms of data, projections, and fiscal forecasting.

Persuasion is the final traditional political and legislative skill we address in this section. Presidents can persuade by using either "inside" or "outside" influence. Inside influence is shaped by factors like personal relationships, as well as policy and procedural knowledge. Outside influence might include using the speeches—the so-called bully pulpit—to shape public opinion in favor of the White House. Normally, a combination of the two is most effective or at least attempted.

The president's ability to move public opinion to an extent that it persuades Congress—all other things equal—has come under some question in recent years.[6] Quiet diplomacy and compromise seem like more of a recipe for success than major White House–backed public relations campaigns.

During his first year as president, President Trump is including his campaigning skills and techniques of persuasion in his governing strategy. His use of social media platforms such as Twitter has been both unconventional and effective so far. Successful persuasion often needs to be built on a good policy presented in a compelling way both to the Congress and their constituencies. President Obama had threatened to use the resources of his successful campaign strategies in his governing. As we look back over the last years, it does not appear that they were employed in the pursuit of specific policy initiatives. The jury is still out as to whether Trump's wide-ranging tweets will be as successful in policy making as they have been in campaigning and garnering press attention. It could be just the tool that breaks through the arcane and cumbersome processes and customs of the Congress.

Some scholars have discussed the challenges of presidents "going over the head" of Congress to sway public opinion. President Trump, so far, has used social media to often go over the heads of the mainstream media, much to the dismay of traditional journalistic outlets.

In addition to considering how these traditional presidential political and legislative skills impact relations with the Congress, there are two other variables we explore later in this chapter—changes in technology and the increased number of stakeholders in the process. Transformations in both these areas have become more important as polarization has increased and created challenges and opportunities for presidents' interactions and success in managing relations with Congress.

POLARIZATION IMPACTS PRESIDENTS
DIFFERENTLY THAN CONGRESS

As we argue above, the White House is not immune from the forces of polarization. And developing a full understanding of modern presidential-congressional relations requires incorporating the new realities and challenges of hyperpartisanship as a window to view how these two important institutions get along (or not). But polarization does not impact presidents and legislators in exactly the same way. Below we describe some of the differences and outline the reasons why this is the case.

First, and perhaps most obviously, presidents and Congress are on different campaign cycles. Not only are there practical differences between two-, four-, and six-year terms, but once a president wins reelection to a second term, he no longer faces any personal electoral constraints. Most scholars and pundits agree presidents should act quickly after being elected because their political capital inevitably seems to evaporate. But even a newly elected president has four years before he has to face reelection, while all House members and a third of the Senate are up for reelection in two years.

Second, presidents—unlike congressional leaders—do not face a constituency that elected them on a daily basis. Party leaders run for office twice—once with their constituents and then again to win support of their rank-and-file members. The political calculus for being elected leader of one's caucus is often at odds with the constituencies that send them to Congress in the first place, or possibly more broadly, even the popular sentiment of the country. Senators Byrd and Daschle, both popular leaders of the Democratic caucus, drew serious, and in Daschle's case, deadly, reelection challenges, having to balance the needs of a more liberal caucus with the demands of their more conservative state constituencies. This constraint often was a major consideration in managing the demands of a president of their own party or the opposition.

During preelection 2011–2012 budget negotiations with the White House, congressional leaders had to face their respective caucuses every day, a national expectation to address our fiscal problems that would produce real results, and a president who probably could have benefited from a grand bargain. The reality of that scenario would of course need the cooperation of the Republican Speaker of the House and probably some but not all of the Senate Democrats. While the Speaker had his own very complex Republican Conference politics to sort out, Senate leaders faced their own set of challenges.

Senator Reid concluded quickly a "grand bargain" would not be the best path to protecting the largest number of Senate Democratic seats, and thus his majority, that were exposed in the 2012 election. After considerable intraparty haggling behind the scenes, the president decided in the end to align with the Senate Democratic leader and pull the plug on grand bargain negotiations with the Republicans. President Obama conceivably had more political latitude than Senator Reid to decide whether a deal was in the Democratic Senate's long-term interest or not. President Clinton in the late 1990s chose the opposite option in continuing to work out a ten-year budget deal with the Republican leaders, to the chagrin and political detriment of his own congressional party. The grand bargain of that time produced a landslide reelection for Clinton, and expanded majorities in both houses for Republicans at the expense of congressional Democrats.

President Trump is still early in his tenure but appears to be aligning his agenda with the current Republican leadership in many policy areas such as energy and taxes. However, there are several issues where there is not clear policy alignment that may cause serious intraparty fissures if not addressed. The most prominent is in the area of trade; another might be how to fund an infrastructure initiative, and still another might be in the US-Russia relationship.

Third, there are other constituency differences. Presidents report to a national constituency, not a congressional district or state. Obviously a lawmaker from rural Kansas faces a different kind of constituent pressure and interest than the current occupant of the White House. While the tip of that pressure sharpens as a president's reelection comes in focus, his political math gives him many more options to weave together a path to victory than a member of Congress representing a single state or district. While there are some circumstances in the country for which the president deservedly gets the blame or credit, a member, even of his own party, may escape without any negative consequence. The 2012 election demonstrates President Obama was able to use his most popular positions on immigration, auto bailout, and concern about the middle class to stitch together a string of like-minded states, leading to his own electoral victory. Yet at the same time, House Republicans were able to appeal enough to their smaller congressional districts to retain a majority. President Trump, while performing well in traditionally red, Republican states, also won stronger than normal support among white, working-class Democrats from traditionally blue states in the upper Midwest that had little or no Republican representation on a statewide basis. He will be contemplating how he makes good to those constituencies, who are interested in jobs, trade policies, and protecting entitlements.

Fourth, presidents can stay close or far away from the lawmaking process. There are times when a president is knee-deep in the congressional process, going so far as to host negotiating sessions at the White House or sending senior emissaries to Capitol Hill. Or the president may choose to keep his distance and only engage at the last minute, or not at all. These are tactical choices each White House must make, *but the point is there is a choice.* Legislators engaged in the lawmaking process don't have the same ability to calibrate their engagement with the process. Like President George W. Bush and President Obama, whose vice presidents (Cheney and Biden, respectively) had substantial congressional experience, President Trump seems to be relying a lot on Vice President Pence to engage in daily negotiations and relationship building on Capitol Hill. Presidents who have selected vice presidents with deep congressional experience can sometimes take a step back and leave the daily back-and-forth to someone else. Presidents who do this can stay above the fray of the daily "sausage-making" process.

Fifth, presidents have more tools at their disposal. For example, even if the White House is stymied in terms of its relations with Capitol Hill, individual actions, such as executive orders or other decisions by cabinet-level agencies, can produce powerful policy outcomes. President Obama chose to pursue the regulation of carbon at the Environmental Protection Agency (EPA) with a series of policy proposals after cap-and-trade legislation failed to pass the Congress. President George Bush liberally used signing statements that often indicated that he would not comply with aspects of the legislation he was signing into law.

Sixth, presidents can also attempt to use the power of the bully pulpit to try to convince the public through media appearances, such as televised addresses to the American people. Some political scientists question the direct impact of these tactics. We have been in the conversations as White House staff, trying to determine how to "break through" with their message, even having the president personally delivering it. Nevertheless, there is no doubt the president at least has these opportunities, while congressional leaders only rarely share the chance to "address the nation."[7] And even if these rhetorical forays do nothing but rally core supporters, it's a tactic that no one other than the president can use.

In today's digital media world, President Trump has broken new ground in his ability to be seen and heard by the media and many rank and file. His use of platforms like Twitter has been unprecedented in volume, velocity, and impact, both during the campaign and as president. It is assumed by most that he will continue this practice during his presidency. The question is, will it remain an effective tool over time to shape legislation and American policy more broadly?

POLARIZATION AND DELEGATING
LEGISLATIVE POWER TO PARTY LEADERS

When a president's political goals lead him to keep his distance from Congress, he still needs to make sure lawmakers don't move in a direction adverse to White House interests. We argue that it's easier today—in a more polarized age—for presidents to keep a healthy distance from the lawmaking process (if that is their political goal) because the ideological space between the White House and the president's party in Congress has shrunk. Gone are the days of President Lyndon Johnson when Democrats in the Senate spanned the spectrum from northern liberals like Hubert Humphrey of Minnesota to southern conservatives like Richard Russell of Georgia.

Closing the ideological gap between lawmakers and their leaders, as well as presidents and their own party leaders, has some important consequences. For example, one of the effects of polarization in Congress is that rank-and-file members delegate power to legislative party leaders during periods of partisan polarization.[8] Our thesis is that presidents often do the same—or at least more than they used to in a less partisan age. As we demonstrate below, when policy preferences between a president and his party in Congress line up closely, it's safe for the White House to let its party leaders do its bidding in legislative negotiations.

An example of this approach occurred in 2011 as the deadline for a debt-ceiling increase approached. Instead of refereeing three-way negotiations between Democrats, Republicans, and his White House, President Obama stepped back and allowed his leaders on Capitol Hill to negotiate a bipartisan package. In a polarized age, President Obama could do that, knowing the final product as negotiated by congressional Democrats would not stray too far from his preferred policy positions on key issues like cuts to Medicaid and other important priorities.

But there are also times when tensions still exist—even between a president and his own legislative leaders. In these cases something has to give. Either the president convinces his caucus to follow him or the president chooses a direction consistent with his party's strategy on the Hill. We outline some examples of both below.

The conditional party government theory asserts that when ideological cross pressures decline between the preferences of lawmakers' constituents and the demands of party leadership, legislators choose to delegate power to their leadership.[9] The rationale is straightforward: when congressional leadership preferences are closely aligned with a congressman's constituents, following the leaders' wishes produces both legislative success and electoral dividends. Under these conditions, lawmakers essentially trust their leadership to take the ball and run with it. This produces strong party leadership in Congress. As mentioned above, we've seen this phenomenon reemerge in the last two decades.

As the congressional parties have grown increasingly polarized over the last two decades, Republicans and Democrats alike have transformed into more homogeneous "teams." And as rank-and-file lawmakers have delegated power to party leaders, the clout of leaders has grown.

Our observation of presidential-congressional relations over the past two decades reveals a similar pattern at work between the branches. Just as the rank-and-file members of Congress have increasingly trusted their legislative leadership to do their bidding, so have presidents under some circumstances (President Obama with Senate Democratic Leader Harry Reid and Speaker Nancy Pelosi, President George W. Bush with Speaker Dennis Hastert and Senate Republican Leader Bill Frist).

In other words, as leadership in Congress has been strengthened by the rank and file ceding power, in many ways the White House has followed suit. Congressional leaders are stronger not only because the rank and file delegate power to them but also because presidents do so.

Strong partisan party leaders in Congress almost instinctively reflect the views of a partisan president—they've got his back and he has theirs—a phenomenon that has fundamentally changed many aspects of White House–legislative relations.

Prior to the period of extreme polarization we now find ourselves in, presidents had to do their own bidding—and it was hard to conclude congressional party leaders "had the president's back." Could President Kennedy, for example, trust Sam Rayburn to carry out the White House legislative agenda or would the Texas Speaker of the House attempt to find middle ground between his southern and northern membership?

Kennedy could not let go of his agenda in a congressional environment filled with powerful committee chairs and legislative leaders facing a diverse caucus. He had to win the votes on his own.

Today's environment is very different. When Nancy Pelosi was Speaker there was little daylight between her caucus's agenda and President Obama. She could cut the deals and produce the votes knowing nearly everything she did and supported would be in line with the president's preferences. In an environment like that, presidents can delegate authority to leaders, just like the rank and file does. As a result, lots of negotiating goes on among party leaders to produce legislation without direct White House involvement.

In unified government, this can produce a lot of partisan legislation with polarized public support (for President Obama, for example, the Affordable Care Act, the economic stimulus legislation, and the Wall Street reform known as Dodd-Frank). In divided government it can produce a lot of partisan rancor and polarization, as was the case with President Obama and the Republican House from 2011 to 2016 or earlier between President George W. Bush in 2007 and 2008 with the then-Democratic majority in Congress.

Contrast these more recent examples with the 1986 tax bill, Clean Air Act amendments of 1990, or welfare reform near the end of the Clinton administration in 1998. These are all examples of bipartisan accomplishments in less partisan times, negotiated between the White House and individual lawmakers, not among just congressional leaders.

And there are exceptions still happening today. For example, in 2012, during a period of divided party control, Congress did produce legislation that got signed into law despite the politics and polarization of an election year. Food and Drug Administration (FDA) reform, a highway bill, and a package that included extension of a payroll tax cut and unemployment insurance all passed with broad bipartisan support. All three measures received little direct input from the White House, yet Democratic

Party leaders knew the parameters of the president's policy preferences and could negotiate with Republicans, knowing the end product was acceptable to the president.

President Trump may also provide some exceptions to this rule. While he is still in the first year of his administration at this writing, he campaigned on several issues that are out of step with some traditional Republican views. Trade policy is the most prominent example and obviously important to President Trump. It's unlikely he will allow the Republican Congress to move ahead with legislation in this area that doesn't include his more populist views on the issue. He has also effectively positioned himself as the sole arbiter of whether it meets these undefined criteria or not. A similar comment could be made about his views on drug pricing and immigration reform, where he has staked out more populist views than represented by more conventional recent Republican policies.

WHEN DOES THE WHITE HOUSE CHOOSE *NOT* TO CEDE POWER TO PARTY LEADERS?

Sometimes furthering political goals means presidents do not cede power to party leaders. Even though polarization has reduced the amount of ideological difference between presidents and their party leaders in Congress, there are several reasons why a president's political goals might lead him not to pursue this strategy.

For example, during periods of divided government, it's nearly impossible for presidents to cede power to their party leaders in Congress because the minority party (at least in the House) can accomplish little on its own. President Clinton clearly decided to forgo intraparty alignment in the months leading up to his reelection in 1996. While he started out marching in step with congressional Democrats in opposition to the Republicans' budget that they proposed after their congressional victories in 1994, he abandoned that approach once he saw the Republicans were willing to compromise after their government-shutdown strategy failed in 1995. Congressional Democrats would have preferred to have allowed the embarrassment of the shutdown to hang around the Republicans' necks through the 1996 election. But Clinton chose to compromise from a position of strength and got legislative deals on the budget, small-business tax relief, and children's health insurance, to his electoral advantage and theirs. This was very upsetting to congressional Democrats, who lost further seats in both the House and Senate.

Yet often the old institutional tensions still exist. In these cases, the White House needs to sort through its strategy and interests with its own party leaders and determine a path forward. But even under these conditions of

institutional give-and-take, today they are done in a more partisan atmosphere—rather than some kind of bipartisan summit.

IS TWITTER THE NEW BULLY PULPIT?

The speed of modern communications and the fragmentation of the media
also provide new challenges and opportunities regarding how presidents
manage relations with Congress. The news cycle used to be a daily occurrence, capped by the evening news program on one of the major networks
or the morning headlines generated by a wire service or nationally read
daily newspaper. In the Clinton administration, there was a daily ritual of
several senior staff gathering in the White House chief of staff's office every
day at around 6:00 p.m. to watch each of the three networks' nightly news
feeds. In doing so the team assessed the progress they made that day by
monitoring the movement of good stories up and bad ones down among
the top three leads of each network. Today the back-and-forth can and does
occur many times during the day, some say in two-hour news cycles or even
more, before the network anchor shows up for work in New York.

Using technology to educate, organize, and mobilize supporters is another new tactic available for presidents to lobby Congress. This new strategy was put to the test in the 113th Congress for the first time as President
Obama attempted to use the database that proved so successful in identifying and motivating his supporters in 2012, and to translate this electoral
support into legislative advocacy. It's unclear this strategy did anything but
educate and energize some existing supporters.

President Trump's use of Twitter is the latest iteration in this evolving
media landscape. Much to the dismay of the mainstream media and his
opponents, the forty-fifth president seems to have discovered an effective
way to communicate with many Americans who used to rely on other
media outlets to communicate the White House message. It's still too
early to tell how this phenomenon will impact congressional persuasion
and President Trump's legislative results, but it is already reshaping the
political landscape and narrative and impacting nonelected leaders and
other domestic institutions.

FROM SANDLOT TO YANKEE STADIUM:
EXPANDING THE NUMBER OF PLAYERS

Modern-day interest-group politics also test the president's legislative and
political skills. White House–congressional relations used to occur in closed

settings—lubricated by bourbon and branch in the White House private residence, a frank negotiation in the Oval Office, or a handshake in a Senate hideaway. No more. Today there are both more players and more spectators. The number of individuals and stakeholders used to be small and manageable. But over the past thirty years, the roster of players has grown exponentially. These outside agents dramatically shape the tone, content, strategies, and tactics of White House–congressional relations. The game has expanded from small to big—from the sandlot to Yankee Stadium.

The larger number of entrants on the playing field provides both challenges and opportunities for how presidents advance their legislative agendas. Successful presidents can exploit these opportunities, mobilizing outside groups such as individual lobbyists, business trade associations, consumer groups, unions, environmental activists, or corporations to advance the White House agenda.

One of the best recent examples of a White House activating outside groups was President Obama's efforts with parts of the health-care community when it came to passage of the Affordable Care Act (aka Obamacare).

Groups like the pharmaceutical manufacturers (PhRMA), the American Medical Association, and the American Hospital Association could have presented major obstacles to passage of the new health-care law. Instead, the White House recognized the importance of bringing these groups into the fold early to ensure they did not mobilize active opposition to the bill.

Working with politically aligned stakeholders (for Democrats, unions, environmental groups, and consumer groups; for Republicans, business associations and conservative social and economic groups) is another area that tests a president's legislative and political skill. Unlike the example above, where the White House had to actively lobby health interests to help with passage of the legislation, there are many stakeholder groups or even more ideological think tanks that lean Democratic or Republican that are ready, willing, and able to help their team in the White House.

As the number of interest groups has expanded, it's become increasingly important for the White House to identify those that are politically aligned with Republicans or Democrats and move quickly to win their support for the president's legislative agenda, or to enlist these groups' support in fighting off hostile proposals from Capitol Hill—particularly in mixed-party government situations.

Here's the bottom line. Management, persuasion, and leveraging outside groups was not a prerequisite to presidential success in managing relations with Capitol Hill in the past because the number of groups was much smaller and their communications channels less robust. Today that has all changed. How presidents manage the expansive array of outside groups is a major test of their political and legislative skill.

CONCLUSION

As we complete the writing of this chapter, Donald Trump has just begun his first term as the forty-fifth president of the United States. We can best understand how he will operate in his first term by using the model we have outlined.

Constraints and Opportunities

President Trump, like recent presidents such as Clinton in 1993–1994, Obama in 2009–2010, and Bush in 2001–2006, has the luxury of unified party government. This creates a series of opportunities to move his agenda through a partisan-friendly environment. And like Clinton, Bush, and Obama, President Trump must also solidify party unity and overcome the Senate filibuster on many issues that don't have the procedural protections like budget reconciliation (where only a fifty-one-vote threshold is necessary). Maintaining party unity and the Senate filibuster are his constraints, while unified party control is an opportunity.

Unified party control should help enact many of his legislative initiatives, assist in getting judges and other political appointees confirmed, and avoid Congress passing a lot of measures that the president would have to veto. In sum, President Trump's constraints are few and opportunities numerous given his institutional circumstances. His constraints would mainly be self-inflicted to the extent he would insist on straying from the conventional Republican agenda and insisting, at least in part, on the more populist policies on which he campaigned. This would potentially divide his Republican congressional support, with hopes to make up the difference with receptive Democrats.

Presidential Goals

President Trump's legislative goals were spelled out often during the 2016 campaign. He talked repeatedly about "making America great again." According to President Trump, this translated to negotiating better trade deals; repealing and replacing Obamacare; ensuring the American jobs don't go overseas; simplifying the tax code and lowering tax rates; tightening immigration laws, including the construction of a "wall" at the Mexican border; building more infrastructure projects; and loosening energy and environmental laws to spur more development.

Many of these goals should be achievable in the House of Representatives given the current 241–194 Republican majority. The Senate will be the tricky institution for President Trump, as Senate Democrats could stall his goals with unified and determined opposition, given that institution's supermajority rules. However, the prospects for getting business done in

Washington could change dramatically if the Republican leadership decides to use the "nuclear option." This would entail modifying the filibuster rules to require a simple majority instead of sixty votes to pass legislation in the Senate. This has already been done for some executive branch officials. The agenda of a party with unified control could then be adopted in full.

Political and Legislative Skills

President Trump is a political novice when it comes to the ways of Washington. Yet his choice of Mike Pence, a former congressman and member of the House leadership, will help compensate for some of his lack of experience dealing with Congress. But despite his limited legislative experience, Trump's unconventional style and skillful use of social media could prove extremely helpful as he navigates the congressional relations terrain.

President Trump is fortunate to be president under positive institutional conditions (unified party government), his legislative goals seem not extensive and manageable, and he has compensated for no legislative experience by picking a vice president who formerly served in the House leadership. He has also discovered a method to overcome much of the filter of the mainstream media by using platforms like Twitter to both make news and communicate his views.

While partisanship will no doubt impact the Trump White House in significant ways, the forty-fifth president also has a unique relationship with his party leadership in Congress. Many rank-and-file Republican voters ultimately supported President Trump in the 2016 general election, while many congressional leaders were slower to back him and more tentative in their support during the campaign. How this dynamic plays out in White House–congressional relations is still unknown at this writing. In light of the many Democrats who supported his candidacy, and several of his policy proposals that are nominally attractive to some Democrats, he might decide to do as President Clinton did two decades earlier and triangulate his own party as he moves in a more postpartisan, populist direction. This will likely put him at odds with some in his own party, causing party unity and polarization to ebb. However, given the power of partisanship in politics in the twenty-first century, polarization and party unity might persist and even increase to higher levels, while continuing to dramatically shape the relationship between presidents and Congress for the foreseeable future.

NOTES

1. Frances E. Lee, *Insecure Majorities: Congress and the Perpetual Campaign* (Chicago: University of Chicago Press, 2016).

2. Sean M. Theriault, *Party Polarization in Congress* (New York: Cambridge University Press, 2008); Lee, *Beyond Ideology*.

3. John F. Manley, "The Conservative Coalition in Congress," *American Behavioral Scientist* 17 (1973): 223–47.

4. Nicholas Confessore and Jo Craven McGinty, "Obama, Romney and Their Parties on Track to Raise $2 Billion," *New York Times*, October 25, 2012.

5. LBJ Presidential Library, http://www.lbjlib.utexas.edu/johnson/archives.hom/dictabelt.hom/content.asp.

6. George C. Edwards, *On Deaf Ears: The Limits of the Bully Pulpit* (New Haven, CT: Yale University Press, 2003).

7. Edwards, *On Deaf Ears*.

8. See, for example, John Aldrich, *Why Parties? The Origins and Transformation of Party Politics in America* (Chicago: University of Chicago Press, 1995); Gary Cox and Mathew McCubbins, *Legislative Leviathan: Party Leadership in the House*, 2nd ed. (New York: Cambridge University Press, 2007); David Rhode, *Parties and Leaders in the Post-Reform House* (Chicago: University of Chicago Press, 1991).

9. Cox and McCubbins, *Legislative Leviathan*.

CHAPTER 8

Presidential and Congressional Cooperation

A Provisional Partnership

Ross K. Baker

In the last decade of the twentieth century, Jon R. Bond and Richard Fleisher wrote that "In their efforts to promote programs of the national party, the president's party leaders typically assume the role of administration lieutenants in Congress."[1] The writers went on to cite examples of congressional leaders of the recent past saying such things as "I'm a servant of the president," "I like being a good soldier," or "I'm the president's spear in the Senate." They then reflected on the quaintness of such pledges and added, "Party leaders from the president's party . . . are not always so strongly committed to the administration. Leaders in Congress are constrained by institutional interest and loyalty. They may be the administration's lieutenants but they are leading an undisciplined army that makes its own demands on them."[2]

The former chief of staff to then Senate Democratic Leader Harry Reid recalled an incident in which his boss made it abundantly clear where he stood on the matter of his relationship to the president:

> There's a famous quote that Reid got a lot of shit for when he said it. It was before Obama got inaugurated. Reid had a meeting in his office with Obama. There was a big do. [Obama's Chief of Staff] Rahm Emanuel also came up. Somebody asked a question and Reid answered, "I don't work for the president." Well, the media lit Reid up on that comment. But Reid wasn't wrong in saying that. He didn't say it in a mean way, you know. "I don't work for him. I have my own duties." It was just a factual statement.[3]

What startled the reporters in Reid's statement was that it was widely known that Reid had encouraged freshman Illinois senator Barack Obama to consider seeking the Democratic presidential nomination in 2008. As Reid's former chief of staff recalled:

Reid told me one day that Obama was on the floor speaking early in his career and Reid called him in afterwards and said to him, "I've seen a lot of people come through here and I've heard a lot of people speak and you are very gifted. I listened to what you had to say." Then Reid said, "Have you given any thought to possibly running for president?" It wasn't the first time Obama had heard that, but it was a validation the first time somebody was saying it not just for the sake of saying it. This was the leader of the party saying "Have you thought about this?" So it was more like, "Wow! I'm being taken seriously." Reid was the validator that Obama needed. It wasn't just somebody blowing smoke up Obama's ass.[4]

In light of Democratic leader Reid's personal fondness for the president and the role he played in encouraging Obama in what might have seemed at the time an improbable quest, it would not be surprising to learn that Reid behaved much the way the party leaders of years past behaved, as a loyal lieutenant.

Reid's deputy chief of staff for policy, Bill Dauster, saw an unusual closeness between the two Democrats.

He was in Obama's camp early and he encouraged him. Reid was smart about it. It was the right choice. And he always felt a personal attachment and personal proprietary interest in Obama's success. And when President Obama would call him, Senator Reid would try not to waste the president's time. He would try to help him out whenever he possibly could.

When Senator Reid would call President Obama, he would plan very carefully what he was going to ask for, try not to ask for too much and try to be deferential to the president. And I do believe that they have had a deep friendship and it has mattered. They have been able to work together to get great things done. Most of the great Obama things were great Reid things. I think about the Affordable Care Act, the stimulus, and Dodd-Frank.[5]

It is understandable that the Democratic leader's chief aides would emphasize the role of their boss in the signal achievements of President Obama's time in office. The president of course lobbied members heavily for their passage. Reid and Obama were certainly key players, but, as journalists reported, "it could not have passed without [House Speaker Nancy] Pelosi."[6]

There is a strong case to be made then, that personal fondness played an important role in the relationship between President Obama and the Democratic leaders of Congress. But as much as good personal chemistry can sometimes lubricate the dealings among politicians, conflicts arise that not even friendship can entirely quell. So while Pelosi "praised Obama for constantly pushing for a comprehensive approach to [health-care reform] and refusing to embrace a scaled-back bill . . . she said the White House could have been far more helpful in pushing back against Republican critics, and she [made] clear she had disagreements with the president's top advisers."[7]

These comments should alert us to the tensions that can underlay the nominally friendly relationships that generally prevail between a president and the leaders of his party in Congress. These tensions are of an institutional and political nature and arise from several sources:

1. *Divergent bargaining strategies*: Presidents, especially first-term presidents, move quickly to develop a record that they can run on when seeking a second term. Once they have achieved a second term, they work to build a legacy that will bear witness to their time in the White House. Both of these prod presidents to be much more inclined to make deals even if it involves circumventing their own party leaders in Congress and cutting deals with the political opposition.

   Barack Obama was certainly not unique in these impulses. His predecessor, George W. Bush, worked closely with Democrats to gain passage of the "No Child Left Behind" law that sought to promote educational accountability and to broaden Medicare to include coverage of prescription drugs. Achievement of legislative goals for members of Congress, even party leaders, is the product of collective action in which credit must necessarily be shared. It is not that members of Congress are oblivious to signal achievements and legacies, but few members even in lengthy careers on the Hill can lay claim to important legislation that bears their name.

   This proclivity of presidents to want to strike deals may involve bargains with the opposition party that can create friction between the president and his own party in Congress. The furtherance of these presidential goals involves the interaction of White House officials such as chiefs of staff and members of the legislative affairs team (the president's lobbyists) with congressional leadership. This interaction varies greatly in quality. Governments of law, we must remind ourselves, are also governments of men (and women).

2. *The institutional complexity of Congress*: The party's leader in the Senate presides over a collectivity. And although the battle lines between the parties are as sharply drawn as they have ever been and though "[a]ll the evidence on parties in government in recent years points to very high unity within and sharp ideological and policy differences between the two major parties,"[8] one congressional party is less homogeneous than the other, especially in the Senate. Harry Reid, for much of Obama's term, presided over a caucus that, while overwhelmingly liberal, could be susceptible to divisions on certain issues and vulnerable to moves by the Republicans to use parliamentary devices to induce defections. On occasion, what the president wanted created problems for the members of his party in Congress.

3. *The close-run nature of majority control*: As Frances E. Lee has so convincingly argued,[9] the very narrow margins of majority control in recent years have injected an intensity into Senate elections, and inflated the value of even a single seat to heights unknown in the 1960s when Democrats were always comfortably in control and seated on well-padded margins. As Lee observed, "In today's environment of intense two-party competition for control of Congress, the political stakes are higher. Members remain concerned about their individual careers, of course. But they are also far more likely to consider how their actions might affect their party's prospects for retaining or gaining power in the chamber."[10] In the 113th Congress (2013–2015) red-state Democrats such as Louisiana's Mary Landrieu and Alaska's Mark Begich found it politically risky to endorse environmental legislation favored by most Senate Democrats. Yet they, and North Carolina's Kay Hagan, had also provided the margin of majority control enjoyed by the Democrats. Their defeat in the 2014 election contributed to the loss of the Democrats' majority.

COMBAT OR COMPROMISE:
EXECUTIVE EAGERNESS AND HILL HARDBALL

Early in 2010, not long after the successful effort to pass the Affordable Care Act, a bipartisan group of senators met in the White House with presidential chief of staff Rahm Emanuel, a former member of Congress himself, to discuss legislation that would transform the energy industry in the United States to take account of the effects of burning fossil fuels on the environment.

Exhausted by the fight for the Affordable Care Act, some of President Obama's principal aides were not certain that they wanted to take on a battle that could reshape the US economy while the nation was still recovering from the financial crisis that began in 2008. The president's chief strategist, David Axelrod, was lukewarm about the plan known as "cap and trade." Emanuel wanted another big win but was unsure whether the votes were there to pass it.[11]

Each of the three senators in the bipartisan group, Joseph Lieberman, an Independent, formerly a Democrat from Connecticut; John Kerry, a Democrat from Massachusetts; and Lindsey Graham, a Republican from South Carolina, was looking for a signature legislative achievement that had thus far eluded them in their Senate careers. But their eagerness for a signal legislative accomplishment by a small group of senators was not shared by the president himself.

The legislation was complex and required the cooperation, or at least the acquiescence of, normally antagonistic groups such as a collection of environmental groups that did not necessarily see eye-to-eye, the oil and natural gas producers who also were not uniformly in agreement, and renewable energy groups that would stand to gain from a shift away from fossil fuels.

Unfolding, as it did, in the aftermath of the Affordable Care Act, which had received no Republican votes, the timing of cap and trade was not auspicious. Added to that was the emergence in 2009–2010 of the Tea Party movement, which was, by this time, hostile to almost anything coming out of the Obama administration, especially a policy that might be depicted by its enemies as involving a new tax.

Given the stakes involved, concessions were necessary to get the nominally antagonistic groups to agree to a plan. To get the support of certain large oil companies, the three senators were using as a bargaining chip the opening of large stretches of the East and Gulf coasts to oil and gas drilling. In return, the companies would not publicly criticize the cap-and-trade plan.

But just as the negotiation had reached a critical stage, the White House announced the opening of the coastal areas for drilling without getting any concessions from the energy industry. "Obama had now given away what the senators were planning to trade."[12]

There had been an assumption that the president had been working hand in glove with the three senators, but he had decided, perhaps as a gesture to the opponents, to open the tracts for drilling without informing the three senators.

There had been hints from the very beginning that the president was not wholly invested in cap and trade. Environmental groups had been urging him to take a more active role as the negotiations progressed, but the failure of the initiative in the Senate led some to place the blame at the feet of the president. "Several sources in the Senate and in the environmental community . . . privately complained that the administration failed to take a leadership role." This charge was rebutted by Democratic leader Harry Reid, who declared, "For anyone to think the president hasn't been involved in this is simply mistaken."[13]

It is possible, of course, that the decision to "serve the dessert before the children had promised to eat their spinach"[14] was due less to Obama's personal preference than it was the product of disagreement among top White House staff. One faction, led by staffers with Capitol Hill backgrounds, urged Obama to get more deeply involved in the legislative process. Another group, led by political strategist David Axelrod, believed that by involving himself in the give-and-take of legislative bargaining Obama risked appearing just like any other conventional politician.

As Reid's press secretary, Jim Manley, put it, "Obama had a difficult relationship with the Hill and not just with Republicans but with Democrats as well. For whatever reason, he didn't like to get his hands dirty in the legislative process. He didn't like to mix it up. He wanted to hang out at the

64,000-foot level and leave the tough stuff to others including, of course, Harry Reid."[15]

Whether it was this allegedly Olympian disdain for the legislative process on Obama's part, or the remarkable success in enacting the Affordable Care Act that had passed with the faintest White House fingerprints, that convinced the president that he was best served by leaving the heavy lifting to Reid and Pelosi, a laissez-faire attitude characterized the first two years of Obama's approach to his legislative agenda. Accordingly, it was congressional Democrats who were held responsible by the voters in the election of 2010 for Obama's signature accomplishments, most notably Obamacare. Even before the electoral debacle that cost the Democrats sixty-three House seats and four seats in the Senate, personnel changes at the White House were taking place. These changes were to have long-lasting repercussions on the relationship between the president and his closest allies on Capitol Hill.

In the fall of 2010, Rahm Emanuel left Washington to run for mayor of Chicago. His place was taken temporarily by Pete Rouse, who had served as Obama's chief of staff in his short tenure in the Senate. In the White House Rouse had become one of the president's most trusted managers. But in the aftermath of what Obama called "a shellacking" at the hands of the voters in the November 2010 election, he decided that he needed someone of stature to reach out to the business community—not the natural allies of Democrats—and on the recommendation of Emanuel chose for his new chief of staff William M. Daley, a Chicago banker who took up his duties early in 2011.

Daley was no stranger to Washington. He had served as President Bill Clinton's secretary of commerce and was considered an ideal emissary to congressional Republicans and the new Speaker of the House, Rep. John Boehner. Daley had a message that he thought would resonate with Republicans. He believed that entitlement programs such as Social Security and Medicare had grown far too expensive and needed to be reined in. While this was an appealing message for Republicans, it was repugnant to congressional Democrats who saw themselves as the trustees of the handiwork of the two great Democratic presidents, Franklin Roosevelt and Lyndon Johnson.

While Daley seemed to get along well with Boehner, he infuriated Democrats in Congress. In a series of interviews he gave to journalist Roger Simon at the end of October 2011 he was quoted as saying Obama needed to "make a startling end run around not just the Republicans but also the Democrats in Congress."[16] This tactic that is used on occasion by presidents is known as triangulation. This involves siding with the opposition party in Congress against one's own party members. It is an approach that signals that the president wishes to advance his own agenda even at the expense of his own party.

Daley was seen as behind this tactic, and the resentment on the part of congressional Democrats was captured by Reid Chief of Staff David Krone:

> It [the relationship between the White House and the Democratic leadership] had been good but it all went downhill when Daley came in. He was there for only a year but it was a wasted year for the presidency. And the president knew it, and that's why Daley was fired. He started in January of 2011. The first time he came to see Senator Reid was in September of 2011. Nine months had passed before he came to see Senator Reid.[17]

At the president's direction, Daley had embarked upon working out a "grand bargain" with the Republicans whereby the Republicans would (reluctantly) agree to certain tax increases and the Democrats (equally reluctantly) would consent to make changes in entitlement programs.

> Reid finds out that Daley's going up and talking to Boehner about cutting a deal on a so-called grand bargain. Reid wasn't very happy about it, believing correctly that the Speaker could never cut a deal because he couldn't deliver the votes. It got so bad that Reid authorized his staff to publicly criticize Daley in the newspapers. That had never happened before.[18]

Daley seemed all too ready to concede the need for cuts in entitlements, including raising the eligibility age of Medicare, without any firm guarantee that Boehner could deliver tax increases in return, especially in light of the influx of House Republicans elected in 2010 who were determined to cut the federal deficit. With the need for Congress to pass appropriations bills by an April 2011 deadline, Boehner, under pressure from the Tea Party wing of the Republican Party, announced in late January that the Republican majority in the House was going to cut $100 billion in spending from the appropriations bills.[19]

Then, according to Krone, "Daley, unbeknownst to anybody wound up telling Barry Jackson, Boehner's Chief of Staff, 'Well, we'll agree to cut $70 billion right off the bat.' He did that without telling anybody. Reid was so angry that he called Obama to say 'When I need Daley's help, I'll let you know.'"[20]

Daley remained at his post through the tense summer of 2011 when the nation faced the possibility of a credit default for the first time in its history. But by November 2011, he was, in the words of one journalist, "a walking corpse" whose authority had been reduced when the president brought back Pete Rouse with authority to make decisions without Daley's approval. "Daley retained his West Wing corner office, but he was chief of staff in name only."[21]

The default was averted at the last moment in August 2011, but the solu-tion to the crisis would have repercussions throughout Obama's first term and into his second.

Part of the deal to avert default was the creation of a bipartisan "super committee" consisting of members of Congress and economists tasked with coming up with $1.5 trillion in savings over a ten-year period. As an incen-tive to the committee to make those cuts, the Budget Control Act that was a key element in the settlement stipulated that failure to make the cuts would result in a "sequestration" in which across-the-board cuts would take place in every federal government program except entitlements. The committee's effort to make these arbitrary cuts failed because spending reductions of that magnitude would have required tax increases (opposed by Republi-cans) and cuts in entitlement programs (opposed by Democrats). With the sequester coming into force, everything from military aircraft purchases ($4 billion cut) to the Holocaust Memorial Museum ($3 million cut) suffered.[22]

Worse was to come at the end of 2012. In late December, the combined expiration of the 2001 tax cuts initiated by President George W. Bush and the budget cuts enacted pursuant to the August debt crisis were creating what came to be known as "the fiscal cliff." Were both to take effect, the impact would likely be disastrous for an economy just emerging from the financial crisis that began in 2008.

The effort to avert the fiscal cliff produced another situation in which the negotiating strategy of Majority Leader Harry Reid and that of President Obama were not in sync. The president sought a deal and Reid craved a victory over his nemesis, Republican leader Mitch McConnell.

In November 2012 Obama was elected to a second term. Reelected presidents very quickly become legacy-minded. Knowing that only four years remain to achieve a lasting impact on American public policy, this sentiment—common to all presidents—intensified Obama's desire for deal making. This propensity for quick closure we saw in the cases of cap and trade and William Daley's preemptive offer of spending cuts to Republicans that so angered Harry Reid continued into Obama's second term.

Late in 2012, Harry Reid and Mitch McConnell had been in talks to avert the fiscal cliff. It appears that Reid expected the talks to break down and, in fact, wanted them to fail. He calculated that McConnell would get the blame for the inevitable government shutdown that would result. As one observer noted, "[I]t's clear that Reid had a plan for resolving the cliff and considered the breakdown in talks with McConnell very much a part of it."[23] A journalist further recounted: "With his negotiations stalling with his Democratic counterpart, Harry Reid, McConnell called up Vice-President Biden, who had served with him for many years in the Senate. 'Does any-one down there know how to make a deal?' he demanded to know. He and Biden hashed out a deal that, once again, upset many Democrats."[24]

Biden, of course, needed to get the approval of President Obama to engage in talks with McConnell. The success of the talks averted the fiscal cliff but angered many Democrats who faulted Obama's "a deal at any price" approach to negotiations as excessively generous to the GOP and at odds with his party's congressional leadership. Worse still, Obama's dispatch of Biden to parley with McConnell cut the ground out from under Harry Reid. A journalist noted:

> Reid was furious. In a call, he told the president that he or Biden would have to come to the Senate and pitch the deal to the Democrats themselves—Reid wanted no part of it himself. But while other accounts have portrayed Reid's frustration as stemming from the substance of the deal, Reid was just as frustrated over the fact that he'd been in the middle of executing his own plan, which was now moot.[25]

THE POLITICAL MISALIGNMENT BETWEEN MEMBERS OF CONGRESS AND THE WHITE HOUSE

The overall agenda of a president and his party in Congress may appear to be in harmony, but policies favored by the president may place members of his congressional party in awkward positions, especially when this misalignment coincides with upcoming congressional elections. In the Obama years, policies favored by the president were especially problematic for Senate Democrats seeking reelection from states that Obama had not carried in 2008 and/or 2012.

Typical of this group of senators were Claire McCaskill of Missouri, Jon Tester of Montana, and Joe Manchin of West Virginia, all of whom were facing reelection in 2012, and their reaction to the Keystone XL pipeline project. These "red-state" Democrats were in a difficult position. As Democrats, they did not want to advance a bill opposed by environmentalists, a key Democratic constituency. And although it was generally assumed that President Obama also opposed the pipeline, he had deferred taking a stand on it, pending a decision by the State Department, whose approval was necessary due to the fact that the line originated in Canada and was thus an international agreement. But blocking the pipeline was a priority for the Democratic Party's liberal base. Republicans, who backed construction of the pipeline, attempted to accelerate the process of approval early in 2012 by attaching it as an amendment to a transportation bill.

Controversial bills in the Senate are invariably required to get the support of sixty senators in order to be taken up. This occurs when there is an implicit threat to filibuster a bill by its opponents. This generally produces a recognition on the part of a bill's sponsors that if a bill is going to have to ultimately face a sixty-vote threshold on a subsequent cloture vote to defeat the filibuster, they might as well simply agree to the supermajority requirement at the outset.

Sixty votes in a closely divided Senate is an objective not easily attained. Paradoxically, however, this situation can provide political cover for senators like McCaskill, Tester, and Manchin. It enables them to vote for the bill with the reasonable certainty that the sixty-vote threshold will not be reached and thus to appease their pro-pipeline constituents while "doing no harm." But these "atypical" Democratic senators periodically found themselves having to straddle the gap between the policies of a Democratic president and the preferences of constituencies far more conservative than those of the typical Democratic senator. There are other examples—both major and minor—of the lack of fit between Obama's proposals and the political needs of members of Congress.

Another sore point between the White House and some members of the Senate Democratic Caucus was the president's decision to press ahead with a major trade agreement with a number of nations in Asia. Known as the Trans-Pacific Partnership (TPP), it was seen as the descendant of the North American Free Trade Agreement that was enacted during the Clinton administration and was seen by some Democrats from industrial states as having resulted in the loss of manufacturing jobs to countries with lower labor costs such as Mexico. This, combined with the Keystone XL pipeline, put the president and congressional Democrats on a collision course going into the 2014 congressional elections.[26]

At the time that Obama was making overtures to the business community, the Republican-controlled House passed with Democratic support legislation labeled "the JOBS bill." The word "jobs" was an acronym for "Jumpstart Our Business Startups." The bill was designed to facilitate start-up companies' initial public offerings (IPOs), including the use of crowdsourcing. Most Republicans supported it. Democrats were badly split.

Senator Charles Schumer, who would ultimately succeed Harry Reid as Democratic leader in 2017, favored it. Reid couldn't even bear to call it anything but "the IPO bill." Reid's whip (deputy majority leader), Richard Durbin, opposed it, as did Michigan's Carl Levin, even more vehemently. Both senators considered the bill an open invitation to fraud.

The bill enjoyed enough support to be seen as a "vehicle"—a popular piece of legislation likely to pass. Members welcome such bills because, if they seem headed for passage, they can add amendments that might not pass on their own. While Reid might have been leery of the bill, he reasoned that he could bargain with Republicans to modify it and to add amendments for consumer protections sought by Democrats. He had reason to believe that Minority Leader Mitch McConnell was eager to pass it to give a victory to House Speaker John Boehner. This put Reid in the enviable position of modifying the bill to suit the preferences of liberal Democrats, and if McConnell would not accede to the changes, he would request that President Obama veto it.[27]

President Obama, to the surprise and dismay of Democrats, came out in favor of the bill in his 2012 State of the Union address, thus eliminating the veto threat and greatly decreasing Reid's leverage on McConnell. It was the view of leadership staff in the Senate that Obama saw the JOBS bill as an opportunity to burnish his bipartisan credentials and appear high-minded and above the battle. Reid's chief of staff grumbled that it was "a lousy bill" and that the White House had "screwed up" by endorsing it and removing the threat of a veto, thus depriving the Senate Democrats of leverage.[28]

The JOBS bill passed the Senate by a vote of 73–26 on March 23, 2012, despite a valiant last-minute effort by Senator Carl Levin. The bill had caused a deep breach in the ranks of Senate Democrats and between the Senate liberals and the White House.

President Obama signed the JOBS bill, now the Jobs Act, on April 5, 2012, with House Majority Leader Eric Cantor looking on. The signing ceremony was in the White House Rose Garden, a locale reserved for bill signings for which a president wishes to receive the maximum media exposure. A journalish noted: "[T]he White House was mainly celebrating a rare bipartisan achievement on legislation that had been pushed by Republicans and embraced by President Obama in his State of the Union address, [but] most of the administration's legislative program bill had little chance of being passed by a hostile Congress in an election year."[29]

The year of President Obama's reelection was also a good year for Senate Democrats. In contrast to the midterm election of 2010, Democrats held their losses to a single seat (Ben Nelson's in Nebraska) and picked up one seat in Indiana (Joe Donnelly) and one in Massachusetts (Elizabeth Warren). There were five Democratic retirements, but all were kept in the Democratic column. But the Democrats' success in 2012 also revealed vulnerability: victories in Indiana and Missouri and the retention of the North Dakota seat were in states that were either Republican or leaned in that direction. The 2014 election would expose that weakness dramatically with the defeat of six red-state Democrats. Such Democrats have always posed a problem for Democratic leaders. Indeed, a Democratic leader—Tom Daschle—representing the red state of South Dakota went down to defeat in 2002. Pulled in one direction by the conservative politics of their states and in the other by the overwhelmingly liberal Senate Democratic caucus, they often face difficult, even agonizing, choices.

Looking at a map of how the states voted in the last three presidential elections (2016, 2012, and 2008), the Republican and Democratic states break down pretty evenly into twenty-one solidly Republican and twenty predictably Democratic states. The nine remaining states are those that have shown an ability to spring surprises, especially after the 2016 collapse of the vaunted Democratic "blue wall" of midwestern states plus Pennsylvania. These turned from supporting Democratic candidates in 2012 to support-ing Donald Trump for president in 2016. The nine "swing states," with the exception of Iowa and Michigan, send a Democratic and a Republican sen-ator to Washington. These nine are where the Democratic and Republican Senate campaign committees must go prospecting for pickups. This con-tributes to what Frances Lee has characterized as "One of the most striking characteristics of the current era in American politics . . . [the] prolonged evenly-matched contest for party control of National institutions."[30]

While picking up seats in states where the odds of a pickup are more nearly even is a priority for party leaders in the Congress, of even greater importance, once a majority has been attained, is protecting incumbents. This was the challenge faced by Harry Reid in the four election cycles of the Obama presidency.

The cost of winning and retaining these seats is steep. It involves not simply the expenditure of money by the senatorial campaign committees but also using the legislative process to provide accomplishments for these senators and to shield them from having to cast votes on bills and amend-ments offered by the opposition with the express purpose of forcing them to take positions certain to alienate large groups of voters in their states. Both campaign money and legislative strategy loomed large in the relation-ship between the Obama White House and the Democratic leadership in Congress, especially in the Senate.

THE CRISIS OF 2014

By the summer of 2014, members of Congress were going public with their criticisms of the president. Some complained of lack of invitations to the White House and an inattentive, even dismissive attitude on the part of Mr. Obama. At a White House meeting with Harry Reid and his Republican counterpart, Mitch McConnell, for the purpose of discussing security issues, Senator Reid abruptly changed the topic to complain about Republican tactics on blocking Obama's nominations. "Mr. Obama quickly dismissed the matter. 'You and Mitch work it out' Mr. Obama said coolly, cutting off any discussion."[31]

Of greater concern was whether Democratic Senate candidates facing election in November would have enough money to run winning cam-paigns, especially in those states that had been won by Republican presi-dential candidate Mitt Romney in 2012.

Concerned that Democrats would be outspent by super PACs organized by billionaires Charles and David Koch, Reid commissioned the creation of a pro-Democratic super PAC to be headed by his former chief of staff, Susan

McCue. The Senate Majority PAC would augment the campaign funds that Democratic candidates raised on their own or received from the Democratic Senate Campaign Committee. Reid and McCue anticipated that President Obama would participate actively in fundraising for the PAC and would direct money to it from the Democratic National Committee. By late August, the president had scheduled no appearances on behalf of the Senate Majority PAC. Moreover, the White House had laid down a series of limitations on the availability of the president for events sponsored by the PAC.[32]

Election Day, November 4, 2014, was a disaster for the Democrats. Six Democratic incumbents were defeated and three seats held by retiring Democrats were won by Republicans. This provided the Republicans with a solid majority in the Senate. Twelve House seats also fell to the Republicans. Democrats had no shortage of people to blame.

Obama came in for furious criticism for allegedly obstructing the flow of campaign money to Democratic congressional candidates. Because of his low approval rating, most Democrats were not eager to have him campaign for them, but they were most anxious for him to raise money on their behalf while staying discreetly behind the scenes. Journalists reported:

> At a March 4 [2014] meeting in the Oval Office, Senate Majority Leader Harry M. Reid (D-Nev.) and other Senate leaders pleaded with Obama to transfer millions in party funds and also help to raise money for an outside group [the Senate Majority PAC]. "We were never going to get on the same page," said David Krone, Reid's Chief of Staff. "We were beating our heads against the wall."[33]

The recriminations continued. Krone had picked up from journalists covering the White House that officials close to the president were blaming the legislative strategy devised by him and Senator Reid for the party's poor performance in the election. Krone, with Reid's authorization, then gave an interview to *Washington Post* reporters in which he laid the blame on Obama for not doing more to help the vulnerable Democratic senators.[34]

Reid wanted not only to provide Democratic senators facing the electorate with the money they needed to compete, he also devised what turned out to be a controversial strategy to shield red-state Democrats by blocking politically risky amendments from coming to a vote. Journalists wrote: "With less ammunition to use against their incumbents, Democrats hope that enough of their members will survive."[35]

While he is hardly an impartial judge of Reid's strategy, Republican leader Mitch McConnell's press secretary pronounced it a failure:

> He simply protected them into unemployment. Reid didn't allow any of his members to have two things: one, a split from their party leadership which is important in some states, or even have votes on their own items, their own accomplishments. He didn't give them the things they needed to run on. . . .

He prevented them from having any accomplishments. He didn't protect them at all. He hurt them. It backfired.[36]

It is, of course, arguable whether Reid's strategy to save his majority backfired or whether 2014 was simply a bad year for a Democrat to be running in a red state or even a light blue one, as the fate of Colorado's Tom Udall suggested. President Obama's job approval rating reached its low point—38 percent—in eight polling periods.[37] Being blocked from going on record as opposing an unpopular president might have been a handicap, but just being a Democrat in a red state might alone have been sufficient to get unseated.

PRESIDENTS AND CONGRESSIONAL PARTIES: NOT ALWAYS ON THE SAME PAGE

Presidents and presidential cabinets have, from time immemorial, pleaded with voters not only to elect them but to give them a team of senators and House members that will enable them to achieve their objectives. Recent trends in voting behavior suggest that voters are obliging by supporting presidential and congressional candidates of the same party. Likewise, in midterm elections, congressional candidates either sink or swim depending on the job approval of the president of their party. That was certainly the case in both of President Obama's midterm elections in 2010 and 2014. But this community of shared fate between presidents and members of Congress of their own party and the obvious disposition of those members to support their president on legislation is not to imply that their objectives are always congruent. We have seen this misalignment in the case of President Obama and Congress in this chapter. But it is important to note that this situation is not confined to President Obama. It is true more generally and in 2016–2017 may even extend to presidents-elect.

In the course of assembling a cabinet before his inauguration, Donald Trump received a suggestion from his son, Donald Jr., to consider for the post of secretary of the Interior a Montana Republican congressman named Ryan Zinke. The younger Trump, a member of a sportsmen's organization, Backcountry Hunters and Anglers, had heard favorable reports about Representative Zinke, especially his opposition to selling off federal land. President-elect Trump had already floated the name of Rep. Cathy McMorris Rodgers for the Interior post. Unlike Representative Zinke, Rodgers favored the land sales.[38]

Senate Republican Leader Mitch McConnell had other plans for Representative Zinke. He had approached Zinke over the summer to run for the US Senate against Democratic Senator Jon Tester, a red-state Democrat and, therefore, vulnerable. McConnell, holding only a narrow majority of 52–48 in the 115th Congress, was eager to boost his advantage to sixty seats, and Zinke's election would advance that goal. Zinke, by accepting Trump's nomination, was delivering a blow to McConnell's vision of a sixty-seat GOP majority.

McConnell was further frustrated by his effort to persuade Trump to nominate a red-state Democratic senator to his cabinet. High on the list were Senators Joe Manchin of West Virginia and Heidi Heitkamp of North Dakota. Both states have Republican governors who, in the event of a vacancy created by a senator's departure for the cabinet, would appoint a Republican successor and place that person in a strong position to retain the seat for the Republicans. Again Trump acted contrary to the wishes of the man who would be his party leader in the Senate.

Donald Trump is certainly an unconventional president, but in his desire to shape a cabinet to suit his own preferences the needs of his congressional party do not top his list of priorities. In this one respect, at least, Donald Trump may be a quite conventional president.

NOTES

1. Jon R. Bond and Richard Fleisher, *The President in the Legislative Arena* (Chicago: University of Chicago Press, 1990), 124.

2. Bond and Fleisher, *The President in the Legislative Arena*, 124.

3. Telephone interview with David Krone, October 4, 2016.

4. Telephone interview with David Krone, October 4, 2016.

5. Telephone interview with Bill Dauster, October 28, 2016.

6. Bob Cusack, Sarah Ferris, and Peter Sullivan, "The Chaotic Fight for Obama Care," *The Hill*, February 10, 2016.

7. Cusack, Ferris, and Sullivan, "The Chaotic Fight for Obama Care."

8. Thomas E. Mann and Norman J. Ornstein, *It's Even Worse Than It Looks* (New York: Basic Books, 2012), 44–45.

9. See Frances E. Lee, "Making Laws and Making Points: Senate Governance in an Era of Uncertain Majorities," *The Forum* 9, no. 4, article 3 (2011).

10. Lee, "Making Laws and Making Points," 3.

11. Ryan Lizza, "As the World Burns," *The New Yorker*, October 11, 2010.

12. Lizza, "As the World Burns."

13. Evan Lehmann, "Senate Abandons Climate Effort, Dealing Blow to President," *New York Times*, July 23, 2010.

14. Lizza, "As the World Burns."

15. Telephone interview with Jim Manley, September 30, 2016.

16. Roger Simon, "Exclusive: Bill Daley, Unplugged," *Politico*, October 28, 2011.

17. Telephone interview with David Krone, October 4, 2016.

18. Telephone interview with Jim Manley, September 30, 2016.

19. Michael O'Brien, "Boehner Takes Pressure from the Right on Spending Cuts," *The Hill*, January 24, 2011.

20. Telephone interview with David Krone, October 4, 2016.

21. Paul Starobin, "The Rise and Fall of Bill Daley: An Inside Account," *The New Republic*, January 18, 2012.

22. Dylan Matthews, "The Sequester: Absolutely Everything You Could Possibly Need to Know, in One FAQ," *Washington Post*, February 20, 2013.

23. Noam Schreiber, "The Inside Story of How Obama Could Have Gotten a Better Tax Deal without Biden," *The New Republic*, January 9, 2013.

24. Alec MacGillis, *The Cynic: The Political Education of Mitch McConnell* (New York: Simon & Schuster, 2014), 118.

25. Schreiber, "The Inside Story of How Obama Could Have Gotten a Better Tax Deal without Biden."

26. Janet Hook and Peter Nicholas, "Fractures Emerge Between Obama, Congressional Democrats," *Wall Street Journal*, February 3, 2014.

27. Author's notes, March 19 and 20, 2012.

28. Conversation between the author and David Krone, March 21, 2012.

29. Mark Landler, "Obama Signs Bill to Promote Start-Up Investments," *New York Times*, April 5, 2012.

30. Lee, "Making Laws and Making Points," 3.

31. Carl Hulse, Jeremy W. Peters, and Michael D. Shear, "Obama Is Seen as Frustrating His Own Party," *New York Times*, August 18, 2014.

32. Hulse, Peters, and Shear, "Obama Is Seen as Frustrating His Own Party."

33. Philip Rucker and Robert Costa, "Battle for the Senate: How the GOP Did It," *Washington Post*, November 5, 2014.

34. Jason Horowitz, "Reid Is Unapologetic as Aide Steps on Toes, Even the President's," *New York Times*, November 21, 2014.

35. Manu Raju and Burgess Everett, "Reid's Plot to Keep the Senate," *Politico*, September 18, 2014.

36. Telephone interview with Donald Stewart, press secretary to Senator Mitch McConnell, December 13, 2016.

37. http://www.gallup.com/poll/116479/barack-obama-job-approval.aspx.

38. Jonathan Martin and Alexander Burns, "McConnell Eyed Zinke for a Senate Seat. Donald Trump Had Other Ideas," *New York Times*, December 16, 2016.

CHAPTER 9

Rivalry for Power in the Judicial Appointment Process

John Anthony Maltese

The death of Justice Antonin Scalia on February 13, 2016, focused public attention on the political rough-and-tumble of the Supreme Court appointment process. About an hour after Scalia's death had been confirmed, Senate Majority Leader Mitch McConnell (R-KY) announced that the Senate should not consider any nominee put forward by President Barack Obama to fill the seat because of the upcoming presidential election. As he put it, "The American people should have a voice in the selection of their next Supreme Court justice. Therefore, this vacancy should not be filled until we have a new president."[1] Within twenty-four hours, other Republicans fell into line.

According to Article II, Section 2 of the US Constitution, the power to appoint justices to the Supreme Court is shared between the executive and legislative branches: the president nominates individuals to serve on the court, but those nominations are subject to the "Advice and Consent of the Senate." In other words, the Senate has the power to confirm or reject nominees. Still, the Constitution leaves many questions unanswered. What exactly constitutes "advice"? Under what circumstances may the Senate reject a nominee? Does confirmation require a simple majority vote of the Senate, or is it permissible to filibuster judicial nominees? May the Senate take no action whatsoever on a nominee, or does the clause require some sort of action? If it does require action, how quickly must that action be taken? Without specific guidance from the Constitution, such questions can lead to conflicting answers by those involved in the process. That is precisely what happened in the wake of Justice Scalia's death.

Democrats viewed the Republican threat to ignore any nominee put forward by President Obama as a political ploy designed to deprive the president of a court appointment. They also argued that the Senate has a constitutional responsibility to act on a nominee when the president presents one. It can choose to reject that nominee, they noted, but the Senate should not simply ignore a nomination by refusing to hold hearings or to allow a timely vote on the nominee. And so, on March 16, President Obama nominated Merrick Garland, the chief judge of the US Court of Appeals for the District of Columbia Circuit, to fill the vacancy left by Justice Scalia's death. Obama urged the Senate to act on the nomination, saying, "Presidents do not stop working in the final year of their term; neither should a senator."[2]

Republicans responded by pointing to Vice President Joe Biden's own words as a US senator in a floor speech on June 25, 1992. At that time, he served as the Democratic chairman of the Senate Judiciary Committee—the body that holds hearings on Supreme Court nominees. Speaking then, with Republican president George H. W. Bush running for reelection, Biden suggested that if a Supreme Court justice were to retire after that date, the president should refrain from making a nomination until after the election. Should a justice retire and the president nominate someone anyway, Biden said, "the Senate Judiciary Committee should seriously consider not scheduling confirmation hearings on the nomination until after the political campaign season is over."[3] Now, with Garland, Republicans said, they were simply following the "Biden Rule."

In fact, both parties have employed obstructionist tactics to block nominees they oppose, but have then turned around and accused obstructionists of shenanigans when one of their nominations was at stake. At root, the process is a political one. Merrick Garland proved to be just the latest casualty of that process. But Garland is a useful springboard for discussing the rivalry for power that Supreme Court vacancies can engender—particularly when the White House and the Senate are controlled by opposing political parties. The reason for such rivalry is clear. The Supreme Court is the final arbiter on difficult constitutional questions involving many of the most contentious issues of public policy, including abortion, same-sex marriage, gun control, voting rights, the Affordable Care Act ("Obamacare"), and a wide array of issues related to free speech, the separation of church and state, and the rights of criminal defendants, to name a few. Moreover, once confirmed, Supreme Court justices enjoy life tenure. Thus, they have the potential to impact public policy for generations to come.

CONSTITUTIONAL AMBIGUITY

Reaching definitive conclusions about precisely what the process should entail is difficult, if not impossible, because the constitutional language in question is ambiguous. Like so much of the Constitution, that ambiguity reflects the fact that the Constitution was a jointly drafted document. Delegates to the Constitutional Convention held widely differing views about a broad range of issues, including the appointment process. For example, there were those who favored a strong legislature proposed appointment by Congress, either by both chambers or by the Senate alone. On the other hand, advocates of a strong executive opposed legislative appointment and called for executive appointment instead. The convention remained deadlocked on the issue until the Committee on Postponed Matters finally came up with the compromise language that ended up becoming part of the Constitution.[4] Great debate preceded that compromise language, so it is reasonable to assume that the ambiguities in the advice and consent clause were intentional. It allowed various framers to cling to differing interpretations of that language, just as rival political parties do today.

For example, the Constitution does not specify when the Senate should withhold its consent of a president's nominee. Should the Senate generally defer to the president and only reject a nominee for extraordinary reasons, such as lack of qualifications or some sort of impropriety? Or may the Senate take a more aggressive role and block nominees for political or ideological reasons? Alexander Hamilton, a proponent of a strong executive, argued in "Federalist No. 76" for senatorial deference, explaining that the Senate's power to withhold consent is primarily "a check upon the spirit of favoritism in the President" designed to prevent individuals from being appointed because of "family connection" or "personal attachment."[5] But that did not prevent Hamilton from encouraging the Senate to reject George Washington's 1795 nomination of John Rutledge to be chief justice of the Supreme Court on political grounds—because Rutledge opposed the Jay Treaty between the United States and Great Britain.[6] George Washington himself suggested that the Senate could reject nominees for whatever reason it might choose. In a 1789 message to a Senate committee on treaties and nominations, he wrote that just "as the President has a right to nominate without assigning reasons, so has the Senate a right to dissent without giving theirs."[7]

In practice, the degree of deference displayed by the Senate has evolved with changing political circumstances. Support for an aggressive senatorial role has come variously from both ends of the political spectrum depending upon the exigencies of the moment. Thus, when economic conservatives controlled the Supreme Court in the first part of the twentieth century, progressives and economic liberals demanded aggressive vetting of Supreme Court nominees. For example, when President Herbert Hoover nominated Charles Evans Hughes to be chief justice in 1930, Senate opponents called for his defeat because they feared he would promote "judicial activism" by reading economic rights into the Constitution. Conservative supporters of Hughes, such as the *New York Herald Tribune*, decried such opposition as "a ridiculous approach to an examination of a man's fitness for judicial office" and concluded: "The primary requisites for such an office are integrity, wide experience, capacity and intellectual independence. Mr. Hughes has all these."[8]

However, the situation reversed itself in the 1950s and 1960s when the Supreme Court moved in a more liberal direction under Chief Justice Earl Warren. Then it became conservatives who accused liberals on the court of engaging in "judicial activism" by reading personal liberties, such as a right of privacy, into the Constitution. They became the ones urging aggressive vetting of nominees. As a young attorney in 1959, William Rehnquist—who would go on to serve as both an associate justice (appointed by Richard Nixon) and chief justice (appointed by Ronald Reagan)—urged the Senate to restore its practice of "thoroughly informing itself on the judicial philosophy of a Supreme Court nominee before voting to confirm him" because if "greater judicial self-restraint is desired, or a different interpretation of the phrases 'due process or law' or 'equal protection of the laws', then men sympathetic to such desires must sit upon the high court." The only way to assure such restraint, Rehnquist concluded, is for the Senate to inquire.[9] Armed with such inquiry, the majority of the Senate could presumably use it to reject nominees who embraced an interpretation of the Constitution that ran counter to theirs.

BLOCKING SUPREME COURT NOMINEES

The failure rate of Supreme Court nominees is the highest for any appointive post requiring Senate confirmation.[10] Excluding consecutive nominations of the same individual by the same president for the same seat on the court and Ronald Reagan's 1987 nomination of Douglas Ginsburg (which he announced but then withdrew before formally submitting it to the Senate), presidents had submitted 153 Supreme Court nominations to the Senate as of January 1, 2017. Out of these, seven individuals declined after being nominated, one died before taking office, and one expected vacancy failed to materialize. President George W. Bush withdrew yet another nomination (John Roberts) for an associate justice seat and resubmitted it to fill the newly vacated chief justice seat. Of the remaining 143 nominations, 116 were confirmed by the Senate. The other twenty-seven may be classified as "failed" nominations because Senate opposition blocked them. If one includes Douglas Ginsburg, the number rises to twenty-eight, with eight occurring in the past fifty years. (See table 9.1.)

An outright rejection of a nominee entails a vote by the Senate, but the Senate has also passively blocked nominees through inaction, as it did with Merrick Garland. Prior to Garland, however, it had been a long time since the Senate did this. Not counting instances when the president withdrew a nomination before Senate action began (as President George W. Bush did

Table 9.1. Failed Supreme Court Nominees

Nominee and Date of Nomination	President and Party	Composition of Senate	Action/Date
John Rutledge, 12/10/1795[a]	Washington	16 PA, 14 AA	Rejected 10–14; 12/15/1795
Alexander Wolcott, 2/4/1811	Madison (DR)	27 DR, 7 F	Rejected 9–24; 2/13/1811
John J. Crittenden, 12/17/1828	J. Q. Adams (AJ)	27 J, 21 AJ	Postponed 23–17; 2/12/1829
Roger B. Taney, 1/15/1835	Jackson (J)	26 J, AJ, 2 other	Postponed 24–21; 3/3/1835
John C. Spencer, 1/9/1844 (renominated 6/17/1844)	Tyler (I)[b]	29 W, 23 D	Rejected 21–26; 1/31/1844 (renomination withdrawn 6/17/1844)
Reuben H. Walworth, 3/13/1844 (renominated 12/4/1844)	Tyler (I)	29 W, 23 D	Postponed 27–20; withdrawn; 6/17/1844 (renomination withdrawn 2/4/1845)
Edward King, 6/5/1844 (renominated 12/4/1844)	Tyler (I)	29 W, 23 D	Postponed 29–18; 6/15/1844 (renomination withdrawn 2/7/1845)
John M. Read, 2/7/1845	Tyler (I)	29 W, 23 D	No action
George W. Woodward, 12/23/1845	Polk (D)	34 D, 22 W	Rejected 20–29; 1/22/1846
Edward A. Bradford, 8/16/1852	Fillmore (W)	36 D, 23 W, 3 other	No action
George E. Badger, 1/3/1853	Fillmore (W)	36 D, 23 W, 3 other	Withdrawn; 2/14/1853
William C. Micou, 2/14/1853	Fillmore (W)	36 D, 23 W, 3 other	No action
Jeremiah S. Black, 2/5/1861	Buchanan (D)	38 D, 26 R, 2 other	Rejected 25–26; 2/21/1861
Henry Stanbery, 4/16/1866	A. Johnson (D)	39 R, 11 D, 4 other	No action[c]
Ebenezer R. Hoar, 12/14/1869	Grant (R)	62 R, 12 D	Rejected 24–33; 2/3/1870
George H. Williams, 12/1/1873	Grant (R)	47 R, 19 D, 7 other	Withdrawn; 1/8/1874
Caleb Cushing, 1/9/1874	Grant (R)	47 R, 19 D, 7 other	Withdrawn; 1/13/1874
Stanley Matthews, 1/26/1881	Hayes (R)	42 D, 33 R	No action
William Hornblower, 12/5/1893	Cleveland (D)	44 D, 40 R, 4 other	Rejected 24–30; 1/15/1894

(*continued*)

Table 9.1. *Continued*

Nominee and Date of Nomination	President and Party	Composition of Senate	Action/Date
Wheeler H. Peckham, 1/22/1894	Cleveland (D)	44 D, 40 R, 4 other	Rejected 32–41; 2/16/1894
John J. Parker, 3/21/1930	Hoover (R)	56 R, 39 D, 1 other	Rejected 39–41; 5/7/1930
Abe Fortas, 6/26/1968[d]	Johnson (D)	64 D, 36 R	Withdrawn; 10/4/1968
Homer Thornberry	Johnson (D)		Withdrawn; 10/4/1968
Clement Haynsworth Jr., 8/21/1969	Nixon (R)	57 D, 43 R	Rejected 45–55; 11/21/1969
G. Harrold Carswell, 1/19/1970	Nixon (R)	57 D, 43 R	Rejected 45–51; 4/8/1970
Robert H. Bork, 7/7/1987	Reagan (R)	55 D, 45 R	Rejected 42–58; 10/23/1987
Harriet Miers, 10/7/2005	G. W. Bush (R)	55 R, 44 D, 1 other	Withdrawn; 10/28/2005
Merrick Garland, 3/16/2016	Obama (D)	54 R, 44 D, 2 other	No action

Notes: AA = Anti-Administration, AJ = Anti-Jackson (which later became the National Republicans), D = Democrat, DR = Democratic-Republican, F = Federalist, I = Independent, J = Jacksonian Democrat, PA = Pro-Administration, R = Republican, W = Whig. Tyler, Fillmore, and Andrew Johnson had been vice presidents who ascended to office when the president died, so they had not been elected president in their own right. Political parties did not formally exist in 1795. President Washington had no political affiliation. Sixteen members of the Senate at that time are typically identified as supporting Washington (Pro-Administration) and thirteen as opposing him (Anti-Administration).

[a] Rutledge had previously served as an associate justice. The Senate rejected his nomination to be chief justice.

[b] Tyler had been elected vice president as a Whig. When he assumed the presidency he effectively acted as an Independent. Thus, while Whigs controlled the Senate, the situation amounted to divided government.

[c] The Judicial Circuits Act of 1866, signed into law on July 23, 1866, reduced the size of the Supreme Court, thereby eliminating the vacancy.

[d] Fortas sat as an associate justice when Johnson nominated him to be chief justice.

Sources: Party division in the Senate is based on https://www.senate.gov/history/partydiv.htm. Dates of nomination and Senate action, as well as Senate votes, are based on http://www.senate.gov/pagelayout/reference/nominations/Nominations.htm.

with the nomination of Harriet Miers in 2005), the Senate had not, prior to Garland, blocked a nominee through inaction since 1881. In that instance, President Rutherford B. Hayes, with only a little over a month left in his term, nominated Stanley Matthews on January 26, 1881. He did so after his successor—James Garfield—had already been elected president. Even that block proved only temporary. Garfield renominated Matthews and the Senate confirmed him two months later.

In general, Senate inaction typically occurred when presidents submitted nominations late in their term of office. A notable exception came in the tumultuous period immediately after the Civil War. Radical Republicans, who then controlled the Senate, took no action on President Andrew Johnson's nomination of Henry Stanbery on April 16, 1866. Then, just over three months later, Congress passed and President Johnson signed the Judicial Circuits Act of 1866, which reorganized federal circuit courts and also reduced the number of justices on the Supreme Court from the ten that had been authorized in 1863 to seven. (In another compromise, Article III of the Constitution established the Supreme Court but left it to Congress to determine the specific number of justices on the court through simple legislation.) Since justices have life tenure, the act allowed the reduction to take place by attrition: the next three justices who left the court would not be replaced. The Radical Republicans thereby took away the seat that Stanbery would have filled and deprived President Johnson of further opportunities to appoint Supreme Court justices who might oppose Reconstruction. Johnson remained in office until March 4, 1869, but never appointed a Supreme Court justice. Once Johnson left office, Congress passed the Judiciary Act of 1869, which increased the size of the court to nine justices, where it has stayed ever since.

Prior to Obama's nomination of Merrick Garland, the longest it had taken any successful Supreme Court nominee to be confirmed was 125 days (the record set by Woodrow Wilson's nomination of Louis Brandeis in 1916). Garland broke that record on July 20, 2016, but inaction on his nomination continued through the end of President Obama's term on January 20, 2017. That is why the White House argued that the Senate had plenty of time to consider the Garland nomination when the president made it. As the White House noted on its webpage when Scalia died and Senate Majority Leader McConnell threatened inaction: "The Senate has almost a full year to consider and confirm a nominee. In fact, since 1975, the average time from nomination to confirmation is 67 days." For the Senate to refuse to act, the White House insisted, "would be an unprecedented dereliction of duty."[11] From the day President Obama nominated Garland, over three hundred days remained in his term.

Nevertheless, the vacancy left by the death of Justice Scalia is far from the longest vacancy on the Supreme Court. Even though 125 days is the longest it has taken a *successful* nominee to be confirmed, the process has been littered with unsuccessful nominees who have slowed down the process. In addition to the seat left vacant by Scalia's death, 10 other seats on the Supreme Court have remained vacant for over 300 days. Only 1 vacancy lasted that long in the twentieth century, however: the seat vacated by Justice Abe Fortas's resignation on May 14, 1969. President Richard Nixon, a Republican, first nominated Clement Haynsworth to fill the seat, but the Democrat-controlled Senate rejected his nomination by a vote of 55–45. Then Nixon nominated G. Harrold Carswell. After revelations that Carswell had given a speech supporting segregation, the Senate rejected him by a 51–45 vote. Finally, Nixon nominated Harry Blackmun. A weary Senate confirmed him by a vote of 94–0 on May 12, 1970. That vacancy lasted 391 days. But that pales in comparison to the vacancy left by the death of Justice Henry Baldwin on April 21, 1844, which dragged on for 841 days across two presidential administrations. In all, five nineteenth-century nominations to the Supreme Court took over 500 days; two others took over 400 days.[12]

What about the argument that presidents should not make and the Senate should not consider Supreme Court nominations in a presidential election year, particularly in a terminal election year when it is clear that there will soon be a new president? Whatever the strengths and weaknesses of that claim may be, the historical record shows a long tradition of presidents nominating Supreme Court justices in presidential election years. Even in years when elections that chose their successor, presidents have routinely nominated justices and the Senate has often confirmed them. In the calendar year of a presidential election that chose their successor, presidents prior to Obama nominated thirteen individuals (three of them twice) from 1800 to 1968. Six of those individuals were confirmed. (See table 9.2.)

Until 1937, presidents had a longer lame-duck period after the election because inaugurations used to take place in March rather than January. As unfathomable as it may seem in today's environment, nine different lame-duck presidents have nominated a total of fourteen people to serve as Supreme Court justices after the election of their successor. (See table 9.3.) Eight of the fourteen were confirmed (although two of those confirmed, John Jay in 1800 and William Smith in 1837, declined their seat). Eleven of those nominations actually took place in the year after their election (between January 1 and the inauguration of their successor on March 4), with the Senate confirming six of them. Andrew Jackson went so far as to make two Supreme Court nominations on his last day in office. The Senate confirmed both (although one declined his seat). In Jackson's case, a fellow Democrat, Martin Van Buren, succeeded him. Adding nominations made by presidents in the calendar year prior to the election but still within 365 days of the election of their successor adds six more nominations to the list. The Senate confirmed all six, four of them in the year of the election (including Ronald Reagan's nomination of Anthony Kennedy by a vote of 97–0 on February 3, 1988). (See table 9.4.)

All told, presidents have nominated thirty-one individuals to the Supreme Court in the period ranging from 365 days prior to the election of their

Table 9.2. Supreme Court Nominations Made in the Same Calendar Year as the Election of the President's Successor

Date of Nomination	President	Nominee	Action/Date
December 18, 1800	Adams	John Jay	Confirmed (voice vote); 12/19/1800; but declined by Jay
December 17, 1828	J. Q. Adams	John Crittenden	Postponed 23–17; 2/12/1829
January 9, 1844 (renominated June 17, 1844)	Tyler	John Spencer	Rejected 21–26; 1/31/1844 (renomination withdrawn; 6/17/1844)
March 13, 1844 (renominated December 4, 1844)	Tyler	Reuben Walworth	Tabled 27–20; 6/17/1844 (renomination withdrawn; 2/4/1845)
June 5, 1844 (renominated December 4, 1844)	Tyler	Edward King	Postponed 29–18; 6/15/1844 (renomination withdrawn; 2/7/1845)
August 16, 1852	Fillmore	Edward Bradford	No action
December 15, 1880	Hayes	William Woods	Confirmed 39–8; 12/21/1880
April 30, 1888	Cleveland	Melville Fuller	Confirmed 41–20; 7/20/1888
July 19, 1892	Harrison	George Shiras Jr.	Confirmed (voice vote); 7/26/1892
February 19, 1912	Taft	Mahlon Pittney	Confirmed 50–26; 3/13/1912
February 15, 1932	Hoover	Benjamin Cardozo	Confirmed (voice vote); 2/24/1932
June 26, 1968	L. B. Johnson	Abe Fortas	Withdrawn; 10/4/1968
June 26, 1968	L. B. Johnson	Homer Thornberry	Withdrawn; 10/4/1968
March 16, 2016	Obama	Merrick Garland	No action

Source: Data drawn from http://www.senate.gov/pagelayout/reference/nominations/Nominations.htm.

successor to the day their successor was inaugurated. The Senate confirmed eighteen of those nominations. It is correct to say that in such instances the Senate has been more aggressive than usual in exercising its power to block nominees (blocking roughly 42 percent of the nominees as opposed to the roughly 19 percent failure rate for Supreme Court nominees overall). Nonetheless, the record shows that presidents have consistently nominated Supreme Court justices in the last year of their term when vacancies have occurred. Over the past 100 years, however, only three presidents have had an opportunity to nominate justices during the calendar year of the election of their successor: Herbert Hoover in 1932, Lyndon Johnson in 1968, and Barack Obama in 2016. The Senate confirmed only one of those nominees: Benjamin Cardozo in 1932.

Table 9.3. Supreme Court Nominations Made by Lame-Duck Presidents after the Election of Their Successors

Date of Nomination	President	Nominee	Action/Date
December 18, 1800	Adams	John Jay	Confirmed (voice vote); 12/19/1800; but declined by Jay
January 20, 1801	Adams	John Marshall	Confirmed (voice vote); 1/27/1801
December 17, 1828	J. Q. Adams	John Crittenden	Postponed 23–17; 2/12/1829
March 3, 1837	Jackson	William Smith	Confirmed 23–18; 3/8/1837; but declined by Smith
March 3, 1837	Jackson	John Catron	Confirmed 28–15; 3/8/1837
February 26, 1841	Van Buren	Peter Daniel	Confirmed 25–5; 3/2/1841
February 4, 1845	Tyler	Samuel Nelson	Confirmed (voice vote); 2/14/1845
February 7, 1845	Tyler	John Read	No action
January 3, 1853	Fillmore	George Badger	Withdrawn; 2/14/1853
February 14, 1853	Fillmore	William Micou	No action
February 5, 1861	Buchanan	Jeremiah Black	Rejected 25–26; 2/21/1861
December 15, 1880	Hayes	William Woods	Confirmed 39–8; 12/21/1880
January 26, 1881	Hayes	Stanley Matthews	No action
February 2, 1893	Harrison	Howell Jackson	Confirmed (voice vote); 2/18/1893

Source: Data drawn from http://www.senate.gov/pagelayout/reference/nominations/Nominations.htm.

Table 9.4. Supreme Court Nominations Made by Presidents in the Calendar Year Prior to a Presidential Election but within 365 Days of the Election of Their Successors

Date of Nomination	President	Nominee	Action/Date
December 28, 1835	Jackson	Philip Barbour	Confirmed 30–11; 3/15/1836
December 28, 1835	Jackson	Roger Taney	Confirmed 29–15; 3/15/1836
December 11, 1851	Fillmore	Benjamin Curtis	Confirmed (voice vote); 12/20/1851
December 6, 1887	Cleveland	Lucius Lamar	Confirmed 32–28; 1/16/1888
November 28, 1975	Ford	John Paul Stevens	Confirmed 98–0; 12/17/1975
November 30, 1987	Reagan	Anthony Kennedy	Confirmed 97–0; 2/3/1988

Source: Data drawn from http://www.senate.gov/pagelayout/reference/nominations/Nominations.htm.

EVOLUTION OF THE SUPREME COURT
APPOINTMENT AND CONFIRMATION PROCESS

Many aspects of the Supreme Court appointment and confirmation process are based on tradition, rather than being dictated by the Constitution. Starting in 1853, the Justice Department took on the formal responsibility for identifying and recommending potential nominees to the president, but the White House has also developed its own staff units to vet nominees. Recent presidents have relied heavily on the Office of White House Counsel, a unit created by President Harry Truman, but nothing dictates precisely how the selection process should work. Likewise, the confirmation process has evolved. For example, the Senate Judiciary Committee took on an important role in the process by holding hearings on nominees and voting on their acceptability prior to a full Senate vote. In the nineteenth century those hearings—along with Senate debate on Supreme Court nominees—routinely took place in secret.

Many aspects of the confirmation process, such as nominee testimony before the Judiciary Committee, are modern developments. Not until 1925 did a Supreme Court nominee (Harlan Fiske Stone) testify, and such testimony did not become the norm until 1955. Earlier nominees believed it to be improper to speak publicly in any way during the confirmation process, either through testimony or any other form of public comment. When the *New York Sun* pressed Louis Brandeis to say something about his nomination in 1916, he replied: "I have nothing to say about anything, and that goes for all time and to all newspapers, including both the *Sun* and the moon."[13] Today, televised testimony by nominees is commonplace—a practice that began with Sandra Day O'Connor's testimony in 1981.

Routine interest group involvement in the process is also a relatively recent development. The earliest example of an organized interest group lobbying to defeat a Supreme Court nominee came in 1881, when groups such as the National Grange and the Anti-Monopoly League opposed the nomination of Stanley Matthews. Despite sporadic involvement in the coming years, interest group involvement in the Supreme Court appointment process did not become routine until well into the twentieth century. Three institutional changes in the twentieth century helped to spur interest group activity. First, the ratification of the Seventeenth Amendment to the Constitution in 1913 led to the direct election of senators. Prior to that, senators were chosen by state legislators, rather than being popularly elected. That undermined the potent threat of electoral retaliation against senators that interest groups now enjoy. The Seventeenth Amendment removed that impediment. Second, Senate rules changes in 1929 made open-floor debate on nominations the norm. Prior to that, floor debate had remained closed unless two-thirds of the Senate voted to open it—a rare occurrence—so all aspects of the Supreme Court confirmation process had usually been cloaked in secrecy. Opening the process made senators more publicly accountable for their actions, likewise increasing the leverage of interest groups. Third, the televising of the Senate Judiciary Committee's confirmation hearings, which began in 1981, gave representatives of interest groups a free platform to express their views.[14]

Other developments in the late twentieth century also affected the Supreme Court appointment process. Among these were unusually long periods of "divided government," with one party controlling the White House and another party controlling the Senate. From 1969 through 2016, the same party controlled both the White House and the Senate for only twenty-two out of forty-eight years. In contrast, the same party controlled the White House and the Senate for fifty-eight out of sixty-eight years from 1901 through 1968. Since confirmation is much less likely during periods of divided government, it should not be surprising that nominations have been so contentious in recent years.

Another development that has affected the process is an increase in partisanship. Republicans have replaced conservative southern Democrats, and Democrats have replaced liberal Republicans, making the parties in Congress more monolithic. Partly as a result of this, the parties became more polarized and the ideological gap between them widened, leading to a dramatic increase in partisan voting—even on Supreme Court nominees. With relatively rare exceptions, Supreme Court nominees used to be confirmed by bipartisan majorities. As recently as the 1980s, the Senate demonstrated overwhelming bipartisan support for both Antonin Scalia (confirmed by a vote of 98–0 in 1986) and Anthony Kennedy (confirmed by a vote of 97–0 in 1988). In contrast, Senate votes on more recent nominees have tended to break along party lines. The Senate confirmed George W. Bush's two nominees, John Roberts and Samuel Alito, by votes of 78–22 and 58–42 in 2005 and 2006, respectively, and Barack Obama's first two nominees, Sonia Sotomayor and Elena Kagan, by votes of 68–31 and 63–37 in 2009 and 2010, respectively. It would be hard to imagine either Scalia or Kennedy being confirmed with no negative votes in the current environment.

THE APPOINTMENT AND CONFIRMATION PROCESS FOR LOWER FEDERAL COURT JUDGES

The confirmation of lower federal court judges has also become much more contentious in recent years. Lower court nominees tend to get less attention than Supreme Court nominees, but they are also important. After all, over 99 percent of all federal court cases end there. Indeed, the power to appoint the more than 850 judges who make up the lower federal judiciary is arguably among the most important powers of the president. The appointment process for lower court judges is the same as for Supreme Court justices: the president nominates and the Senate offers its advice and consent. However, presidents have traditionally had less control over the initial selection of lower federal court judges than they do over the selection of Supreme Court justices. This is because of an informal rule that has existed since the presidency of George Washington known as "senatorial courtesy." That is, the Senate will usually refuse to confirm nominees who do not have the support of the senators from the state where the vacancy occurs. Thus, presidents have traditionally sought advice from home-state senators about whom to nominate. Once the president nominates someone, the chair of the Senate Judiciary Committee formally seeks advice from home-state senators by sending a form on a blue piece of paper for them to fill out and return. This is a practice that became routinized in the 1940s. Failure to return the "blue slip" or returning it with a negative response amounts to a veto that prevents hearings on the nominee.

Political polarization has led to Senate obstruction of lower federal court nominees, with the blue slip procedure serving as one of the tools. Both political parties have engaged in such obstruction, leading to public rebukes from two chief justices of the Supreme Court. In the last six years of the administration of Bill Clinton, Republicans mounted a slowdown to obstruct Clinton's nominees. This prompted Chief Justice William Rehnquist to write in his 1997 Year-End Report on the Federal Judiciary: "The Senate is surely under no obligation to confirm any particular nominee, but after the necessary time for inquiry, it should vote him up or vote him down."[15] Chief Justice John Roberts made a similar point in his 2010 report, saying: "Each political party has found it easy to turn on a dime from decrying to defending the blocking of judicial nominations, depending on their changing political fortunes." This, he added, had created "acute difficulties" for the federal judiciary and "an urgent need for the political branches to find a long-term solution to this recurring problem."[16]

Republicans were particularly aggressive in blocking Obama's lower court nominees during his last year in office. As of January 1, 2017, 84 of the 678 district court judgeships authorized by Congress were vacant (roughly 12 percent), as were 14 of the 179 court of appeals judgeships authorized by Congress (roughly 8 percent).[17] The entire 114th Congress confirmed only 18 district court nominees and 2 court of appeals nominees, and failed to act on 52 nominations that Obama had submitted for those courts. In comparison, the 100th Congress confirmed 67 district court nominees and 17 court of appeals nominees during the last 2 years of Ronald Reagan's presidency, the 106th Congress confirmed 58 district court nominees and 15 court of appeals nominees during the last 2 years of Bill Clinton's presidency, and the 110th Congress confirmed 58 district court nominees and 10 court of appeals nominees during the last 2 years of George W. Bush's presidency.[18]

Twenty-three of the 52 Obama nominations on which the Senate failed to act received positive votes from the Republican-controlled Judiciary Committee but did not receive a vote by the full Senate.[19] Thirty-eight of these vacancies were deemed "judicial emergencies" (that is, any court of appeals vacancy where adjusted filings are greater than 700 per panel or, if the vacancy lasts more than 18 months, between 500 and 700 per panel, or any district court vacancy where weighted filings are greater than 600 per judgeship or, if the vacancy lasts more than 18 months, between 430 and 600 per judgeship).[20] Even before the slowdown in Obama's last year, a 2012 Brookings Institution report by Russell Wheeler found that the time from nomination to confirmation for district court judges more than doubled from President Clinton's first term (during which nominees took an average of 93 days to be confirmed) to President Obama's first term (during which nominees took an average of 223 days to be confirmed). Likewise, the length of time for court of appeals nominees to be confirmed rose from 127 days during Clinton's first term to 240 days during Obama's first term.[21]

WHAT TO EXPECT UNDER PRESIDENT TRUMP

In addition to being able to fill the vacancies left at the end of the Obama administration, President Trump will likely have many more vacancies to fill during his term because of anticipated retirements of sitting judges.[22] With unified government, it is also conceivable that efforts will be made to expand the number of federal judges—a power that belongs to Congress through simple legislation. At the Supreme Court level, Trump will likely have the opportunity to appoint at least one justice in addition to filling the vacancy left by Scalia. After all, two of the justices are already in their eighties as of January 2017 (Ruth Bader Ginsburg and Anthony Kennedy), and Stephen Breyer, at seventy-eight, is getting close. Retirement is certainly a possibility for any of the three. Although Trump's replacement for Scalia should not significantly change the ideological composition of the court, a replacement for either Ginsburg or Kennedy has the potential to give conservatives on the court a solid 5–4 majority.

With the Senate controlled by fellow Republicans in the 115th Congress, Trump has a distinct advantage in the appointment process. But with only fifty-two Republicans in the Senate, he did not initially enjoy a filibuster-proof majority. Whether or not senators should be able to filibuster Supreme Court and other federal judicial nominees had been another hotly contested question. They had done so—though not often. The first time senators seriously considered using a filibuster to block a Supreme

Court nominee came in 1930, when a coalition of progressive Republicans and Democrats flirted with the idea of using a filibuster against President Hoover's nomination of Charles Evans Hughes to be chief justice. When it became clear that they did not have the votes to sustain a filibuster, they decided not to use the tactic. Republicans mounted the first successful filibuster of a Supreme Court nominee in 1968, forcing President Lyndon Johnson to withdraw his nomination of Abe Fortas to be chief justice. The 1917 cloture rule in effect during both the Hughes and Fortas nominations required a two-thirds vote to end a filibuster. The Senate changed the cloture rule to require a three-fifths vote of the Senate in 1975, so it now takes sixty votes to end a filibuster. This means that Republicans in the 115th Congress would need support from at least eight Democrats to end a filibuster.

During the 2016 presidential campaign, when it looked like Hillary Clinton would win, Republican senator John McCain (R-AZ) promised a talk radio host in Philadelphia that Republicans "will be united against any Supreme Court nominee that Hillary Clinton, if she were president, would put up."[23] Although a McCain spokesperson subsequently walked back that remark, his comments seemed to suggest that Republicans were willing to use the filibuster against nominees put forward by a Democratic president. Given the hyperpartisanship and sharp polarization that bedevils politics today, Democrats would surely be willing to use it as well.

In fact, Senate Democrats mounted a symbolic filibuster against George W. Bush's nomination of Samuel Alito in 2006 (which then-senator Barack Obama joined), even though they did not have the votes to succeed. They also used the filibuster to block ten of Bush's first-term court of appeals nominees. Republicans responded by threatening to change the rules to prevent filibusters of judicial nominees, but a compromise brokered by seven moderate senators from each party put off any formal changes to the filibuster rule by allowing them only in "extraordinary circumstances" rather than as a routine tool to obstruct nominees.[24] However, when Republicans started to employ filibusters against lower court nominees more routinely at the outset of President Obama's second term—a precursor to their obstruction of Merrick Garland—Democrats, who still controlled the Senate, enacted a rules change in November 2013 to allow a simple majority of senators present and voting to end debate and proceed to a vote on most executive and judicial nominations. Significantly, the rules change left in place the opportunity to filibuster Supreme Court nominees.[25] Once they were in control of the Senate and Trump had taken office, Republicans revisited that rules change and disallowed filibusters of Supreme Court nominees in order to secure the confirmation of Neil Gorsuch, the Tenth Circuit Court of Appeals judge that Trump had nominated to fill the seat vacated by Scalia.

The highly charged polarization that characterizes contemporary politics all but guarantees that the judicial confirmation process will be contentious for the foreseeable future. However, Republicans have the clear upper hand in the rivalry for power during the 115th Congress. Whether the midterm elections will solidify or undermine the Republican advantage remains an open question, but even two years will give Trump a significant opportunity to put his stamp on the federal judiciary.

NOTES

1. Burgess Everett and Glenn Thrush, "McConnell Throws Down the Gauntlet: No Scalia Replacement under Obama," *Politico*, February 13, 2016, http://www.politico.com/story/2016/02/mitch-mcconnell-antonin-scalia-supreme-court-nomination-219248.

2. Quoted in Michael D. Shear, Julie Hirschfeld, and Gardiner Harris, "Obama Chooses Merrick Garland for Supreme Court," *New York Times*, March 16, 2016, http://www.nytimes.com/2016/03/17/us/politics/obama-supreme-court-nominee.html.

3. Quoted in C. Eugene Emery Jr., "In Context: The 'Biden Rule' on Supreme Court Nominations in an Election Year," *Politifact*, March 17, 2016, http://www.politifact.com/truth-o-meter/article/2016/mar/17/context-biden-rule-supreme-court-nominations.

4. For a detailed discussion of the different proposals, see Michael J. Gerhardt, *The Federal Appointments Process: A Constitutional and Historical Analysis* (Durham, NC: Duke University Press, 2003), 16–25.

5. Alexander Hamilton, James Madison, and John Jay, *The Federalist Papers* (New York: New American Library, 1961), 457.

6. For a discussion of the Rutledge nomination, see John Anthony Maltese, *The Selling of Supreme Court Nominees* (Baltimore: Johns Hopkins University Press, 1995), 26–31.

7. W. W. Abbot, ed., *The Papers of George Washington* (Charlottesville: University Press of Virginia, 1989), 401.

8. "The Senate at Its Worst," *New York Herald Tribune*, February 14, 1930.

9. William H. Rehnquist, "The Making of a Supreme Court Justice," *Harvard Law Record*, October 8, 1959, 7, 10. Reprinted in the *New York Times*, November 11, 1971, 47.

10. P. S. Ruckman Jr., "The Supreme Court, Critical Nominations, and the Senate Confirmation Process," *The Journal of Politics* 55 (August 1993): 794. In comparison to twenty-seven failed Supreme Court nominations, only nine cabinet nominees in the entire history of the United States had been voted down by the Senate as of January 20, 2017 (see: Nathaniel Rakich, "It's Really Hard to Block a Cabinet Nominee," *FiveThirtyEight*, January 10, 2017, https://fivethirtyeight.com/features/its-really-hard-to-block-a-cabinet-nominee).

11. www.whitehouse.gov/scotus, retrieved December 27, 2016.

12. Drew Desilver, "Long Supreme Court Vacancies Used to Be More Common," Pew Research Center, February 26, 2016, http://www.pewresearch.org/fact-tank/2016/02/26/long-supreme-court-vacancies-used-to-be-more-common.

13. Quoted in Alpheus Thomas Mason, *Harlan Fiske Stone: Pillar of the Law* (New York: Viking, 1956), 181.

14. For a full account of all of this, see Maltese, *The Selling of Supreme Court Nominees*, chapters 3 and 6.

15. John H. Cushman Jr., "Senate Imperils Judicial System, Rehnquist Says," *New York Times*, January 1, 1998, A1, http://www.nytimes.com/1998/01/01/us/sen ate-imperils-judicial-system-rehnquist-says.html.

16. Chief Justice John Roberts, "2010 Year-End Report on the Federal Judiciary," 7–8, https://www.supremecourt.gov/publicinfo/year-end/2010year-endreport.pdf.

17. The status of judicial vacancies is updated every Friday at http://www.amer icanbar.org/advocacy/governmental_legislative_work/priorities_policy/indepen dence_of_the_judiciary/judicial_vacancies.html.

18. Figures for the 100th and 106th Congresses drawn from table 5 of Denis Steven Rutkus and Mitchel A. Sollenberger, "Judicial Nomination Statistics: U.S. District and Circuit Courts, 1977–2003," *CRS Report for Congress*, updated February 23, 2004. Figures for the 110th Congress drawn from "List of Federal Judges Appointed by George W. Bush," https://en.wikipedia.org/wiki/List_of_federal_judges_appointed_by_George_W._Bush. Figures for the 114th Congress from: https://www.justice.gov/archives/olp/114th-congress-judicial-nominations-list.

19. The American Bar Association provides up-to-date statistics on judicial vacancies on its website: http://www.americanbar.org/advocacy/governmental_legisla tive_work/priorities_policy/independence_of_the_judiciary/judicial_vacancies.html.

20. http://www.uscourts.gov/judges-judgeships/judicial-vacancies/judicial-emer gencies/judicial-emergency-definition.

21. Russell Wheeler, "Judicial Nominations and Confirmations in Obama's First Term," *Governance Studies at Brookings*, December 13, 2012, 9, https://www.brookings .edu/wp-content/uploads/2016/06/13_obama_judicial_wheeler.pdf.

22. Joe Palazzolo, "Obama's Successor Will Likely Fill Dozens of Judicial Vacancies," *Wall Street Journal*, March 18, 2016, http://www.wsj.com/articles/obamas-suc cessor-will-likely-fill-dozens-of-judicial-vacancies-1458340351.

23. David Taintor, "McCain: GOP Will Be 'United Against Any' Clinton Supreme Court Nominee," NBC News, October 17, 2016, http://www.nbcnews.com/card/ mccain-gop-will-be-united-against-any-clinton-supreme-court-n667816.

24. "Senators Compromise on Filibusters," *CNN.com*, May 24, 2005, http://www .cnn.com/2005/POLITICS/05/24/filibuster.fight.

25. Susan David and Richard Wolf, "U.S. Senate Goes 'Nuclear,' Changes Filibuster Rules," *USA Today*, November 21, 2013, http://www.usatoday.com/story/news/ politics/2013/11/21/harry-reid-nuclear-senate/3662445.

CHAPTER 10

The President, Congress, and Domestic Policy Making

James A. Thurber

Campaigning for president, Donald Trump promised an immediate revolution in domestic policy—to repeal and replace the Affordable Care Act, to quickly rebuild America's infrastructure, to overhaul the tax code, to build a wall on our southern border, and to deport millions of illegal immigrants. Like all presidents, Trump ran into the slow deliberative processes of American democracy. "Every new president confronts Washington's sluggish culture, but Trump's more grandiose and hardline ideas could face unprecedented challenges—logistical and even constitutional."[1] The business of Washington is democratic government, not top-down business decision making. At the beginning of his administration, President Trump responded to the slow deliberative processes with an unprecedented number of executive orders and pronouncements, all but ignoring Congress.

After a divisive antiestablishment campaign, President Obama entered the White House with his party having a 60-seat majority in the Senate and a 257-seat majority in the House. After the 2016 election the White House–Hill relationship had changed, with congressional Democrats and Republicans closer to parity than before the election and a president who acted unilaterally. It was a change election, but it did not change the congressional leadership or the polarization on the Hill. The same party controlled the 115th Congress as the 114th with the same leadership (save Senate Minority Leader Harry Reid's retirement) and the same domestic policy agendas. Continuity within the congressional parties and the two chambers helps to explain the politics and processes of Congress, but President Trump, a tweet-using newcomer to Washington, who had not served in government or the military, created an unpredictable factor in well-established historic deliberative processes between Congress and the president. President Trump is the major unknown factor in the future of presidential-congressional relations, but the Republican and Democratic

Party leaders are virtually the same. Mitch McConnell of Kentucky remains Senate Majority Leader and Paul Ryan of Wisconsin remains Speaker of the House. With the retirement of long-term leader Harry Reid of Nevada, Chuck Schumer of New York was selected as the Democratic leader of the Senate. Democrats in the House reelected Minority Leader Nancy Pelosi after some confusion and competition.

With the same congressional leadership, the Republican Party established a clear domestic policy agenda: repealing and replacing the Affordable Care Act, tax reform, deregulation, investment in America's infrastructure, and a wall with Mexico. They also wanted to reduce the deficit and replace or restructure social programs such as Social Security, Medicare, and Medicaid. The congressional Republican domestic policy agenda was often at odds with candidate and President Trump. Like many Republican members of Congress, Speaker Ryan disassociated himself from Trump in the 2016 campaign and Senate Majority Leader McConnell did not enthusiastically endorse Trump. After the election, Republican members of Congress and their leaders moved rapidly to support the Trump presidency, but pushed their own domestic policy agenda. But President Trump often issued a flurry of executive orders, fresh tweets, and announcements without collaborating with the Republican leadership, which caught members of Congress by surprise and undermined their capacity to move on their domestic policy agenda.

Underlying tensions from the campaign continued between Trump and congressional leaders after he was inaugurated. Trump's campaign attacks on the Washington establishment (including Republican leaders) and his direct criticism of the Congress in his inaugural address did not help build a bridge to congressional leaders. With the "change" election, Trump continued a radical agenda that disrupted and undercut long-fought policy goals of the Republican leadership. If President Trump continues his confrontation with congressional Republicans as well as Democrats, he will have limited impact on domestic policy through the legislative process. Experienced congressional leaders might attempt to limit his unilateral presidential actions. If Trump engages in more conventional strategies with Congress, by pursuing the Republican Party's agenda and helping to build cross-party compromise, he could succeed in achieving the longer-lasting domestic policy changes that he promised in his campaign.

Ironically, Trump might force Congress to take back domestic policy-making power from the presidency. They could take the lead in addressing major domestic policy issues facing the United States and improving policy making on the Hill. Former Republican congressional leader Mickey Edwards argues that Congress is the last bastion against Trump: "For the next four years, Donald J. Trump will be America's president, but what effect his presidency will have on the country will depend largely on what happens not in the White House but 16 blocks away where, constitutionally, much of the nation's true power rests." Edwards continues, "Because Mr. Trump is so erratic and so prone to acting upon impulse rather than information, the four most important people in America today—at least the four upon whose judgment and character we must now rely—are the ones who hold the leadership positions in the House and Senate."[2] Much depends upon the leadership skills of Paul Ryan, Nancy Pelosi, Mitch McConnell, and Chuck Schumer and how they respond to President Trump.

Understanding and explaining the impact of the 2016 election on domestic policy and the dynamic relationship between President Trump and Congress is a major challenge for scholars of presidential-congressional relations. The impact of President Trump's unique, unpredictable, and sometimes bizarre behavior on Congress is difficult to predict, but partisan polarization will likely be the norm on the Hill.[3] Congressional organizations, committees, rules, the Senate filibuster, and regular policy processes will help structure the interaction between the two branches.[4] Most important, the well-established policy agendas of both parties will fundamentally influence the rivalry between the president and Congress. Some politics will be bipartisan, other policies will be strictly partisan, others will need cross-party coalitions, and many will continue the partisan gridlock that has prevailed for the last decade. Whether there is presidential-congressional cooperation, compromise, conflict, or deadlock in domestic policy making may depend on the nature of the policy under consideration. As seen with other presidents and Congresses, the nature of the problems and solutions to those problems drives different kinds of dynamics. When there is a clear threat or widely agreed-upon problem facing the United States, the rivalry between the president and Congress is often mitigated. When there are long-standing differences between the parties and their supporting voters, there is often conflict and gridlock between the president and Congress. I will review the dynamics of presidential-congressional relations related to the economy and the battle over the federal budget, and then review those dynamics in debates over health-care reform, during the Obama administration and the beginning of the Trump presidency. The conflicts over these major issues are domestic policy-making examples of how the White House and Congress relate to each other differently during unified and divided party government. They also illustrate the extent to which polarization has dominated policy making on core national issues in recent years.

PRESIDENT OBAMA, CONGRESS, THE ECONOMY, AND THE BATTLE OVER THE BUDGET

Early in his presidential transition, Obama led a brainstorming session with his policy team about first-term accomplishments. Tim Geithner offered a downer of a reality check: "Your accomplishment is going to be preventing a second Great Depression." "That's not enough for me," the president-elect shot back. "I'm not going to be defined by what I prevented."

Indeed, with unified party government in his first two years in office, President Obama's domestic-policy legislative accomplishments were wide-ranging (yet controversial): the Lilly Ledbetter Fair Pay Act, the American Recovery and Reinvestment Act (the economic stimulus legislation), health-care reform (the Affordable Care Act), Wall Street/financial institutional reform (Dodd-Frank), reauthorization and funding of the Troubled Asset Relief Program (TARP), a major tax bill, extension of unemployment compensation, and food safety reform, to name just a few of more than three hundred laws signed into law.[5]

Nevertheless, the budget and its effects on the economy were at the center of President Obama's first two years in office. At the beginning of 2009, the Congressional Budget Office predicted "a recession that will probably be the longest and deepest since World War II."[6] President Obama summarized the economic and budgetary state he inherited as follows:

> We are inheriting an enormous budget deficit . . . (of) over a trillion dollars. That's before we do anything. And so we understand that we've got to provide a blood infusion into the patient right now, to make sure that the patient is stabilized, and that we can't worry short-term about the deficit. We've got to make sure the stimulus is large enough to get the economy moving.[7]

With the support of Congress, President Obama took bold moves in his first two years to help the economy and to control increased spending on health care.[8] President Obama's stimulus package was fifty times larger than the $16 billion that President Clinton had failed to enact in 1993.[9] It was also larger than the entire New Deal in real dollars.

The economic stimulus is now widely credited by economists with helping to end the Great Recession with a massive short-term economic boost. It directly lifted 13 million Americans out of poverty; gave record educational aid to states that averted 300,000 teacher layoffs; and funded "shovel-ready" projects that upgraded 42,000 miles of road, 2,700 bridges, and 6,000 miles of rail. The stimulus also created $300 billion worth of tax cuts for businesses and families. In order to gain support for the stimulus he built a cross-party coalition, relying on three GOP senators to avoid a filibuster. He compromised and gave in to their demands, including an $800 billion cap on spending and the removal of a $10 billion initiative to renovate America's schools.

President Obama found the challenge of pulling the economy out of recession as well as dealing with the looming deficits and debt particularly difficult, especially after the massive 2010 electoral loss for the Democratic Party and the return to divided party government. Obama's policy choices in his first two years were ambitious and successful: the stimulus bill and health-care reform.

President Obama's relationship with Congress was first driven by the economic crisis he inherited and the politics of unified party government and later by deficits, debt, and a polarized, divided party government. President Obama took office when the consequences of the financial system breakdown had only begun to spread through the economy, unlike President Franklin Delano Roosevelt's well-engrained Great Depression. At the beginning of his administration, Obama's budget and policy preferences were carefully crafted with the congressional Democratic Party leadership. The Democratic Party policies of more spending and reduced revenues caused the deficit and the debt to get significantly worse than before the recession hit. President Obama viewed deficit reduction as an essential part of the "new era of responsibility" (announced in his first inaugural address). He promised to "get serious about fiscal discipline," which meant getting serious about entitlement reform. He used a special commission on debt and deficits to help set the policy agenda to address entitlements, which created conflict with Democratic Party members of Congress. It was a pledge that led to conflict and deadlock in Congress over the budget and appropriations.

President Obama's battle with Congress over the budget (spending and taxing) is typical of a common phenomenon that is fundamental to the rivalry between the two branches. That battle has been especially turbulent over the last forty-three years since the passage of the 1974 Budget and Impoundment Control Act.[10] The Congressional Budget and Impoundment Control Act of 1974 (BICA) created a new fiscal year and a centralized budget process, a House and Senate Budget Committee, the Congressional Budget Office, and a procedure for controlling presidential impoundments. The bill overhauled the Budget and Accounting Act of 1921, which had been intended to assist Congress in its appropriations role by requiring the president to submit an annual budget. As the budget process grew more institutionalized, members of Congress sought to exert greater control over federal spending. Frustrated with President Richard M. Nixon's impoundment of congressionally appropriated funds, Congress reasserted its budget authority through the 1974 act. By shifting the federal government's fiscal year from July 1 to October 1, Congress gained the time to respond to the president's annual budget message and to legislate federal spending in a timely fashion. The 1974 act created both the House and Senate Budget Committees with the responsibility of passing an annual Concurrent Budget Resolution (CBR) with the support of the Congressional Budget Office (CBO). The CBO is charged with gathering data and estimates and supplying the committees with proper information to assist the federal budget process. Since passage of BICA, there have been constant federal budget challenges and spectacular changes in the rules of the congressional budget process in attempts to control spending and limit the president's power. The CBR has only passed on time four times since 1976, the first year of implementation of BICA. Congressional attempts to express stronger constitutional "powers of the purse" are founded in constant battles with the president over spending and revenue policies.

President Obama's battle over the budget changed when the Democrats lost their majority in the House and Senate in the 2010 election. His battle over the budget highlights the rivalry between the president and Congress. This history of the relationship between the president and Congress over the budget from 1974 through the Obama administration has been almost predestined to conflict and failure, especially in controlling deficits and the debt, even during the four years of budget surpluses during the Clinton presidency. Since passage of the Congressional Budget and Control Act of 1974 through recent reforms such as the Budget Control Act of 2011, there seems to be avoidance behavior related to making hard choices on long-term spending cuts and tax reforms, and a lack of resolve to reduce the growth in the deficit and debt. With multiple failures, whether with unified or divided party government, Congress and the president have succeeded in delaying changes to spending and taxing policies that lead to budget deficits. An example of congressional budget process impotency during the Obama presidency is the failure of the "super committee" in 2011.[11]

The electorate reacted to President Obama's policy agenda with an historic "wave election" bringing in eighty-seven new conservative freshmen (eighty-six signed a no new taxes pledge, half were associated with the Tea Party movement) into the House of Representatives. The election was partially about Obama's "expansive government," but also about the federal government budget debt and deficit. With renewed alarm about the ballooning deficit and debt in 2010, President Obama created the Fiscal Responsibility Commission (cochaired by former senator Alan Simpson and former White House Chief of Staff Erskine Bowles). The purpose of the commission was to come up with a balanced bipartisan way to turn around the growth of the deficit during a recession. The Simpson-Bowles commission report recommended tough proposals along the lines of what President Obama originally wanted, such as cuts in entitlement programs like Social Security and Medicare, an end to popular tax deductions, and higher taxes for the wealthy. Both Democrats and Republicans objected to the commission's recommendations. Even Democratic leaders objected to the commission's report; in Nancy Pelosi's words, it was "simply unacceptable."[12] President Obama was not about to push the plan without Republican support in Congress and with strong opposition from his own party.

After the midterm election, President Obama agreed to extend all the 2001 and 2003 Bush income tax cuts for two years. The estate tax was not abolished, but was cut substantially below 2009 levels for 2011 and 2012. In return, President Obama received a thirteen-month extension of unemployment benefits, continuation of some of the stimulus tax credits for two years, a temporary tax cut for business investment, and a temporary cut in the Social Security payroll tax. The entire package grew the deficit. Ultimately, it would cost $900 billion over two years, adding substantially to the national debt.[13]

Throughout all of 2011 a series of negotiations and confrontations between the White House and the Hill occurred over the spending and taxing in the budget. Congress by law sets a debt ceiling, a limit on the amount of money the US government can borrow in order to pay its bills. During the 2010 election Eric Cantor and his "Young Guns" demagogued the issue of the debt and said they would not vote for an increase in the debt limit. It was a "wedge issue" in the 2010 campaign, but Republican leaders Boehner and McConnell knew they could not let a default happen. It would be devastating for the economy. After averting a federal government shutdown in May 2011, subsequent negotiations over the debt limit between Vice President Biden and House Majority Leader Eric Cantor failed. The rejection of the Bowles-Simpson Commission recommendations and the failure of the Biden-Cantor two-month negotiations led President Obama and Speaker John Boehner to work directly together into July 2011 to try to reach a "grand bargain" of modest tax increases, entitlement reforms, and other spending cuts.[14] These negotiations also failed and led to President Obama and Republicans agreeing to raise the debt limit enough for about eighteen months more of government borrowing and to create a bipartisan super committee to deal with the deficit.

The Super Committee and the Budget Control Act of 2011

The Joint Select Committee on Deficit Reduction (the "super committee") was established on August 2, 2011, after months of conflict and the abortive negotiations between President Obama and congressional leaders over how to slow the growth of the government's deficit and debt.[15] House and Senate Democratic and Republican leaders selected super committee members with an equal number from each party in the House and the Senate, with the goal of building a bipartisan agreement to reduce the deficit. The twelve super committee members were generally part of and reflected the views of the leadership; they were experienced and individually and collectively had extensive knowledge about issues surrounding attempts to reduce the deficit.[16] Republicans and Democrats who were selected for the super committee represented key powerful committees and constituencies in the House and Senate and were loyal to the party leadership.

The Budget Control Act (PL 112-25) raised the federal debt ceiling by $2.5 billion, thus preventing the debt default of the federal government; cut spending; and created the super committee, granting it extraordinary scope and power.[17] The immediate increase in the debt ceiling was accompanied by $1.2 trillion in cuts in defense and domestic discretionary spending over ten years. The super committee's powers included the charge of crafting a recommendation by November 23, 2011, encompassing at least $1.5 trillion in additional deficit reduction over a ten-year period, beyond the $917 billion cuts made as a first installment in the Budget Control Act. Everything was supposed to be "on the table" for negotiation: tax increases; tax reforms, such as simplifying the tax code and eliminating some tax breaks and loopholes; and reforms to slow down the growth of entitlement programs, such as Social Security, Medicaid, and Medicare. Should the super committee not agree on a recommendation or the full Congress fail to pass the super committee's recommendation, a "trigger mechanism" requiring enactment of $1.2 trillion in automatic spending cuts was included. The super committee was given the power to operate entirely outside the budget, appropriations, and authorizing process. It could receive recommendations from relevant committees, but was not bound by anything the panels submitted. Obama got an increase in the debt limit, enough to get beyond the 2012 election, and some protection for some domestic programs that Democrats cared about.

Under the Budget Control Act, the $1.2 trillion across-the-board spending cuts had to be split between the national security and domestic programs, with some of the biggest entitlement spending, Medicaid, food stamps, jobless benefits, and veterans' pensions excluded, thus setting up for the super committee an array of choices, but removing the largest targets from the automatic cuts. It took the regular legislative process entirely out of deciding the federal government budget priorities. The threat of the automatic across-the-board spending cuts—known as sequestration—was intended to be sufficiently "distasteful to lawmakers" to provide a strong incentive for them to adopt a bipartisan agreement, but the chance to avoid action was a major factor in dooming the super committee's deliberations and outcome.[18] The automatic spending cuts proved insufficiently draconian to guarantee action in a highly polarized Congress.

The compromise did not occur. The twelve members met on September 8, 2011, to begin work. It was their only public meeting outside of four hearings used to question budget experts on ways to control the federal debt. However, the members met in small groups and as a whole dozens of times in private, trying to strike a deal to meet the statutory goal of at least $1.2 trillion in deficit reduction over the next decade. Members of both parties maintained their polarized "Democrat" or "Republican" identity throughout the process.

Inevitably, the proposals from Democratic and Republican members failed to bridge the vast partisan divide between the two parties on deficit reduction through tax increases and spending cuts. Democratic panel members proposed a combination of spending cuts and revenue increases of between $2 and $3 trillion over 10 years. The Republican proposals focused on saving over $2 trillion primarily through cuts in spending. Both sides attempted to compromise, with Republicans offering $300 billion in new tax revenue, a proposal that was untenable to their own members who had taken a "no new tax" pledge. Democratic members proposed to cut hundreds of billions of dollars from federal health-care programs, a proposal that angered the base of the congressional Democrats. Ultimately, the Republican members, influenced by their colleagues who had made a no new tax pledge, were unable to make tax reform offers that were large enough to satisfy Democrats. Democratic committee members did not make proposals to cut entitlement programs (Medicare and Medicaid) sufficient to please the Republicans, and the super committee gave up.[19] The super committee, even with its extraordinary potential powers and pressure from the president, could not overcome the partisan gridlock that has prevailed over deficit reduction for years.

The president offered his own package of tax hikes and spending reductions, but did not put the personal weight of his office behind it. In fact, he left the country as the super committee talks came down to the wire. House Speaker John Boehner and Senate Minority Leader Mitch McConnell were neither vocal nor visible during the final negotiations. Senate Majority Leader Harry Reid and House Democratic Leader Nancy Pelosi were also unwilling to use political capital and work hard for a deal. The leaders did not push for public agreement, and if they exerted private pressure, it was not effective. This seeming inaction can be interpreted several ways: the leadership believed the super committee would function best if left alone; they exerted their influence through private meetings and phone calls to no avail; the leaders either did not care or did not want a deal; or the president and congressional leaders felt their party would have an advantage in the 2012 election by blaming the other party for the failure. Whether President Obama and the congressional party leaders were weakened by the procedural power of the super committee, took a pass on the super committee negotiations because of previous failures, or wanted to delay the tough budgetary decisions about cuts and tax increases until after the 2012 election, is not known, but it is clear the president and the congressional leaders did not play a leadership role with the super committee in building a successful bipartisan solution to deficit reduction.

The super committee failed in its mission, informing Congress, President Obama, and the public on November 21, 2011, that they had been unable to reach agreement on a deficit reduction plan by the statutory deadline.[20] The super committee issued the following rather lame statement:

After months of hard work and intense deliberations, we have come to the conclusion today that it will not be possible to make any bipartisan agreement available to the public before the committee's deadline.[21]

After the failure of the super committee to propose a deficit reduction plan, there were partisan statements from both congressional parties condemning the failed outcome. President Obama and congressional leaders immediately raised the specter of new taxes and cuts in popular domestic programs and defense. President Obama accused congressional Republicans of rejecting a "balanced approach" to deficit reduction, arguing that the deficit reduction plan should have included tax increases for the wealthy. He said,

Despite the broad agreement that exists for such an approach, there are still too many Republicans in Congress that have refused to listen to the voices of reason and compromise that are coming from outside of Washington.[22]

Senate Majority Leader Harry Reid defended Democrats, stating they

were prepared to strike a grand bargain that would make painful cuts while asking millionaires to pay their fair share, and we put our willingness on paper. . . but Republicans . . . never came close to meeting us halfway.[23]

Senate Republican Minority Leader Mitch McConnell of Kentucky argued that an agreement

proved impossible not because Republicans were unwilling to compromise, but because Democrats would not accept any proposal that did not expand the size and scope of government or punish job creators.[24]

Republican presidential candidates in 2012 also argued that President Obama failed to use his leadership to build an agreement to cut the deficit.

The primary reasons for the failure of the super committee were both internal and external to Congress. The president and party leaders learned a hard lesson: conciliation and compromise were losing strategies both in policy and election terms. Boehner could not deliver to his members any big deal that Democrats could accept. Voters were not enthusiastic about the sacrifices that any grand bargain would require, interest groups wanted to preserve the status quo in many areas (meaning no change for their favorite spending and tax programs), and the ideological gaps between the two parties were insurmountable and supported by their respective party voters. Obama thought compromise with the Republicans would only make him look weak and might well lead to a reelection defeat.

Public interest in and support of a realistic budget agreement waned. A *National Journal* survey found that only slightly more Americans favored a

Democratic proposal to reduce the deficit with cuts and revenue increases on the wealthy than the Republican cuts-only approach.[25] By a margin of just 5 percent, 49 percent to 44 percent, the public favored the Democratic plan suggested in October 2011 that would have included "$4 trillion in deficit reduction through a combination of federal spending cuts and tax increases on wealthier Americans" over "a Republican plan that calls for $3 trillion in deficit reduction through spending cuts alone, with no tax increases."[26] The survey of voters showed that the American people seemed no more unified than the members of Congress and the super committee members on deficit reduction solutions. The poll and many other surveys showed a decided lack of confidence in Congress to get anything done with historic low evaluations of Congress shortly after the super committee failure. A Quinnipiac University poll conducted November 14–20, 2011, revealed that 44 percent of voters blamed the looming impasse on congressional Republicans and 38 percent blamed it on President Obama and congressional Democrats, a mere 6 percent difference. Public opinion might have been used as a partial justification by the congressional participants to do nothing. It also provided President Obama's justification to avoid being heavily invested in another failed congressional deficit reduction process.

In the end, there was not overwhelming public support for a balanced plan of tax increases and cuts in popular entitlement programs. Without strong public support for a balanced deficit reduction plan of cuts and tax increases and with the public blaming Congress for the super committee's failure, there was political cover for President Obama and fresh political fodder for the 2012 campaign.

Strong interest groups were also not pushing hard for change through cuts and tax increases. Generally, they were silent or they were lobbying for no change, the status quo, for their programs.[27] The AARP, health-care organizations, and unions were prime examples of this; they expended large sums of money for advertising, grassroots, and direct lobbying on Capitol Hill to stop cuts in popular programs for elderly Americans, health care, and union workers. There were few groups or think tanks pushing for the hard choices that needed to be made to have real reduction in the growth of deficits and debt. One exception was the Center for a Responsible Federal Budget, with its board of directors made up of former Budget Committee chairs and former directors of the Office and Management and Budget and CBO who all pushed to "Go Big" ($4 trillion or more in deficit reduction in 10 years) on a deficit reduction plan through entitlement spending cuts and tax increases.

But maybe none of this mattered because of the lack of bipartisanship and ideological polarization in the Congress and among the voters they represent. Maybe there was never a chance for success because the schisms fundamentally undermined the capacity of the super committee to find

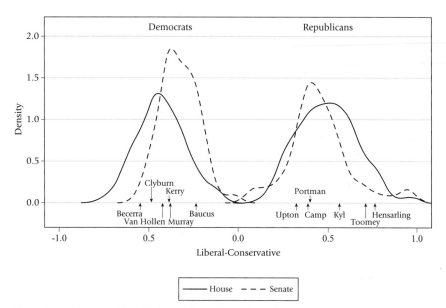

Figure 10.1. Ideological Distribution of Super Committee Members

Note: This figure depicts where each member of the super committee fell on a left-right ideological spectrum, and how their ideological distribution compared to the ideological distribution of all congressional Democrats and Republicans in the 112th Congress.

Source: http://enikrising.blogspot.com/2011/08/supercommittees-ideal-points.html. Used with permission from Keith Poole.

common ground. The graph of the DW-NOMINATE Common Space Scores for House and Senate Democrats and Republicans in the 112th Congress and for their representatives on the super committee summarizes and illustrates the ideological divisions. (See figure 10.1.) The figure shows that all Republican members of the super committee were considerably more conservative than all Democratic members of the super committee. The missing ideological middle and the widespread partisan differences reveal the underlying problem of finding common ground on a solution to reducing the deficit and budgeting generally.

The president and Congress continued to engage in partisan gridlock and ideological warfare over the deficit, spending, and taxes after the failure of the 2011 budget reform effort. Deficit reduction and the automatic cuts scheduled to take effect in January 2013 were issues in the 2012 presidential election.[28] President Obama stated that he would veto any attempt by Congress to cancel the required $1.2 trillion sequester, giving rise to campaign issues and a major confrontation between Congress and the president and between the parties.[29] The issue of solutions to deficit reduction, of major spending cuts and tax increases, was moved to the campaign trail and left for a "lame-duck" Congress and the new Congress in 2013 to resolve. The drive for reelection by members of Congress made it unlikely they would agree on the realistic spending cuts and tax reforms needed to stop the increase in the deficit during the 2012, 2014, and 2016 campaigns.

Indeed, there is little common ground between the parties with regard to the primary issue of the size of the federal government. The issues in the 2016 election show that mainstream Democrats believe government should play an important role in the economy and provide a safety net for the disadvantaged. They also want high-income people to pay more taxes to fund those programs. President Trump and a majority of Republicans disagree. They want to limit government's many domestic administrative actions and deregulate, characterizing a wide range of regulations as interference in markets. They disagree with many social safety net programs, such as the Affordable Care Act, and they believe taxes are too high. They promise smaller government and no new taxes, while cutting the deficit and reducing the debt. There is little chance members of Congress can agree to compromise or ever get the votes from their party members to bridge that chasm without strong leadership.

The ideological divide was most evident in Republicans' refusal to shift or budge on their no-tax pledge and Democrats' insistence on tying spending cuts to tax hikes in the super committee. In the end, this was almost certainly the biggest single factor influencing the committee's failure. Little has changed after the 2016 election except a new president who has not been engaged in budget negotiations. As long as the president and GOP leadership remain trapped in their commitment to never raise taxes, there will be no serious fiscal agreement. Any Republican who dares to stick his head out of the "no new tax" foxhole and hint at a willingness to consider revenues will be barraged with friendly fire. Democrats were never going to agree to cuts in the Affordable Care Act, Medicare, and Medicaid without significant GOP concessions on taxes. However, with enough political cover from President Trump, Republicans might reluctantly move tax reform in exchange for some entitlements reform. An observation by David Axelrod, President Obama's senior aide, applies to the president's inability to lead on this issue. Axelrod believed there was a miscalculation about the president's ability to bridge the ideological gap between the two parties. He reflected that, "Perhaps we were naïve, but Obama believed that in the midst of crisis you could find partners on the other side of the aisle to help deal with it. I don't think anyone here expected the degree of partisanship we confronted."[30]

Lessons can be learned for the Trump presidency from the experience of the super committee. Its purpose was to force Congress to make the hard choices to trim the deficit through a spending cut trigger, but with bipartisanship and compromise missing, members continued to look for loopholes rather than a balanced deal, continuing the primary pattern of the last forty years.[31] That may continue under the Trump-Congress relationship.

The future of the congressional budget process in post-2016 American politics is closely linked to the relationship between the president and Congress and ultimately the polarization of American voters. The lack of will of the American people to support hard spending and taxation choices directly affects presidential-congressional relations. Whatever presidential and congressional decisions are made or not made about budget, both will have a significant impact on voters. As always, the final say about spending, taxing, and deficits will lie with the American electorate.

HEALTH-CARE REFORM: THE PATIENT PROTECTION AND AFFORDABLE CARE ACT

President Obama made health-care reform the top priority after his stimulus legislation. He believed enacting health-care legislation that controlled health-care costs, expanded access, and instituted greater quality control was essential for the country. Obama did not submit a detailed plan to Congress; instead, he let the Hill take the lead, with the White House negotiating with key lobbying groups as the process unfolded.

Senator Max Baucus (D-MT), chair of the Senate Finance Committee, and Senator Ted Kennedy (D-MA), chair of the Health, Education, Labor and Pensions Committee, had worked on health-care legislation before the 2008 election. Immediately after the election, they organized a bipartisan group of senators and proposed a mandate requiring Americans to have health insurance, a national marketplace to purchase insurance, and a government-run option for individuals to buy insurance in competition with private insurance plans.

President Obama wanted to "change the way Washington works" by bringing a postpartisan strategy to relationships with Congress. Obama convened a health-care summit to which he invited Republican and Democratic congressional leaders. "Over seven hours of civil and substantive discussion, Obama made the case for thorough going reform and showed that the Republicans lacked a plan."[32] As health-care reform negotiations on the Hill became a marathon and his summer 2009 deadline for enacting health-care legislation passed, President Obama used the bully pulpit. He toured the nation in a PR initiative trying to get support for the reform, giving cover to the Hill negotiators. He also continued to negotiate with key interest groups. He created the Office for Health Care Reform (OHCR) that acted as a liaison between the executive and the Congress. "Its purpose was to relay White House positions and priorities to Congress and try to influence the direction the bill was taking, but not to write the bill itself."[33]

The OHCR met with the relevant committees weekly until they were meeting daily in the summer of 2009. Obama initially attempted a bipartisan outreach strategy to the Republicans. But after a sharp fall in the president's approval ratings and a refusal by congressional Republicans to cooperate on health-care legislation, Obama shifted his strategy to a strictly partisan approach on the Hill. He relied on Speaker Pelosi and Majority Leader Reid to write bills in their office (not following the regular order).

On Christmas Eve 2009, the Senate passed a health-care reform bill on a straight party-line vote of 60 to 39. It took intense coordination and effort for the White House, other members of the administration, and the president with close coordination with the Democratic leadership and its organization to pass a bill in the House. On March 21, 2010, the House first passed the Senate bill by 219 to 212 and then passed the reconciliation bill that fixed the Senate bill by a 220 to 211 vote. Finally, following the House agreement with the Senate version and creative procedural maneuvering, Obama signed the Patient Protection and Affordable Care Act (PPACA) on March 23, 2010.[34] On March 25, the Senate passed the reconciliation bill 56 to 43 that included the main changes the House Democrats needed to the PPACA. The president signed it on March 30. The president relied entirely on Democratic votes to pass the legislation. No Republican in the House or Senate supported any of the measures.

The PPACA, also called the Affordable Care Act (ACA) or Obamacare, revolutionized health care in America but caused an uproar by Republicans, especially the Tea Party members. Six months after its passage, concerns over the program's cost and the mandated insurance requirement helped Republicans win control of the House of Representatives in the historic 2010 midterm election. Thus began the war in Congress over Obamacare and its repeal and replacement. This war included over fifty votes to repeal the act in the House from 2011 through 2016. However, with Obama in the White House and in control of the veto power, congressional Republicans had no realistic prospect of repealing the legislation during his presidency.

After the 2016 election, President Trump, Speaker Ryan, and Majority Leader McConnell declared repealing and replacing Obamacare their first order of business, with a target date for action within three months. The congressional leaders laid out a three-pronged plan to undermine Obamacare with a combination of new legislation, executive action, and regulatory changes. They were strong on repeal and weak on replacement. They acknowledged a replacement law would require some Senate Democratic support, and were slow to issue a clear proposal for such a law in the House. Their struggle to come to an agreement over a replacement for Obamacare revealed that it is much easier to criticize a law than to take responsibility for changing it, particularly when changing it could mean the loss of health benefits for millions of Americans.

CONCLUSIONS

President Trump has unified party government, making it easier to enact his domestic legislative agenda, but he must work closely with the congressional leadership. He can use reconciliation and get judges (e.g., Supreme Court Justice Neil Gorsuch) and other political appointees confirmed without the needed sixty votes to stop a filibuster in the Senate. He can also use his veto if necessary. However, congressional leaders can only go as far as their followers allow. When working with Congress, presidents also must persuade, not just command. Even with unified party government, Congress is prone to partisan gridlock without large majorities. Given weak Republican Party unity on some issues (e.g., trade and tariffs, the deficit, spending on infrastructure); narrow majorities in the House and Senate; Trump's narrow electoral victory (no "coattails"); and the possibility of Senate filibusters on most legislation, Trump needs to work carefully with his Republican colleagues on the Hill. With his propensity to undermine the Republican congressional agenda with provocative tweets, rushed executive orders, and self-inflicted mistakes, Trump must work hard to maintain and grow a governing coalition on the Hill. President Trump may continue unilateral executive action to overcome the slow, deliberative, and messy legislative process on the Hill by ignoring Congress, but that is likely to result only in a short-term victory in his rivalry with the Hill.

It is unlikely with a highly polarized Congress and a legislative amateur in the White House who has ignored and insulted the Republican leadership, but there continues to exist the possibility of building bipartisan coalitions on the Hill. Indeed, Speaker of the House Paul Ryan did this rather effectively in 2015 (see table 10.1). Speaker Ryan's leadership built cross-party coalitions on major legislation that year, including on highly polarized issues. This legislation covered major issues, including education reform (the Every Student Achieves Act), environmental regulation (the Toxic Substance and Chemical Act), international business (reauthorization of the Export-Import Bank), and international trade (granting trade promotion authority to the president).

There remains therefore the hope and possibility of reducing polarization ("changing the way Washington works") through skillful persuasion and civil deliberation by congressional leaders and the president. However, the crowded legislative agenda, high expectations by voters, the limited time for legislative business before each new election, the probability of Democratic Party delaying tactics, and a president who has a tendency to make mistakes and to act in a unilateral, top-down manner without coordination with the Republican leadership all point to continued gridlock on the major issues facing America.

Table 10.1.   Bipartisanship in the House, 2015

	Republicans		Total	Democrats	
Issue/Vote	No	Yes	Yes	No	Yes
Toxic Substance and Chemical Act	1	231	398	0	167
"Doc Fix"	33	212	392	4	180
Every Student Achieves (Conference Report)	64	178	359	0	181
Highway Bill (with Ex-Im Bank Reauthorization)	65	178	359	0	181
Cyber Info Sharing (Homeland Security)	19	220	355	44	135
21st-Century Cures	70	170	344	7	174
USA Freedom Act	47	196	338	41	142
"Tax Extenders"	3	241	318	106	77
FY 16 Omnibus Bill	95	150	316	18	166
Ex-Im Bank Reauthorization	117	127	313	1	186
Cyber Info Sharing (Intelligence)	37	202	307	79	105
Medical Device Tax Repeal	0	234	280	140	46
Continuing Resolution	151	91	277	0	186
Permitting Keystone Pipeline Construction	1	241	270	151	29
2-Year Budget Agreement	167	79	266	0	187
Repeal of Oil Export Ban	6	235	261	153	26
DHS Funding without Shutdown	167	75	256	0	181
Trade Promotion Authority	50	190	218	158	28

Note: Entries in this table refer to the number of House members voting for or against each bill. Since there are 435 House members, approval by 218 or more House members ensures a bill's passage in the House.

NOTES

1. Robert Costa and Philip Rucker, "Reality Check Awaits Trump: Government Not 'Built for Speed,'" *Washington Post*, January 15, 2017, A1. Also see Dan Balz, "How Does Trump Lead? The Way He Campaigned," *Washington Post*, May 3, 2017, Q8.

2. Mickey Edwards, "Congress Is the Last Bastion against Trump," *New York Times*, January 20, 2017.

3. For a discussion of the sources of partisan polarization, see James A. Thurber and Antoine Yoshinaka (eds.), *American Gridlock: The Sources, Character, and Impact of Political Polarization* (New York: Cambridge University Press, 2015).

4. For details on the impact of polarization on Congress, see Thurber and Yoshinaka, *American Gridlock*.

5. For an assessment of President Obama's first two years in office, see James A. Thurber (ed.), *Obama in Office* (Boulder, CO: Paradigm Publishers, 2011).

6. US Congress, Congressional Budget Office, *The Budget and Economic Outlook: An Update* (Washington, DC: CBO, January 2009).

7. Interview with Tom Brokaw on NBC's *Meet the Press*, December 7, 2008.

8. Joseph White, "From Ambition to Desperation on the Budget," in Thurber, *Obama in Office*, 183–98.

9. Ibid., 187.

10. For a history leading to the passage of the Budget and Impoundment Control Act of 1974, see James A. Thurber, "The Dynamics and Dysfunction of the Congressional Budget Process: From Inception to Deadlock," in Lawrence C. Dodd and Bruce I Oppenheimer (eds.), *Congress Reconsidered* (Washington, DC: CQ Press, 2013).

11. For an analysis of the failure of the super committee and the budget process reforms of 2011, see James A. Thurber, "Agony, Angst, and the Failure of the Super-committee," *Extensions: A Journal of the Carl Albert Congressional Research and Studies Center* (Summer 2012): 17–24.

12. Jackie Calmes, "Panel Seeks Social Security Cuts and Higher Taxes," *New York Times*, November 10, 2010.

13. David M. Herszenhorn and Jackie Calmes, "Tax Deal Suggests New Path for Obama," *New York Times*, December 7, 2010.

14. Joseph J. Schatz, "Boehner, Obama Take Over Talks," *Congressional Quarterly Weekly*, June 27, 2011, 1376.

15. The Joint Select Committee on Deficit Reduction was an unusual construct in the history of Congress. Former Senate Historian Donald Ritchie found inexact parallels between the Joint Select Committee and various historical joint committees. The only precedent for the committee's power to write and report legislation is the 1946–1977 Joint Committee on Atomic Energy. All other congressional joint committees have not had the power to write and report legislation.

16. Baucus, Becerra, Camp, and Hensarling had served on the National Commission on Fiscal Responsibility. All four voted against the Simpson-Bowles plan that emerged from the commission.

17. The 2011 Budget Control Act increased the debt ceiling by $400 billion in August 2011. The act required the federal government to make $917 billion in spending cuts over a ten-year period as a first installment. This was based on a Congressional Budget Office estimate using a current-law economic baseline, including the expiration of the Bush tax cuts. Under the act, government revenues were projected to rise after 2012.

18. Robert Pear and Catherine Rampell, "Lawmakers in Both Parties Fear That New Budget Panel Will Erode Authority," *New York Times*, August 5, 2011. "Lawmakers from both parties expressed scorn on Monday for a central feature of the deficit-reduction deal that creates a powerful 12-member committee of Congress to recommend major changes in entitlement programs and the tax code."

19. The end came two days before the panel's November 23, 2011, deadline, in the face of a requirement that before a vote could occur, a plan would have to be available for forty-eight hours after the Congressional Budget Office had scored its fiscal impact. The vote would not have been subject to amendments, House "majority of the majority" blocks, or Senate filibusters, guaranteeing a pure majority vote in both chambers.

20. Under the terms of the August debt limit law, the panel did not officially terminate until January 31, 2012. Nonetheless, its work was finished after it lost its privilege to submit legislation immune from amendment or procedural roadblocks as a consequence of missing its deadline for a vote.

21. "Statement from Co-Chairs of the Joint Select Committee on Deficit Reduction," *deficitreduction.gov*, November 21, 2011, retrieved January 30, 2012.

22. Catherine Dodge and Kathleen Hunter, "U.S. Supercommittee Fails to Reach Agreement as Across-the-Board Cuts Loom," Bloomberg, November 21, 2011.

23. Augustino Fonteecchia, "Deficit Supercommittee Officially Admits Failure," *Forbes*, November 21, 2011.

24. Jim Kuhnhenn, "Supercommittee Failure Complicates Election Year," *Businessweek*, November 23, 2011.

25. Matthew Cooper, "Public Split on Parties' Super Committee Ideas," *National Journal*, November 9, 2011.

26. Ibid.

27. Ibid. Also see Christopher Wlezien, "The Public as Thermostat: Dynamics of Preferences for Spending," *American Journal of Political Science* 39 (4): 981–1000.

28. Mike Dorning, "Both Parties Set to Use Failure of Debt Deal for 2012 Campaign," Bloomberg, November 22, 2011.

29. Barack Obama, "President Obama Makes a Statement about the Supercommittee," retrieved December 14, 2011, from https://www.whitehouse.gov/photos-and -video/video/2011/11/21/president-obama-makes-statement-about-supercommittee.

30. Quoted in Peter Baker, "Education of a President," *New York Times Magazine*, October 17, 2010.

31. John Hudson, "The Super Committee's Great Escapes," *The Atlantic Wire*, November 16, 2011.

32. Barbara Sinclair, "The President and the Congressional Party Leadership in a Hyperpartisan Era," in James A. Thurber (ed.), *Rivals for Power: Presidential-Congressional Relations*, 5th ed. (Lanham, MD: Rowman & Littlefield, 2013), 123.

33. Anne-Laure Beaussier, "The Patient Protection and Affordable Care Act: The Victory of Unorthodox Lawmaking," *Journal of Health Politics, Policy and Law* 37, no. 5 (2012): 775.

CHAPTER 11

Presidential-Congressional Relations in Foreign Policy

Jordan Tama

In the immediate aftermath of America's 2016 presidential election, congressional Republicans highlighted the Republican Party's unity as it prepared to control both the executive and legislative branches of government
for the first time in a decade. The day after the election, Senate Majority
Leader Mitch McConnell said of his plans for working with Donald Trump's
administration, "We're going to be an enthusiastic supporter [of Trump]
almost all the time. When we have differences of opinion, I prefer that we
work them out in private."[1]

Yet Republicans on Capitol Hill soon made it clear that they did not support key foreign policy positions of President-elect Trump. On international
trade, leading Republican lawmakers indicated that they opposed Trump's
call to impose a hefty tariff on US companies that move their production
overseas and then sell goods to the US market. House Majority Leader
Kevin McCarthy said, "I think history has shown that trade wars are not
healthy . . . [We] need to trade around the world."[2]

On other major foreign policy issues, it quickly became clear that
Trump would face opposition from both Republicans and Democrats in
Congress. Just a week after the election, the Republican-controlled House
of Representatives approved with strong bipartisan support a bill that
imposed new sanctions on any government or corporation that provided
Syria with financial, material, or technological assistance.[3] Since Russia
had been giving such aid to Syria, it represented a principal target of the
legislation. The *Washington Post* noted that, in advancing the bill, "the
House risks running afoul of the incoming Trump administration, which
has advanced a friendlier posture toward Russia and espoused a more
hands-off strategy vis-à-vis Syria."[4]

A few weeks later, Congress approved legislation authorizing substantial
increases in US military assistance to Ukraine and NATO allies in eastern

Europe—an effort designed to reassure these countries of US support and deter further Russian aggression in that region.[5] This legislation further challenged Trump's foreign policy platform in that Trump had questioned the value of US security alliances during the presidential campaign and called on US allies to take on more of the burden of providing for their own security.[6]

At the same time, Republican senators John McCain and Lindsey Graham joined Democratic senators Chuck Schumer and Jack Reed in calling for the creation of a select committee to investigate Russian cyberattacks on the United States during the 2016 election.[7] In a statement, the four senators added, "Recent reports of Russian interference in our election should alarm every American. . . . This cannot become a partisan issue. The stakes are too high for our country."[8] This statement and proposal deviated sharply from Trump's repeated suggestions that claims of Russian meddling were not well founded and represented nothing more than an effort to delegitimize his election.[9]

Moreover, influential lawmakers in both parties signaled their intention to advance additional challenges to Trump's oft-stated desire to cooperate more closely with Russia. Graham said during the presidential transition, "My view has not changed even though Trump won. [The Russians] are a bad actor in the world, they need to be reined in. [Trump's] the commander-in-chief but Congress does have a say and a role in all this."[10] Ben Cardin, the senior Democrat on the Senate Foreign Relations Committee, noted, "I don't look at Russia as a partner, I look at it as a bully . . . I think my Republican colleagues agree with me, not with President-elect Trump."[11] Cardin and other senators also signaled that they planned to be aggressive in advancing further sanctions legislation targeting Russia.[12]

Trump defused some of this congressional pressure after taking office by toning down the pro-Russian rhetoric of his presidential campaign and carrying out airstrikes against Syria in response to that country's use of chemical weapons. Nevertheless, the indications that members of Congress in both parties were ready to challenge the new president on foreign policy were striking considering the severe partisan polarization that generally characterizes American politics today. To be sure, foreign policy has not been immune from partisan polarization in recent years. For instance, Congress has been sharply polarized on proposals to address climate change and diplomatic agreements with Iran. But it remains more common on foreign policy than on domestic policy for debates to be characterized by internal divisions within the parties and by clashes between Congress and the presidency that transcend partisan lines.

In what follows, I provide an overview of the extensive scholarly literature on congressional-presidential relations in foreign policy and use examples from the Obama administration to illustrate how the two branches have handled international affairs in recent years. In this discussion, I focus especially on the respective influence of the two branches over foreign policy, as well as the extent and character of bipartisanship in foreign affairs.[13] The chapter provides two main takeaways. First, Congress often constrains the president's ability to carry out his or her foreign policy agenda. Second, while some foreign policy debates are characterized by severe partisan polarization or bipartisan unity, many others are marked by internal divisions within the parties or interbranch disagreement.

OVERVIEW OF MAJOR RESEARCH FINDINGS

The Foreign Policy Influence of Congress and the President

A large literature has analyzed to what extent, how, and in what circumstances each of the two branches shapes US foreign policy. Whereas some scholars have argued that the president dominates foreign policy making, others have shown that Congress influences foreign policy in important ways and have identified conditions that facilitate or impede congressional action on international issues.

The notion that the president dominates foreign policy making took root strongly at the height of the Cold War. In 1966, Aaron Wildavsky showed that presidents are more frequently able to persuade Congress to approve their proposals on foreign than on domestic policy.[14] Wildavsky concluded that this difference is so significant that there exist what he called "two presidencies"—one involving sharply limited presidential power on domestic affairs, and the other involving more expansive presidential power on foreign affairs.

Around the same time, the term "imperial presidency" became commonly used to describe presidential behavior that appeared to deviate from the limits placed by the Constitution on presidential authority. A landmark 1973 book traced how presidents had expanded their power since the Second World War through steps such as entering into international agreements and deploying the military without congressional approval—actions that appeared to be at odds with the Constitution, which grants to Congress the powers to ratify treaties and declare war.[15]

More recently, evidence of a dominant presidency could be found in actions such as:

- military interventions by President Bill Clinton in the Balkans during the 1990s and by President Barack Obama in Libya in 2011 that were not authorized by Congress,

- military strikes by Presidents George W. Bush and Obama on suspected terrorists in a range of countries on which Congress had not declared war,[16]
- the Bush administration's conduct of unauthorized coercive interrogations of detainees and surveillance of Americans' communications after the terrorist attacks of September 11, 2001,[17] and
- Obama's approval of the 2015 Paris climate change agreement without seeking the Senate's advice and consent concerning the accord.

One major study argues that such initiatives by recent presidents represent the emergence of a "new imperial presidency" after a brief uptick in congressional activity on foreign policy during the 1970s.[18] Some scholars further argue that Congress tends to defer to the president on international matters, thereby allowing the president to dominate this area of policy making.[19]

Other studies see the glass as half full (from the standpoint of congressional influence). This alternative perspective blossomed as many lawmakers claimed more authority over foreign policy in the wake of revelations about abuses of power—in both domestic and foreign affairs—by the Nixon administration. Following those revelations, Congress passed a series of laws in the 1970s that were designed to rein in the presidency. These measures included the War Powers Resolution (or War Powers Act), which restricted the president's ability to deploy US troops without congressional authorization, and the Hughes-Ryan Act, which established new requirements for the president to inform Congress of covert intelligence activities.[20] In the 1980s, Congress also challenged a major policy of President Ronald Reagan by passing laws that prohibited the executive branch from providing aid to anti-Communist rebels—known as the Contras—in Nicaragua. In this context, a number of scholars argued that congressional influence on foreign policy was quite substantial, in books with titles such as *Foreign Policy by Congress, Congress Resurgent,* and *The New Tug-of-War.*[21]

More recent studies have demonstrated that Congress constrains the president in a wide range of foreign policy areas, including international trade, human rights, the development of weapons systems, counterterrorism policy, funding of international institutions, diplomatic agreements, civil-military relations, and economic sanctions.[22] Scholars have even showed that lawmakers often influence presidential decisions concerning the use of force—an area where the president has typically been considered dominant.[23] One of the key insights of this scholarship is that congressional influence on foreign policy is often greater than it appears because the president routinely refrains from taking certain international actions based on concern about how lawmakers will react to them. The upshot is that the president is clearly the leading actor in international affairs, but is not usually able to carry out foreign policies that depart sharply from congressional preferences.

At the same time, it is important to recognize that the respective influence of the president and Congress is not the same on all foreign policy issues or in all political circumstances. Studies have found that presidential power relative to Congress tends to be greater during crises and on issues involving the use of military force than on matters involving international economics or most types of foreign policy spending.[24] These differences are driven in part by the greater involvement of interest groups—who can pressure Congress to act assertively—on issues that directly affect the welfare of economic constituencies.[25] Yet congressional activism is not driven only by interest group pressure. For instance, studies of the politics of military deployments have found that the president tends to be more constrained by Congress when the opposition party has more influence in Congress, when a war is relatively costly or unsuccessful, and when the president is relatively unpopular because these conditions give more lawmakers a political incentive to oppose the president's military actions.[26]

Partisanship and Bipartisanship on Foreign Policy

Scholars have also examined extensively the extent of partisan polarization and bipartisanship among US elected officials on foreign policy. One of the most well-known expressions about foreign policy states that "politics stops at the water's edge." This phrase conveys the idea that elected officials put aside—or should put aside—partisan considerations when it comes to the conduct of foreign affairs.[27]

Yet there exists extensive evidence that increases in partisan polarization in Washington over the past several decades have not been limited to domestic affairs. In particular, bipartisan congressional voting on international issues has become less common since the Vietnam War.[28] Moreover, scholars have found that partisanship even frequently shapes congressional behavior on the most important national security issues, such as decisions concerning war and peace.[29] This infusion of partisanship into foreign policy making is alarming because it can make it more difficult for the president to maintain domestic support for a foreign policy centered on constructive international engagement.[30]

Nevertheless, foreign policy making generally remains less polarized than domestic policy making. Lawmakers still vote with members of the other party more often on international than on domestic matters.[31] In addition, a strong reservoir of support for international engagement exists among voters and elites in both parties—suggesting that foreign policy bipartisanship may remain alive for some time to come.[32]

In my own work, I have shown that contemporary foreign policy biparti-sanship regularly takes multiple forms. Whereas much of the literature on foreign policy bipartisanship defines bipartisanship as broad support for the president's policies among lawmakers in both parties, I have found that many foreign policy issues are characterized by (a) internal splits within the parties generating competing bipartisan coalitions in Congress or (b) law-makers in both parties joining forces to challenge the president's policies.[33] In such cases, Republican and Democratic lawmakers often cooperate, even if broad bipartisan unity does not exist.

MAJOR FOREIGN POLICY DEBATES UNDER OBAMA

Many of the patterns highlighted in the preceding discussion are illustrated well by congressional debates and action concerning major international issues during the Obama presidency. In what follows, I briefly discuss the influence of Congress as well as the degree and character of partisanship or bipartisanship in major Obama-era decisions concerning the use of military force, economic sanctions, trade, and climate change.

The Use of Military Force

The Obama years featured several debates on the use of force, including debates over withdrawing troops from Iraq, deploying new troops to and then withdrawing troops from Afghanistan, using drones as a counterter-rorism tool, intervening in Libya, intervening against the Syrian government of Bashar al-Assad, and intervening in Iraq and Syria against ISIS. While Obama largely set the course of US policy in these cases, a brief discussion of the Afghanistan, Syria, and ISIS cases shows how congressional opinion can influence the president's decision making concerning military intervention and how use of force debates can feature a variety of political alignments.

The Afghanistan Surge

On Afghanistan, Obama inherited from George W. Bush a war effort that included the deployment of roughly 50,000 US troops. During his first year in office, Obama twice decided to deploy more troops to Af-ghanistan—ordering the deployment of roughly 17,000 new troops early in 2009 and about 30,000 additional troops at the end of the year. These decisions were consistent with campaign pledges that Obama had made as a presidential candidate to devote more resources to a war that Obama said the United States had to win—in contrast to the war in Iraq, which Obama had called "dumb."[34]

Congressional opinion appeared to influence an important aspect of Obama's decision making on the Afghanistan surge. When announcing his second surge decision, Obama also indicated that he would begin withdrawing US troops from Afghanistan in July 2011. In-depth reporting suggests that this withdrawal timeline—which Obama subsequently followed—was influenced by the Obama White House's concern that support for the war was eroding in Congress, particularly within the Democratic caucus.[35] Indeed, in 2010, 153 House Democrats joined 9 House Republicans in voting for an amendment to an emergency supplemental appropriations bill that would have mandated a withdrawal of US troops from Afghanistan.[36] Although this amendment was not approved, such measures might have gained more momentum in Congress if Obama had not effectively preempted them by announcing a withdrawal timeline of his own.[37] It is also notable that the principal congressional opposition to Obama's Afghanistan surge came from Obama's own party, illustrating how many foreign policy debates do not break down simply along partisan lines.

Intervention against Bashar al-Assad

Congressional opinion posed even greater challenges for Obama with respect to the prospect of intervention in the conflict that broke out in Syria in 2011. In that conflict, the government of Bashar al-Assad brutally repressed a political opposition that emerged in the context of the Arab Spring, leading the opposition to begin arming itself and resulting in a bloody civil war.

Although Obama signaled as early as 2011 that Assad should leave power, he did not want the United States to become involved militarily in another conflict in the Middle East and was skeptical that the United States could influence events in Syria positively through some form of intervention. In Congress, both parties were internally divided, with many of the most prominent congressional foreign policy voices advocating more forceful US action against Assad and other lawmakers in both parties sharing Obama's reluctance to intervene.[38] Congressional advocates of more forceful action pressed, in particular, for the United States to provide arms to Syrian groups fighting against Assad. This pressure appears to have influenced a decision by Obama to authorize a covert program to give weapons to some Syrian rebels.[39]

Ironically, congressional opinion played the opposite role—contributing to a decision by Obama to avoid becoming more directly involved in Syria—after Assad's military crossed a "red line" that Obama had established by killing more than 1,000 Syrian civilians with chemical weapons in August 2013. In response to this attack, most of Obama's advisors agreed that the president's credibility would be damaged if he did not enforce his red line through some form of punitive action.[40] Yet Obama was reluctant to venture into a new military engagement without congressional backing, and so he asked Congress to authorize a limited set of air strikes on Syrian government facilities.[41]

The subsequent congressional debate revealed that Congress was deeply divided over the prospect of direct intervention in Syria. While hawkish lawmakers in both parties strongly supported air strikes, many other lawmakers expressed a reluctance that was shared by most American voters to become directly involved in another conflict in the Middle East.[42] It soon became clear that the use of force resolution would not gain enough votes to be approved by the House and Senate.[43] In this context, Obama negotiated a deal with Russia—a close ally of Syria—in which Assad agreed to give up all of Syria's chemical weapons in exchange for the United States refraining from a military strike. While Obama may have reached this deal even if congressional opinion had been more supportive of intervention, the limited congressional support for air strikes gave Obama greater incentive to avoid going forward with the strikes.

Intervention against ISIS

In 2014, a new policy debate emerged in Washington, as ISIS—which had become the most powerful group fighting against Assad—gained control of large swaths of territory in Iraq and Syria, beheaded several American citizens, and began to carry out larger terrorist attacks outside the Middle East. In this case, Obama did not wait for Congress to authorize intervention before ordering military action against ISIS in the form of air strikes and the deployment of military advisors to help partners in Iraq and Syria counter what Obama described as a direct threat to the United States.[44]

Although most members of Congress agreed with Obama that the United States should take military action against ISIS—a position that was shared by most of the American public—lawmakers were divided about whether or how to authorize the intervention.[45] Some of this division reflected genuine policy disagreement: hawkish members of Congress favored granting the president much broader authority to fight ISIS than did most liberal lawmakers.[46] But political motivations also greatly shaped how Congress approached the issue. While the policy differences among members of Congress could probably have been bridged through legislative compromise, Republican congressional leaders—who controlled the House and Senate during Obama's final two years in office—had little incentive to hand Obama an apparent political victory by authorizing the military action that he had initiated.[47] As a result, a resolution to authorize the use of force against ISIS was never brought to the House or Senate floor. This failure of Congress to act did not clearly limit Obama's ability to prosecute the war against ISIS, but it shows how partisanship can weaken the ability of Congress and the president to work together effectively on foreign policy.

Economic Sanctions

While Congress was divided and unable to act in some key use of force debates during the Obama years, the institution was marked by greater bipartisanship and productivity in some major recent debates involving economic sanctions. Indeed, Congress passed numerous laws imposing sanctions on other countries by overwhelming margins under Obama and his predecessors, even as overall polarization and gridlock reached record levels. Yet in many of these cases, the president opposed the sanctions bills out of concern that the legislation would harm US relationships with other countries or make it more difficult to achieve broader foreign policy goals.[48] At the same time, Congress has not been entirely immune to polarization in sanctions debates, as partisan behavior has increased when a sanctions debate has been linked to a top presidential priority. In what follows, I illustrate these patterns through a brief discussion of recent debates over sanctioning Iran and Russia.

Sanctions on Iran

It would be difficult to find a foreign policy issue that has been the subject of greater congressional activity and bipartisanship over the past three decades than the placement of sanctions on Iran. From 1996 to 2012, Congress repeatedly imposed new sanctions on Iran based on concerns about Iran's nuclear program, support for terrorism, and domestic repression. These pieces of legislation—some of which represented stand-alone bills and some of which represented amendments to annual defense authorization bills—were all approved by unanimous, nearly unanimous, unanimous consent, or voice votes in the House and Senate.

Presidents Clinton, George W. Bush, and Obama generally shared the concerns of members of Congress about Iran, and at times sought to impose sanctions on Iran. But each of these presidents wanted to maintain control over sanctions policy making and worried that the highly punitive measures mandated by Congress—many of which targeted countries and firms that did business with Iran—would alienate US allies and generate other costs to the United States. Nevertheless, the presidents signed nearly all of the Iran sanctions bills approved by Congress since the bills typically granted the president some flexibility in applying the sanctions and the bills were generally backed by influential domestic interest groups and favored by American voters.[49]

Congress became more polarized on Iran policy, however, as Obama entered into intensive diplomatic negotiations with the Iranian government, which culminated in a 2015 agreement in which Iran agreed to accept certain restrictions on its nuclear activities in exchange for the lifting of various sanctions.[50] Research has shown that members of Congress have more incentive to engage in partisan combat on issues that represent top presidential priorities—because the president's success or failure in addressing top priorities will tend to burnish or harm the reputation of the president's party, thereby affecting the electoral fortunes of members of Congress in both parties.[51] Since Obama's Iran agreement represented a major foreign policy achievement for the president, it gave Democratic lawmakers a strong incentive to support it and gave Republican lawmakers a strong incentive to try to undermine it.

In this context, a series of congressional votes on whether to reject the agreement—which Obama negotiated as an executive agreement, rather than a treaty—or to restrict the president's ability to lift sanctions on Iran generated sharp polarization, with nearly all Democrats lining up on the opposite side as nearly all Republicans.[52] Given the Senate's sixty-vote filibuster threshold and the president's possession of veto power, this political alignment ensured that the Iran deal would not be overturned by Congress while Obama held the presidency.

Sanctions on Russia

More consistent congressional bipartisanship—coupled with some substantial disagreement between Congress and the president—characterized US policy making concerning sanctions on Russia during the Obama administration. This pattern marked both an effort to impose sanctions on Russian officials who committed human rights abuses and efforts to impose sanctions on Russia following that country's invasion of Ukraine.

During Obama's first term in office, a bipartisan coalition of members of Congress advanced legislation mandating travel and financial restrictions on individuals responsible for gross violations of human rights in Russia. At a time when Obama was trying to maintain a productive relationship with the Russian government, Obama opposed this legislation out of concern that it would trigger Russian retaliation and reduce Russian cooperation with the United States.[53] Nevertheless, the House and Senate approved the legislation in overwhelming bipartisan votes in late 2012.[54] Given the bill's strong congressional support and the difficulty of justifying a veto of legislation designed to hold human rights abusers accountable, Obama signed the legislation.[55] His administration subsequently imposed the mandated sanctions on at least forty-four Russian officials.[56]

Russia retaliated by imposing travel sanctions on certain US officials and prohibiting Americans from adopting Russian children.[57]

A new sanctions debate emerged in 2014 after Russia's military intervention in Ukraine and annexation of Crimea. By this point, US-Russian relations had deteriorated for a variety of reasons, and Obama and most members of Congress in both parties agreed that the United States should penalize Russia for its aggression. However, Obama was more concerned than lawmakers with keeping the United States in sync with US allies in Europe on the issue. Although Obama imposed a number of important sanctions on Russia through his executive authority, he expressed concern when the House and Senate neared approval of a bill mandating additional sanctions that went beyond what European allies were willing to support.[58] Obama nevertheless signed the legislation after Congress approved it.[59] A journalist noted: "The Congress passed the bipartisan measure without opposition, making a veto politically untenable."[60] These examples illustrate how bipartisanship can challenge as well as support presidential foreign policies.

As noted in this chapter's introduction, Congress also prepared as Trump took office to take further bipartisan actions targeting Russia, and continued interbranch conflict over Russia sanctions appears likely.

International Trade

Debates about international trade agreements generally have been marked in recent decades by greater polarization than debates over the use of force or sanctions, but they have also generated alliances between Democratic presidents and congressional Republicans. Although all recent presidents other than Trump have supported liberalized trade, the reduction of trade barriers has consistently generated more support among Republicans than among Democrats on Capitol Hill. These patterns reflect two main factors. First, the greater electoral accountability of the president than of members of Congress for overall national welfare gives the president a stronger incentive than lawmakers to favor trade agreements, which typically boost the economy on the whole but harm certain pockets of Americans.[61] Second, pro-free-trade interest groups (such as many business associations) have close ties to most Republican lawmakers, whereas protectionist interest groups (such as many labor unions) have close ties to most Democratic lawmakers.[62]

The result is that the president and Congress typically divide mostly along partisan lines on trade under Republican presidents, while Democratic presidents tend to get more support for their trade agenda from the opposition party than from their own party in Congress. Consider the following examples from the George W. Bush and Obama presidencies. In 2005, under Bush, 88 percent of House Republicans and 78 percent of Senate Republicans voted in favor of a free trade agreement negotiated by Bush with the Dominican Republic and five Central American countries, but just 7 percent of House Democrats and 25 percent of Senate Democrats voted for the accord.[63] In 2015, under Obama, 79 percent of Republican representatives and 90 percent of Republican senators voted to grant the president trade promotion authority (TPA) sought by Obama, while only 15 percent of Democratic representatives and 30 percent of Democratic senators voted for the measure.[64]

Given the Republican majorities in the House and Senate in 2005 and 2015, these vote results were sufficient to give Bush and Obama legislative victories, but it is notable that congressional Republicans provided the bulk of support for the president in both cases. At the same time, it is worth noting that these congressional votes were not entirely polarized, as a significant minority of lawmakers voted with the other party's majority in each case. This crossover voting reveals that congressional positions on trade are driven not only by party identities, but also by the economic characteristics of states and districts. In particular, members of Congress representing states or districts that are relatively abundant in skilled labor generally have a greater incentive to be pro-trade than members representing states or districts that are relatively abundant in unskilled labor, because reduced barriers to trade tend to benefit skilled workers more than unskilled workers.[65]

The TPA vote was particularly important because the granting of TPA to the president was necessary in order to enable Obama to complete the negotiation of the Trans-Pacific Partnership (TPP), a major trade deal involving twelve countries. Obama and the leaders of those countries reached agreement on the TPP in February 2016. However, Trump's staunchly anti-trade campaign platform—which departed sharply from the Republican orthodoxy on trade—reduced support for the TPP among congressional Republicans and made it more difficult politically for pro-trade Republican leaders on the Hill to bring the agreement to the floor of the House or Senate for a vote.[66] Moreover, Republican congressional leaders had an incentive to deny Obama a legislative victory that would join the Iran agreement as one of his major foreign policy accomplishments. The result was that Obama's presidency ended with the TPP left as unfinished business. This made it relatively easy for Trump to announce during his first week as president that he was withdrawing the United States from the agreement.

Climate Change

Recent debates over policies to address climate change have also been marked by relatively high levels of congressional polarization, without trade policy's mitigating dynamic of Republican members of Congress typically siding with Democratic presidents. In particular, Democratic lawmakers and presidents have generally been much more supportive than Republican lawmakers and presidents of policies that would restrict the emission of greenhouse gases in the United States. As with trade debates, however, differences in the economic characteristics of states and districts have prevented Congress from being entirely polarized, as lawmakers in both parties representing states or districts that produce large amounts of fossil fuels have tended to be strongly opposed to emissions restrictions.

During Obama's first two years in office, one of his top priorities—alongside health-care reform and financial sector reform—was the enactment of legislation that would reduce US greenhouse gas emissions dramatically.[67] When the House voted in 2009 on a bill supported by Obama that would set a national ceiling on greenhouse gas emissions and establish a system for firms to trade emissions permits, just 5 percent of Republicans joined 83 percent of Democrats in voting for the bill.[68] While these voting percentages were sufficient for the bill to pass the House at a time when the Democrats held a large majority, the defection of some Democratic lawmakers from the party's prevailing position spelled trouble for the legislation's prospects in the Senate, where it would need sixty votes to overcome a Republican filibuster. Once several Senate Democrats came out in opposition to the Senate's version of emissions reduction legislation in 2010, Senate Majority Leader Harry Reid chose not to advance the bill.[69]

The prospect of congressional action on climate change further dimmed when the Republican Party took control of the House in 2011. Subsequently, Obama relied entirely on regulations and international agreements that he could issue or negotiate without congressional approval to advance his climate agenda. With respect to regulations, Obama ordered the Environmental Protection Agency to issue an array of rules that mandated emissions reductions in various sectors of the economy—from automobiles to power plants—which helped the United States reduce its greenhouse gas emissions by 9.5 percent from 2008 to 2015.[70] Internationally, Obama negotiated an international accord—known as the Paris Agreement—under which the United States committed to further reduce its greenhouse gas emissions, by at least 26 percent below 2005 levels by 2025.[71] Since Obama knew that the Senate would not ratify such a deal, he signed it as an executive agreement, rather than as a treaty subject to the Senate's advice and consent.

While Obama's greenhouse gas regulations and the Paris accord represent major achievements, his inability to gain congressional approval for meaningful action on climate change makes his long-term legacy in this area somewhat uncertain. During his presidential campaign, Trump said he would pull out of the Paris Agreement and rescind Obama's major emissions reduction rules.[72] However, Trump was more equivocal about the Paris Agreement during his presidential transition, and as he took office, it remained unclear how thoroughly he would pursue the very time-consuming and litigious process of revoking Obama's climate regulations.[73] It seemed most likely that Trump would reverse some of Obama's most important emissions regulations, but would not be able to fully undo his predecessor's record on this issue.

CONCLUSION

Although the president tends to have greater capacity to dictate policy and act without Congress on international than on domestic issues, Congress often exerts considerable influence on the president's ability to achieve his or her foreign policy goals. Bipartisan congressional support makes it easier for the president to pursue new international initiatives—from military interventions to global treaties—and makes it more likely that those initiatives will be sustained and successful. By contrast, a divided Congress can make it difficult or impossible for the president to advance key policies— particularly on issues, such as trade liberalization, where the president needs congressional approval in order to move forward.

While the broader trend of increased congressional polarization has led to more frequent partisan division on Capitol Hill on foreign policy, it is also important to recognize that congressional challenges to the president on international issues regularly take several forms. On sanctions, for instance, bipartisan majorities on the Hill regularly mandate the placement of penalties on other countries despite the president's opposition to the legislation. The actions and statements of lawmakers on Russia and Syria as Trump prepared to take office suggest that this pattern will not change anytime soon.

On still other foreign policy issues, the parties are often internally divided, and this pattern is also persisting under Trump. In his inaugural address, Trump expressed a foreign policy vision centered on placing "America first," stating, "We must protect our borders from the ravages of other countries making our products, stealing our companies, and destroying our jobs." This populist and protectionist foreign policy agenda is supported by some members of Congress in both parties, but opposed by others in both parties. In short, when it comes to foreign policy, unified party government under Trump will not translate into unified Republican support and unified Democratic opposition.

At the same time, it is worth noting that presidents are not powerless to influence congressional behavior on foreign policy. Although the president's ability to influence public opinion is limited,[74] some presidents have been quite skillful at using a variety of strategies to build support for their international agenda on Capitol Hill. For instance, Dwight Eisenhower met often with lawmakers and enlisted the advocacy help of nongovernmental organizations when seeking to persuade Congress to boost foreign aid spending, which he considered essential in the fight against communism.[75] Other presidents have gained congressional buy-in by involving lawmakers directly in international negotiations. For example, Franklin Roosevelt included key members of Congress in the US delegation to the international conference that designed the United Nations, and Jimmy Carter involved some senators in negotiations with Panama over the transfer of the Panama Canal from US to Panamanian control.[76]

Still other presidents have brought members of Congress to their side by incorporating concessions to those members into their policies. Bill Clinton did this when negotiating the North American Free Trade Agreement by including in the agreement provisions designed to protect certain vulnerable US industries from Mexican competition,[77] and Barack Obama did it when seeking Senate approval of a nuclear arms reduction treaty with Russia by pairing the arms reduction with a dramatic increase in spending on US nuclear facilities.[78]

Donald Trump has long touted his deal-making ability; indeed, he wrote a best-selling book about it three decades before he became president.[79] During the 2016 campaign, he argued that he would be able to negotiate better international agreements for the United States than past presidents. Yet Trump's ability to succeed in foreign policy will depend as much on his ability to build congressional backing for his international agenda as it depends on his ability to negotiate effectively with foreign leaders. Indeed, if he departs sharply from congressional preferences on foreign policy, he is likely to find, as past presidents have found, that partisan affinity will not prevent members of his own party from joining with congressional Democrats to challenge key parts of his foreign policy agenda.

NOTES

1. Jennifer Steinhauer, "Republicans in Congress Plan Swift Action on Agenda with Donald Trump," *New York Times* (November 9, 2016).

2. Sam Frizell, "Donald Trump's Tariffs Proposal Faces Pushback from Republicans," *Time* (December 5, 2016).

3. H.R. 5732, Caesar Syria Civilian Protection Act of 2016.

4. Karoun Demirjian, "House Passes Two Sanctions Bills, Sending Foreign Policy Message on Iran and Syria," *Washington Post* (November 15, 2016).

5. S. 2943, National Defense Authorization Act for Fiscal Year 2017; Aaron Mehta, "Congress Reassures Baltic Representatives of NATO Commitment," *Defense News* (December 9, 2016).

6. David E. Sanger and Maggie Haberman, "Donald Trump Sets Conditions for Defending NATO Allies from Attack," *New York Times* (July 20, 2016).

7. Seung Min Kim and Rebecca Morin, "McCain, Schumer Double Down on Russia Probe," *Politico* (December 18, 2016).

8. "McCain, Graham, Schumer, Reed Joint Statement on Reports That Russia Interfered with 2016 Election," December 11, 2016, http://www.armed-services .senate.gov/press-releases/mccain-graham-schumer-reed-joint-statement-on-reports -that-russia-interfered-with-the-2016-election.

9. BBC News, "Trump Condemns CIA Russia Hacking Report," *BBC News* (December 12, 2016).

10. Josh Rogin, "Congress May Spoil Trump's Russian Reset," *Washington Post* (November 20, 2016).

11. Karoun Demirjian, "Republican Lawmakers Move to Restrain President-Elect Trump on Russia," *Washington Post* (November 16, 2016).

12. Demirjian, "Republican Lawmakers Move to Restrain President-Elect Trump on Russia"; Jordain Carney, "Senators Vow to Counter Trump on Russia," *The Hill* (November 20, 2016).

13. I define foreign policy broadly, to include national security issues as well as other international matters.

14. Aaron Wildavsky, "The Two Presidencies," *Transaction* 4, no. 2 (1966): 7–14.

15. Arthur M. Schlesinger Jr., *The Imperial Presidency* (Boston: Houghton Mifflin, 1973).

16. For more detail, see Shoon Kathleen Murray, "Stretching the 2001 AUMF: A History of Two Presidencies," *Presidential Studies Quarterly* 45, no. 1 (2015): 175–98.

17. For more detail, see Louis Fisher, "National Security Surveillance," in David P. Auerswald and Colton C. Campbell, eds., *Congress and the Politics of National Security* (Cambridge: Cambridge University Press, 2012), 213–30; and James Pfiffner's chapter in this book.

18. Andrew Rudalevige, *The New Imperial Presidency: Renewing Presidential Power after Watergate* (Ann Arbor: University of Michigan Press, 2005).

19. Barbara Hinckley, *Less Than Meets the Eye: Foreign Policy Making and the Myth of an Assertive Congress* (Chicago: University of Chicago Press, 1994); Stephen R. Weissman, *A Culture of Deference: Congress's Failure of Leadership in Foreign Policy* (New York: Basic Books, 1995); Louis Fisher, *Congressional Abdication on War and Spending* (College Station: Texas A&M University Press, 2000).

20. See Douglas Kriner's chapter in this book for more information on the impetus for congressionally driven intelligence reform in the 1970s.

21. Thomas M. Franck and Edward Weisband, *Foreign Policy by Congress* (New York: Oxford University Press, 1979); Randall B. Ripley and James M. Lindsay, *Congress Resurgent: Foreign and Defense Policy on Capitol Hill* (Ann Arbor: University of Michigan Press, 1993); Jeremy D. Rosner, *The New Tug-of-War: Congress, the Executive Branch, and National Security* (Washington, DC: Carnegie Endowment for International Peace, 1995).

22. Lisa L. Martin, *Democratic Commitments: Legislatures and International Cooperation* (Princeton, NJ: Princeton University Press, 2000); Ralph G. Carter and James M. Scott, *Choosing to Lead: Understanding Congressional Foreign Policy Entrepreneurs* (Durham, NC: Duke University Press, 2009); Glen S. Krutz and Jeffrey S. Peake,

Treaty Politics and the Rise of Executive Agreements: International Commitments in a System of Shared Powers (Ann Arbor: University of Michigan Press, 2011); Kathryn C. Lavelle, *Legislating International Organization: The U.S. Congress, the IMF, and the World Bank* (Oxford: Oxford University Press, 2011); James M. Scott and Ralph G. Carter, "The Not-So-Silent Partner: Patterns of Legislative-Executive Interaction in the War on Terror, 2001–2009," *International Studies Perspectives* 15, no. 2 (2014): 186–208; Jack Goldsmith, *Power and Constraint: The Accountable Presidency after 9/11* (New York: W. W. Norton, 2012); Colton C. Campbell and David P. Auerswald, eds., *Congress and Civil-Military Relations* (Washington, DC: Georgetown University Press, 2015); Jordan Tama, "Bipartisanship in a Polarized Age: The U.S. Congress and Foreign Policy Sanctions," School of International Service Research Paper No. 2015-2.

23. David P. Auerswald, *Disarmed Democracies: Domestic Institutions and the Use of Force* (Ann Arbor: University of Michigan Press, 2000); William G. Howell and Jon C. Pevehouse, *While Dangers Gather: Congressional Checks on Presidential War Powers* (Princeton, NJ: Princeton University Press, 2007); Douglas L. Kriner, *After the Rubicon: Congress, Presidents, and the Politics of Waging War* (Chicago: University of Chicago Press, 2010).

24. James M. Lindsay, *Congress and the Politics of U.S. Foreign Policy* (Baltimore: Johns Hopkins University Press, 1994); Helen V. Milner and Dustin Tingley, *Sailing the Water's Edge: The Domestic Politics of American Foreign Policy* (Princeton, NJ: Princeton University Press, 2015).

25. Milner and Tingley, *Sailing the Water's Edge.*

26. Howell and Pevehouse, *While Dangers Gather;* Kriner, *After the Rubicon.*

27. The phrase entered the foreign policy lexicon during the Cold War—an era that is commonly associated with high levels of foreign policy bipartisanship. The historical record tells a more complex story: while lawmakers provided bipartisan backing for most core foreign policy positions of US presidents during the Cold War, quite a few foreign policy debates in Congress were very heated even when tensions between the United States and Soviet Union were high. See Robert David Johnson, *Congress and the Cold War* (Cambridge: Cambridge University Press, 2006); and James Gibney, "Politics Never Really Stopped at Water's Edge," Bloomberg (September 17, 2015). For information on the history of the expression "politics stops at the water's edge," see Linda Fowler, *Watchdogs on the Hill: The Decline of Congressional Oversight of U.S. Foreign Relations* (Princeton, NJ: Princeton University Press, 2015), 173.

28. C. James DeLaet and James M. Scott, "Treaty-Making and Partisan Politics: Arms Control and the U.S. Senate, 1960–2001," *Foreign Policy Analysis* 2, no. 2 (2006): 177–200; Charles A. Kupchan and Peter L. Trubowitz, "Dead Center: The Demise of Liberal Internationalism in the United States," *International Security* 32, no. 2 (2007): 7–44; Frances Lee, *Beyond Ideology: Politics, Principles, and Partisanship in the U.S. Senate* (Chicago: University of Chicago Press, 2009); John Lapinski, *The Substance of Representation: Congress, American Political Development, and Lawmaking* (Princeton, NJ: Princeton University Press, 2013).

29. Howell and Pevehouse, *While Dangers Gather;* Kriner, *After the Rubicon.*

30. Kupchan and Trubowitz, "Dead Center."

31. Peter Trubowitz and Nicole Mellow, "'Going Bipartisan:' Politics by Other Means," *Political Science Quarterly* 120, no. 3 (2005): 433–53; Laurel Harbridge, *Is*

Bipartisanship Dead? Policy Agreement and Agenda-Setting in the House of Representatives (New York: Cambridge University Press, 2015).

32. Joshua W. Busby and Jonathan Monten, "Without Heirs? Assessing the Decline of Establishment Internationalism in U.S. Foreign Policy," *Perspectives on Politics* 6, no. 3 (2008): 451–72; Stephen Chaudoin, Helen V. Milner, and Dustin Tingley, "The Center Still Holds: Liberal Internationalism Survives," *International Security* 35, no. 1 (2010): 75–94.

33. Jordan Tama, *Bipartisanship in a Polarized Age: When Democrats and Republicans Cooperate on U.S. Foreign Policy*, Book manuscript in progress (on file with author).

34. Mark Landler, "The Afghan War and the Evolution of Obama," *New York Times* (January 1, 2017).

35. For detailed accounts by journalists of Obama's Afghanistan decision making, see Bob Woodward, *Obama's Wars* (New York: Simon & Schuster, 2010); Jonathan Alter, *The Promise: President Obama, Year One* (New York: Simon & Schuster, 2010), 363–94; James Mann, *The Obamians: The Struggle Inside the White House to Redefine American Power* (New York: Viking, 2012), 117–41.

36. House Roll Call Vote 433, July 1, 2010.

37. At the end of Obama's presidency, fewer than 10,000 US troops remained in Afghanistan.

38. Carlo Munoz and Jeremy Herb, "Obama, Congress Inch toward Intervention in Syria Conflict," *The Hill* (March 7, 2012); Josh Rogin, "Democrats and Republicans Unite around Calls for More Aggressive Syria Policy," *The Cable* (March 21, 2013); John Hudson, "Democratic Senator: Obama Has 'No Articulated Strategy' on Syria," *The Cable* (June 24, 2013).

39. Karen DeYoung and Anne Gearan, "U.S. to Scale Up Military Support for Syrian Rebels," *Washington Post* (June 14, 2013).

40. Mark Landler, "After Frantic Week, a Reluctant Obama," *International Herald Tribune* (September 2, 2013).

41. For a detailed discussion of Obama's decision to ask Congress to authorize this intervention, see Douglas L. Kriner, "Obama's Authorization Paradox: Syria and Congress's Continued Relevance in Military Affairs," *Presidential Studies Quarterly* 44, no. 2 (2014): 309–27.

42. David A. Fahrenthold and Paul Kane, "On Strike, Obama Faces a Skeptical Public," *New York Times* (September 4, 2013).

43. Karen Tumulty and Peter Wallsten, "Obama Is Making Little Headway with Congress on Syria," *Washington Post* (September 6, 2013).

44. Juliet Eilperin and Ed O'Keefe, "Obama Announces 'Broad Coalition' to Fight Islamic State Extremist Group," *Washington Post* (September 10, 2014).

45. Jonathan Weisman, Mark Landler, and Jeremy W. Peters, "As Obama Makes Case, Congress Is Divided on Campaign against Militants," *New York Times* (September 8, 2014); Pew Research Center, "Growing Support for Campaign against ISIS—and Possible Use of U.S. Ground Troops" (February 24, 2015).

46. Amber Phillips, "President Obama's Push for Military Authorization to Fight ISIS Won't Go Anywhere in Congress. Here's Why," *Washington Post* (December 7, 2015).

47. See David Jones's chapter in this book for a more detailed discussion of the strategy of congressional Republicans on this issue.

48. Jordan Tama, "The Domestic and International Drivers of Legislative Action on Sanctions," Paper Presented at International Studies Association Annual Meeting (March 2016).

49. Tama, "The Domestic and International Drivers of Legislative Action on Sanctions."

50. Joint Comprehensive Plan of Action, available at https://www.state.gov/e/eb/tfs/spi/iran/jcpoa.

51. Lee, *Beyond Ideology*; David Jones's chapter in this book.

52. Tama, *Bipartisanship in a Polarized Age*.

53. Tama, "Bipartisanship in a Polarized Age."

54. Russia and Moldova Jackson-Vanik Repeal and Magnitsky Rule of Law Accountability Act of 2012 (Public Law 112-208).

55. Jeremy W. Peters, "U.S. Senate Passes Russia Trade Bill, with a Human Rights Caveat," *New York Times* (December 6, 2012).

56. Samuel Rubenfeld, "U.S. Adds More Names to Magnitsky Blacklist," *Wall Street Journal* (January 9, 2017).

57. Masha Lipman, "What's Behind the Russian Adoption Ban?" *New Yorker* (December 21, 2012); Radio Free Europe/Radio Liberty, "Russia Responds to 'Magnitsky List' by Banning Americans" (April 15, 2013).

58. Remarks by Barack Obama at meeting of President's Export Council (December 11, 2014).

59. Ukraine Freedom Support Act of 2014 (Public Law 113-272).

60. Peter Baker, "Obama Signals Support for New U.S. Sanctions to Pressure Russian Economy," *New York Times* (December 16, 2014).

61. On the differing incentives of the president and lawmakers, see Stephen D. Krasner, *Defending the National Interest: Raw Materials Investments and U.S. Foreign Policy* (Princeton, NJ: Princeton University Press, 1978); William G. Howell, Saul P. Jackman, and Jon C. Rogowski, *The Wartime President* (Chicago: University of Chicago Press, 2013); Milner and Tingley, *Sailing the Water's Edge*.

62. On interest group advocacy on trade, see Robert E. Baldwin and Christopher S. Magee, "Is Trade Policy for Sale? Congressional Voting on Recent Trade Bills," *Policy Choice* 105, no. 1 (2000): 79–101; and I. M. Destler, *American Trade Politics*, 4th ed. (Washington, DC: Institute for International Economics, 2005). On interest group lobbying more generally, see Allan J. Cigler and Burdett A. Loomis, eds., *Interest Group Politics*, 8th ed. (Washington, DC: CQ Press, 2012).

63. House Roll Call Vote 443 and Senate Roll Call Vote 209 on H.R. 3045, the Dominican Republic-Central America-United States Free Trade Agreement Implementation Act (July 28, 2005).

64. House Roll Call Vote 374 on the Motion to Concur in the Senate Amendment with Amendment to H.R. 2146 (June 18, 2015); Senate Roll Call Vote 219 on the Motion to Concur in the House Amendment to the Senate Amendment to H.R. 2146 (June 24, 2015).

65. Kenneth F. Scheve and Matthew J. Slaughter, "What Determines Individual Trade-Policy Preferences?" *Journal of International Economics* 54, no. 2 (2001): 267–92; Milner and Tingley, *Sailing the Water's Edge*, 42–44.

66. Eric Bradner, "Obama Pushes Trade in Asia, But Has 2016 Killed the TPP?" *CNN.com* (September 7, 2016).

67. James A. Thurber, ed., *Obama in Office* (Boulder, CO: Paradigm Publishers, 2011).

68. House Roll Call Vote 477 on H.R. 2454, the American Clean Energy and Security Act (June 26, 2009).

69. Evan Lehmann, "Senate Abandons Climate Effort, Dealing Blow to President," *New York Times* (July 23, 2010).

70. See Claudia Thurber's chapter in this book; and Barack Obama, "The Irreversible Momentum of Clean Energy," *Science* (January 9, 2017).

71. For more information on the Paris Agreement, see http://unfccc.int/paris_agreement/items/9485.php.

72. Annie Sneed, "Trump's First 100 Days: Climate and Energy," *Scientific American* (November 29, 2016).

73. Oliver Milman, "Paris Climate Deal: Trump Says He Now Has an 'Open Mind' About Accord," *The Guardian* (November 22, 2016). See also Claudia Thurber's chapter in this book on the difficulty of revoking regulations.

74. George C. Edwards III, *On Deaf Ears: The Limits of the Bully Pulpit* (New Haven, CT: Yale University Press, 2003).

75. Jordan Tama, "From Private Consultation to Public Crusade: Assessing Eisenhower's Legislative Strategy on Foreign Policy," *Congress and the Presidency* 40, no. 1 (2013): 41–60.

76. Lee H. Hamilton, with Jordan Tama, *A Creative Tension: The Foreign Policy Roles of the President and Congress* (Washington, DC: Woodrow Wilson Center Press, 2002), 82–86.

77. Baldwin and Magee, "Is Trade Policy for Sale?"

78. David P. Auerswald, "Arms Control," in David P. Auerswald and Colton C. Campbell, eds., *Congress and the Politics of National Security* (Cambridge: Cambridge University Press, 2012), 189–212.

79. Donald J. Trump, with Tony Schwartz, *Trump: The Art of the Deal* (New York: Random House, 1987).

Index

Page numbers followed by *f* and *t* indicate figures and tables, respectively.

About the Contributors

Gary Andres has served since 2011 as the majority staff director for the House Energy and Commerce Committee. Previously, he served President George H. W. Bush as deputy assistant to the president for legislative affairs (1989–1993) and served President George W. Bush as confirmation coordinator (2001). Before and after his White House appointments, he was a partner, vice president, and vice chairman for research at Dutko Worldwide, a public affairs and lobbying firm. Dr. Andres is the author of the book *Lobbying Reconsidered* (2009). From 2002 to 2010, he wrote weekly columns on politics, legislation, and public opinion for the *Washington Times* and the *Weekly Standard*. He first came to Washington in 1982 as an American Political Science Association Congressional Fellow. He holds a PhD in public policy analysis from the University of Illinois, Chicago.

Ross K. Baker is Distinguished Professor of Political Science at Rutgers University. He is also a member of the board of contributors of *USA Today*. In 2008, 2012, and 2016, while on leave from Rutgers, he was scholar-in-residence in the office of the Democratic leader of the US Senate. His most recent book is *Is Bipartisanship Dead?* (2015).

Sarah Binder is a professor of political science at George Washington University and a senior fellow at the Brookings Institution, specializing in Congress and legislative politics. She is the author or coauthor of four books on Congress: *Minority Rights, Majority Rule: Partisanship and the Development of Congress* (1997); *Politics or Principle? Filibustering in the United States Senate* (1997); *Stalemate: Causes and Consequences of Legislative Gridlock* (2003); and *Advice and Dissent: The Struggle to Shape the Federal Judiciary* (2009). She is also the coauthor of a forthcoming book, *Monetary Politics: Congress and the Federal Reserve, 1913–2016*. She received her PhD in political science from the University of Minnesota in 1995 and her BA from Yale University in 1986. Binder was elected to the American Academy of Arts and Sciences in 2015.

Patrick Griffin is a partner in GriffinWilliams LLC, a management consulting firm. He has thirty years of experience on Capitol Hill, in the White House, and in the private sector. During Bill Clinton's presidency, he served as assistant to the president for legislative affairs. In this capacity, he worked directly with the president, cabinet members, other senior administration officials, and congressional leaders on legislative initiatives and other matters. He has also served as senior policy advisor to two Senate Democratic leaders, Senators Robert C. Byrd and Tom Daschle. In those roles, he advised the Democratic leadership and caucus on policy and strategy. He is the academic director for the Public Affairs and Advocacy Institute in the School of Government at American University. Before coming to Washington, he was an assistant professor at the University of Wisconsin–Milwaukee.

David R. Jones is professor of political science at Baruch College and the Graduate Center, City University of New York. He received his PhD from the University of California, Los Angeles. His research on Congress, political parties, and elections has been published in several scholarly journals. He is also the author of *Political Parties and Policy Gridlock in American Government* (2001) and coauthor of *Americans, Congress, and Democratic Responsiveness: Public Evaluations of Congress and Electoral Consequences* (2009). He has regularly served as an exit poll analyst for CBS News and the *New York Times*.

Douglas L. Kriner is professor of political science at Boston University. He received his PhD from Harvard University in 2006. His research interests include the presidency, Congress, and separation of powers dynamics. He has authored four books, most recently (with Eric Schickler) *Investigating the President: Congressional Checks on Presidential Power* and (with Andrew Reeves) *The Particularistic President: Executive Branch Politics and Political Inequality*, which received the 2016 Richard E. Neustadt Award. His work has also appeared in *American Political Science Review*, *American Journal of Political Science*, and *Journal of Politics*, among other outlets.

John Anthony Maltese is the Albert Berry Saye Professor of Political Science and the associate dean of the School of Public and International Affairs at the University of Georgia. His books include *The Selling of Supreme Court Nominees*; *Spin Control: The White House Office of Communications and the Management of Presidential News*; and (with Joseph A. Pika and Andrew Rudalevige) *The Politics of the Presidency*, currently in its ninth edition. He was named Georgia Professor of the Year by the Carnegie Foundation for the

Advancement of Teaching and the Council for the Advancement and Support of Education. He is a Josiah Meigs Distinguished Teaching Professor, the University of Georgia's highest teaching honor.

James P. Pfiffner is University Professor in the Schar School of Policy and Government at George Mason University. His major areas of expertise are the US presidency, American national government, the national security policy making process, and public management. He has written or edited sixteen books, including *The Strategic Presidency: Hitting the Ground Running; Power Play: The Bush Administration and the Constitution;* and *Torture as Public Policy.* He has also published more than one hundred scholarly articles and chapters in books.

Jordan Tama is associate professor in the School of International Service at American University, research fellow at the Center for Congressional and Presidential Studies, and codirector of the Bridging the Gap Project. He is the author of the book *Terrorism and National Security Reform: How Commissions Can Drive Change During Crises* and coauthor of the book *A Creative Tension: The Foreign Policy Roles of the President and Congress.* He has also published more than two dozen articles and book chapters on US foreign policy and American politics. In 2012, he served in the House of Representatives as an American Political Science Association Congressional Fellow. His research has been supported by the Social Science Research Council, Woodrow Wilson Center, and IBM Center for the Business of Government.

Claudia H. Thurber, a consultant in occupational safety and health, is a veteran of over twenty-two years of federal government service. She served as the Occupational Safety and Health Administration's (OSHA) counsel for health standards until her retirement from government service in 2006. She is an expert on the regulatory process, having worked on some of OSHA's most important and far-reaching standards that protect workers from hazards. Ms. Thurber has spoken at numerous government and professional meetings on current issues in regulation, particularly occupational safety and health, mine safety, and environmental issues. She has lectured to academics, government managers, and graduate students in the United States and abroad. She has also taught political science courses at American University and courses in evidence-based thinking and writing and rulemaking for OSHA. She holds a JD from the Washington College of Law at American University, an MA in government and politics from the University of Maryland, and a BA in history from Washington State University.

James A. Thurber is University Distinguished Professor of Government and founder (1979) and former director (1979–2016) of the Center for

Congressional and Presidential Studies at American University in Washington, DC. His research focuses on American politics, and he is the author or editor of numerous books and scholarly articles, including *American Gridlock: The Sources, Character and Impact of Political Polarization* (with Antoine Yoshinaka, 2015); *Campaigns and Elections, American Style* (with Candice J. Nelson, 2013, fifth edition); *Obama in Office* (2011); *Congress and the Internet* (with Colton Campbell, 2002); *The Battle for Congress: Consultants, Candidates, and Voters* (2001); *Crowded Airwaves: Campaign Advertising in Elections* (with Candice J. Nelson and David A. Dulio, 2000); and *Campaign Warriors: Political Consultants in Elections* (2000). Dr. Thurber was an American Political Science Association Congressional Fellow and is a fellow of the National Academy of Public Administration.